The **DENZEL** Principle

The DENZEL *Principle*

Why Black Women Can't Find Good Black Men

JIMI IZRAEL

St. Martin's Press ≉ New York

www.stmartins.com

Design by Patrice Sheridan

LIBRARY OF CONGRESS CATALOGING-IN-PUBLICATION DATA

Izrael, Jimi.
    The Denzel principle: why black women can't find good black men / Jimi Izrael.
        p. cm.
    ISBN 978-0-312-53485-1
    1. Man-woman relationships.   2. Relationship quality.   3. African American
men—Psychology.   4. African American women—Psychology.   I. Title.
    HQ801.I97 2010
    306.73'408996073—dc22

                                                            2009033709

First Edition: February 2010

10   9   8   7   6   5   4   3   2   1

DISCLOSURE: Names, places, and distinguishing characteristics of some folks have been changed. And trust me, that is for the best.

After much thought, this book is dedicated to my grandfather, a hard man who took a hard line on most things, but was always quick to remind me:

"The main thing is . . . that you know I love you."

Contents

Acknowledgments
and Such

I want to thank my long-suffering agent, Claudia Menza, of the Menza-Barron Agency, and my editor, Monique Patterson.

Gary Dauphin, Kahlil Caldwell, George Kelley, Dmitri Sumbry, Cavana Faithwalker, Delano Massey, Hashim Warren, and David Sedaris, for all the gifts of kindness and wisdom you have given me through the years. Cobbski—I'm still good for that catfish.

Margaret Bernstein, Karen Grigsby Bates, Michel Martin, Kate Tuttle, Stephanie Crockett, Zakia Spalter, Alicia Montgomery, Teshima Walker, Holly Burgess, Cherry Gee, Lynette Clemetson, Natalie Hopkinson, Jam Donaldson, Laine Goldman, Vanessa Gallman, and Lisala Peery—all women who are or have been instrumental in helping me find and fight for my voice and forwarding my career.

Big shout to Mansfield Frazier and Larry Durst.

Gwen Caldwell—I miss you, Mama.

Special thanks to my parents for making me the man I am today.

Paul Springstubb, my friend and colleague, Drs. Dorothy Salem and Carolyn Gordon: thank you. Sam Zalutsky, Brad Ridell,

Charlie Schulman, Mark Galauner, and Sheila Schwartz—thanks. Because good teachers can change lives.

Eric Monte, for being my friend and inspiration. Dackeyia Simmons. My big brother Eugene S. Robinson. My baby sister Liz Burr.

Rita Gatton and the Rev. Evan Golder, for making those jobs so fucking unbearable.

Randy Varcho—thanks.

Special thanks to Scout, Ulley, Atticus (RIP), Murmur Lee, and my Lil Cee—I love you, always.

Erica W., Danielle M., Maura B., Gabrielle T., and Flora E. Yep. That's probably why.

Twaana Reeves, my bestest girlfriend. I love you.

Donna Arceneaux—my dear friend. Always there.

Yolanda Young, who saw all this coming.

Marty and Stephanie, Jimmy, Gwen, and Michael. Ricky and Rafi. And all my cousins (Mookie, et al.).

The Exes—Godspeed.

Rosie Brown—my friend.

Sweetheart—you always knew. Always. I love you so much.

My children—some things are worth fighting for, yes? I love you all.

Grandma Tisdale—I am never as far away as you think, Grandma.

Aunt Margie and Uncle Phil—thank you for everything.

The truly wise woman builds her house up,
even as the foolish one rips hers down with her bare hands.

—*Proverbs 14:1*

Introduction

I pulled up to my four-bedroom colonial and I saw Leslie, my second wife, and her boyfriend loading stuff into a small moving van sitting in the driveway—it's not the kind of thing you see every day. At least, I don't. I took a few minutes to drink it in, this photo of my perfect life, interrupted. It wasn't the portrait of matrimony I'd envisioned: her, looking like she was the next contestant on *The Price Is Right,* as if she'd won some fabulous prize. Him, looking like a jobless yeti—with dreadlocks—ready to be cuckolded, like I unwittingly had been. Yep, there he was: carrying shit I paid for with my hard work, for the love of my family, away to who-knows-where. It didn't seem real. I parked my shitty Escort GT with the broken taillights on the street and watched as they loaded the computer I'd bought for her, the couches we'd picked out together, the appliances her father's people had given us, and all the Coach purses I'd gifted into a U-Haul. It didn't register. Rather, it was some kind of bad Tyler Perry play or awful black romance movie starring Vivica Fox and maybe Tommy Davidson as me, "That Dude." But I couldn't deny my eyes. Was I bitter? Merriam-Webster's defines bitterness at least three different ways, but among the definitions: *bitterness is intense animosity, expression of severe pain, grief, or regret.* Yes. Bingo. *Check.* She was taking the television, the kids, and everything. Those were real Coach purses, not swap-meet bullshit, and those damn purses are not cheap. So, all in, who wouldn't be bitter? Bitter with animus, severe pain, grief, regret, *and* a side of slaw, but not terribly surprised, as I'd kinda been here before, and the déjà vu made me more reflective than anything. Like, how the fuck did I get in this bag . . . again?

Think about it: you never get married thinking about divorce: not if you're really in love. If you are really in love, you leap blindly into the unknown, naked, both feet in the air, like a dip in a hidden swimming hole in the middle of a summer day: you have waited all your life for a love like this; no sense in being practical. Best to jump in whole-hog. That, after all, is love's divine: abandoning all conventional wisdom in order to risk it all and suckle the nectar of the smitten—it is a beautiful intoxication. I've always questioned the point of prenups with all kinds of legalese and early-withdrawal clauses. For all that bullshit, you might as well stay single and just shack up, right? The thing is, your parents would look down on you for that, and you'd never be right with her people either. Not like you'll never be right in their eyes anyway, but why give them more reason to dislike you right out the gate? In-laws are gonna give you the stink-eye, no matter what.

If you are a woman, you are looking for that elusive "happily ever after." If you are a man, chances are good you're like me—a gentleman, and every gentleman wants to make his girlfriend an honest woman. Getting the milk for free without buying the cow is overrated: real men take a chance on love. No sense in playing it safe. Buy the cow, f'r Christ's sake. This analogy fails, of course, when the cow serves you walking papers. Then you got no cow, no milk, and no clue.

Damn.

I'm a product of divorce, and the pain of my parents' separation changed my life forever. I thought we had everything, the three of us in that upstairs apartment. We didn't have a lot of money but to a child, it seemed we had more than enough love to sustain us. Sometimes, kids see their parents always going at it, but not my folks. They seemed to laugh and joke a lot, and genuinely like each other's company. Their divorce came as a complete shock to me. It was traumatizing and it hurts, even today. I miss my nuclear family. Growing into manhood, I never thought about divorce when I got married, and I looked down upon people who did. Divorce sucks. Hopefully, we all get married knowing that no one is perfect, and prepared to weather the storm: that's what all the "for better or for worse" is about, right? I've been married twice, and I can tell you fearlessly that nothing lasts forever, and marriage is no exception. "Tooth and tongue fall out," my grandfather used to say, "and they're God-given." Admittedly, it took me awhile to find the wisdom in his curious axiom, but I got it now, Jack. There are no guarantees and, as the real pimps say in the street, "bitches *come* leavin'." I know—that's kinda raw. Me? I never wanted to be that cynical. Yet, here I am.

I do a lot of online shopping these days because walking the mall, I see young couples at the jewelry stores, poring over rings and some of me wants to be back there: wide-eyed and optimistic, woman by my side, ready to take on the world with a love no man could measure. And I can't help but remember when it was me, broke like two roaches, my tank full on love and cheap wine, trying to wife my girl on the cheap, feeling lucky that she'd ever returned my phone call. Watching her ogle the high-priced ice then edging her gently over to the stuff I could actually afford. Trying on the rings and watching her smile light up the store; I can still feel the lump in my throat, hear my heart sing. Damn, what a lucky guy I was. Her people looked down their nose at me, I didn't have a real job, and we had a serious values disconnect, but so what? Together, we would show the world what true love was. We'd make it happen. I was a young man, with no degree, something like a plan, a lot of hustle, and nothing to fear but the future. Standing there at the junior jewelry counter, I confess: the future couldn't've looked any brighter. I miss those days. They say ignorance is bliss, and it's true: yeah, some of me wants that feeling again. To be hopelessly in love, back when I didn't know better.

Then there is the rest of me: the professional player turned devoted boyfriend then fiancé and husband. The guy who stood watching in-laws, friends, and Oprah Winfrey burn my marriages to the ground while the moving men packed my first wife Frances away; me, sifting through the ashes for clues. I remember watching the men load her life into a cheap rental, and I stood there like that guy you always see on the evening news after a tornado blows through the only home he's ever known. He fights back tears and a burning scream because dignity is the last piece of humanity he has left. Hands at his sides, palms forward, mouth agape, he looks for God in the mayhem, trying hard to understand the wisdom in the wreckage that was his life. There is none, and he cannot fathom the event that has just destroyed the world as he knew it. His won't cry but his eyes say it all:

"What just hit me?"

Yeah. I'm that guy. Confused. Discouraged. PISSED.

Part of me is angry, yes, but just like that guy standing in the ruins of his life, I'm willing to rebuild. After Frances, I was reluctant but willing to give love another shot. I mean, what are the choices? What are we without the hope that love holds? How can you get up and live a day without the idea that you could play the game and win, that you could find love today, if it doesn't find you first? People live that life, but I didn't want it to be me. My life after love was long days, nights that were longer still, spent in drowsy, smoky places where I sat drowning it all, gazing into all the other lonely faces trying to remember love. Any love. Just like me.

There's always the chance you'll get hurt in love, but we live for the moments betwixt first kiss and heartbreak. Well, women pray for it, men die for it, and the elderly lay dying and wish they could taste it one last time. Despite my broken spirit, I would not die that way.

After marrying Frances and then divorce number one, I became a different dude: it was all about me and my needs. I needed women to clean my house, suck my dick, and cook my meals. Lots of them. I didn't rebound, I ricocheted from woman to woman. A lot of those chicks wanted to get married but I was determined never to make the mistake of matrimony again. And this is the endgame for most of the cats I know: black women burn good brothers, use them up, or try to whip them into perfection. I ran the gauntlet. Like so many dudes I know, I fucked up.

Against every instinct, I put my parts together to rebuild a heart I could give to Leslie and her child. Only to be here again, with the familiar smell of smoke and the faces of movers I knew too well, sifting through the ashes of another failed marriage. It was a gamble from the start. I lost. Again. I didn't know then but I know better now. Today, no part of me knows why it all turned to dust, even if I have my suspicions.

I just know after all that, I'm not as inclined to love as I used to be.

It's weird, because I've always thought of myself as a good catch. Why wouldn't I be, right? I mean, I BATHE. Got all of my own teeth, if you don't count the one chomper in the back that I cracked on a girlfriend's cookie (don't ask). Of course, I have my shortcomings, but who doesn't, right? I got bad table manners, and I didn't really hold a steady job until I was in my early twenties. Before then, I was living off a pretty small settlement from a childhood accident. I wasn't lazy, but I just didn't see the point of holding a job if I didn't have to. I got by on my considerable charm and sex appeal. Or at least, I thought it was considerable. I dunno how you quantify these things. Maybe you list them.

Okay so let's give it a shot.

PROS

- Charitable—I give spare change to bums on the regular. Giving to the United Way, most of your donation goes to overhead. Bums just want a beer. I can dig it.
- Loyal—I'm all about My Peeps, often to my detriment.
- Good father—Admittedly hard to do in absentia, but fighting hard for my rights.
- Hardworking—I hustled verbs like a muthafucka to make a living as a writer.
- Honorable—I always try to do the right thing. It's hard to know what that is sometimes.

- Honest, to a fault—It's gotten me in trouble. I know— hard to believe, right?
- Outspoken—Again, too much of a good thing . . .
- Self-made—Nobody handed me shit. And when they did, I was too stupid to know.
- Curious—S'why I read.
- Free thinking—Fuck olde timey Negro black group– think. I'm a G.D.I.—Gott-Damn Individ'jul.
- Independent—We all mostly need people, but some- times, it's been just me. I prefer it that way sometimes.
- Tenacious—Fuck the dumb shit, I gotta get mine. Baby needs a new pair of Jordans.
- Fair and open, mostly—Open for compromise: I'm hard, but I'm fair.
- Unapologetically hetero—Nothing personal.
- Unapologetically black— . . . and I don't owe you any explanations.
- Nice arms—I dunno. Chicks dig the arms.
- Funny—Sometimes.
- Creative—What's life without a dream?
- Animal lover—I love a good catfight.
- Loquacious—Got the gift of rhetoric.
- Respectful of elders, mostly—I hate STUPID old people.
- Tenderhearted—There, but for the grace of God, go I. . . .
- Cocksmith—I'm no novice: I'm in the union. Ask around.

CONS
- Charitable—I'm a sucker for a sob story.
- Standoffish, shy—I don't really fuck with everybody all like that. Sorry.

- Hard on people—I expect the same things from people I expect from myself.
- Sexist—I open doors, pay dinner bills, and occasionally eat pussy. But cooking and cleaning is woman's work.
- Womanizer—Women dig me a little, and I dig women a little too much. S'my cross to bear.
- Unapologetically hetero—What can I say?
- Unapologetically black—It's not everybody's favorite color.
- Not handy around the house—Being raised by a single mom = What's a toolbox?
- Not very domestic—Always had women around to clean up after me. Yeah. I know.
- Doesn't always play well with others—As hard as it may be to believe, I rub some people the wrong way.
- Haven't always been the most responsible father—I opted out once, kinda.
- Funny—Not always at the right times. Like funerals. And fucking.
- Snores—Apnea. Jesus.
- Impatient—Like a seven-year-old.
- Bad temper, when angry—Like Bruce Banner, black. But not physically. Still and all, you won't like me when I'm angry.
- Talks loud—Don't all black people talk loud?
- Selfish—In the end, it's all about me and my kids. No offense.
- Big belly—I'm in good enough shape, but I could use a sit-up Nazi in my life. . . .
- Stubborn—I want it the way I want it. Now.

- Shoe addiction—Love me some nice shoes, man. Jordans. Maddens. Gotta have 'em.
- Flatulent!—I used to fart like a bebop trumpet. I cut out dairy, so now, notsomuch.

I'm no prize, but on balance, you could sure do a lot worse than a hardworking fart-hammer who can't change a tire . . . right? (Not that it matters, because I don't have a car just now either. But I can cook a mean bowl of meatless spaghetti, ladies.)

My second wife, Leslie, lured me in with her kid, truth to tell, because she was a mess of contradictions. She needed fixing—rehabbing in the worst way. She was younger than I, so I was sure she'd grow up. Of course, I loved her, but I fell in love with her son, and his love drew me in and sealed the deal. You'd think a single mother would have a lot of hustle, and when we met, she did. Her shit was right in the pocket. But back when she lied to her manager and told them my mother died just so she could get a few days off of work, it should have rang bells: these were the hints of contradictions. I mean, any one that'll kill off your people in a lie is fucked up to begin with, but just to get some days off . . . Jesus Christ in a Porno, I should have stopped the boat and got off, because this bitch was lazy like a dead rat. Yep—alarms and sirens should have rang in my head: "DANGER, DANGER." Nah. Nothing. No bells. No nothing.

When we first got together I was jobless, with no prospects. I stayed that way for better than a year, and pulled my weight by seeing to the child and cleaning up her place. I started freelance writing, and it took off. I took a part-time gig to complement the hustle, and I was off to the races. Over time, it became clear she resented my work ethic and the moderate success that came with it. On a whim, she found someone not terribly ambitious, a Job Corps scholar with a piece of a job working for a cable company who had a lot of free time to write poetry, do her nails, feed her ego, and make children neither one of them could afford. Her leaving created an upheaval that disrupted my life and shattered my seeds: so much for the innocence of childhood. When I met Leslie, she always had some off-kilter bullshit—too off-kilter for me to write about—going on in her life, and I thought marriage would give her some relief, balance, and stability. I thought, having been a single mom for so long, she had some peace overdue. This placed me in the role that rapper and noted feminist Too Short might call "Captain Save-A-Hoe." Everyone is not cut out for social work, and some folks cannot be changed, and it's not a noble deed to try. It's stupid. It seems some people don't feel complete without some kind of drama in their lives. It's hard to make those people out from the curb, but once you do, best to cut your losses and keep on movin'. Not to cape-up and try to rescue them.

(This is where the camera cuts to Leslie leaving with my beloved stepson and our child together and the yeti, the douche bag carrying her purse.)

When I told my grams what was going down, she said to "send that bitch on with what she brought in, and nothing more." Alas, I didn't see the cause in being petty. Besides, she was taking my kids, and I wanted them to be comfortable, but I didn't see how they'd benefit from our New York porn collection. But there it was—the discreet blue grocery store bag we kept tucked in our bedroom closet—packed into the hull of the truck. She left her work clothes and took the porn. Jesus. Seems like you or I would leave the porn, out of spiteful pity. Instead she takes it, in a move to kind of twist the knife. Insult to injurious insult.

This was my fault, this time. I know that. I probably could have seen it coming. Although because I'm such a light touch, I'm not a great judge of character—I take people how they come and pray they do the same. Most times in my life, this builds strong relationships that last a long time. Sometimes they go looking for what they think must be a better life, and take your kids and all your furniture with them.

What goes around comes around, they say. What a stupid fucking cliché. Love wasn't coming back around for me, this time, or the time before that. Love wasn't good to any part of me. Not the part I gave my stepson, not the part I gave Leslie, and not the part of me sitting in my car, watching my life being carted away from across the street, looking down at my wedding ring. Quietly, this part has become ripe with gangrene and rot: this part sitting in the car wants those years back. This part wants to wrassle that bitch to the ground and take back that diamond ring. Thank God for the Internet, because I'd never buy a pair of shoes or a packet of clean underwear. I'd get to the mall, see that bitch, and find myself ruminating and then get arrested, hiding in the bushes waiting to jump out and snatch back that Coach purse. Like some kind of divorce repo man. Might've started a service, where I went fetching back gifted trinkets for lovelorn men swimming in bitterness and despair.

In aggregate, I have the love of my children and a few nice shirts to show for all the hard work I put into my marriages. And I'm glad they are over—what, with all the lies and bullshit—but at a minimum, part of me wants a refund. I suppress that part. That's not the kind of guy I am, or the kind of guy I want to be. But I can admit it: love has changed me. Love has changed a lot of men I know.

I held the door open for Leslie's boyfriend, the asshat, who was carrying the thirty-six-inch TV I'd given her for Mother's Day for the kids, asking myself, like . . . *what the FUCK?* In me, she'd had a committed, hardworking spouse who loved her— how could you possibly do better than that? I'd paid for this wife's tuition too (maybe word got out I was a mark?), took her child as my own, given her another child, and made her life as a mostly stay-at-home mom pretty comfortable. Didn't matter. She was packing her moving van and moving into a nearly condemned house just to be with this dude, trading me in for someone imagined to be a better man. It didn't matter that he wasn't rich, well-educated, or particularly handsome. Scuttling nearly ten years of a family we'd built together, she left with a man she'd known less than a year. Frances, after I put her through undergrad, waited some two weeks after she got her degree and promptly asked for a divorce. She could "do better" too, she said. We were supposed to take turns in college, but now here I was, left high and dry like a muthafucka. She rolled me for tuition money and bounced. I'd been had.

Wow.

I thought that bitch was crazy. Both of them bitches were crazy. What could they have been smoking? Maybe there was something in the water. Listening to they mama. Maybe a chemical in the hair relaxer. Something. Maybe it was me. Yeah, I had to seriously consider the possibility I wasn't blameless.

I made bad choices, it's not like my environs were brimming with eligible women. By the time I was of a mind to start looking for a wife, the women I hooked up with were the catches of the day in the dating pools I swam in, which isn't saying a lot. I dipped and dabbled in a lot of different circles and most of the women seemed to share the same attitudes. They were all similarly afflicted: they didn't know how to be happy. They wanted a perfect man, someone who would suffer foolishness without objection. I got conned, essentially, into trying to be perfect. Well, I sure as hell am not perfect, and as soon as I stopped trying, I'd get the classic "it's not you, it's me" send-off.

I thought maybe I'd chosen good life partners, but as it turns out, I just have good taste in ex-wives. What went wrong?

After the second split, I moved on, and moved away to take a position with a newspaper in the South as well as further my education. I didn't want to leave my kids behind, but these plans were in motion long before my wife decided to chirp out. She wasn't gainfully employed, so someone had to be an earner and role model for my kids. I wasn't going to let that be her boyfriend, so I got the child support squared away through the court, hired a lawyer, and hit the road. She made overtures about reuniting, but I ain't trust it. Best to just take the loss with as much dignity as possible and keep it stepping. But it was hard to be away from my kids. I sat alone in my flat with the realization that love had alluded me again. Damn, I was hurt. From my toenails on up. The South is a lonely place for a youngish black guy. But it seemed like once word got out that there was a working black man with all his teeth in town, I didn't stay lonely too long. What can I say? Chicks dig me a little. I dig them a little too much.

I tried to stay with my wives despite readily apparent shortcomings and the kind of trifling character flaws that seep deep into the marrow. I overlooked their imperfections, they rejected me because of mine. But there were kids in the mix, this second time around, and they were paying for my bad decision. What just happened to my marriage? What did I do wrong *this* time?

I thought back to the dusty boyfriend running around my house after my wife. She talked to him like hired help: pick up this, haul away that. Lick this up. And he responded like a dutiful, love-starved puppy, wide-eyed, tongue out and all. What a fucking disgrace. This was the man that destroyed my family? What kind of man was this?

"It's not that you're not a *good* man," said Leslie, emptying shrimp, prime rib, chicken breasts, and ice cream bars from our refrigerator. "It's just that you aren't a good man for *me*."

It didn't matter that I begged her not to go. Oprah, *Essence*, Dr. Phil, and all her best girlfriends concurred: I was not the perfect man for her.

I didn't know what she was talking about. A good man is a good man, right? Good, but not good enough? What the fuck was she talking about? She sounded an awful lot like my first wife: like, she thought she was due an upgrade. As if she thought she could do better. But why did she opt to date a string of losers, and here was this one, trading down. What happened to the upgrade?

Then it hit me. This guy, this poor sap? He wasn't much of a man at all. He looks to me like the Punk of the Week, any week of the year. It's as if he'd been waiting all of his life, knowing his lack of honor, self-respect, and integrity would pay off. He was right: the iron was hot, and his time was now. They had so much in common, as they were both looking for the same thing: an empty vessel they could fill with their own ideas and remake in any way they wanted. I question whether they were in love with each other, as much as the idea of each other: the kind of person they could make over into a vision of perfection. Men are stupid enough to fall into that kind of fantasy, but I expected more from my wife. I thought she was too smart to get caught up in the Dizzle.

What's the Dizzle? Glad you asked.

Women are looking for men to turn into something between a girlfriend and a lapdog. Some of them don't know that, but they expect you to know. Especially black women. They want Prince Charming, Mr. Right, or Sir Fucking Lancelot. Some women are drawn not to real men, but to the idea of the ideal man, to watered-down Denzel Washington types who are long on charm and short on manliness.

What do I mean by that? Well, it's not a dig on my dude Denzel, that's for sure: he's worked hard to establish his career. He's not a friend, and we don't do sushi or anything, but from all accounts, he seems to be a helluva guy. Not that anyone knows for sure because he goes through great pains to separate his on-screen life from his personal life. Ironic, given the fact that what lies at the center of his great appeal as a leading man and his paradigmatic charisma is that the characters he plays, from Private Trip in *Glory* to Alonzo Harris in *Training Day* exude a maleness that begs to be captured and tamed. His on-screen macho seems seasoned with just enough of the kind of softness that makes women think he might suddenly call in off patrol, lock up his gun, tie on an apron, wash the dishes, and cook up a casserole. Spend the rest of the evening with the tip of his chin embedded in her asshole as he licks the lining out of her pussy, only getting up to do her toes while he asks about her day. Denzel comes off as not too hard, not too soft, on cue. It's the kind of wishy-washy fantastical reworking of manhood that women embrace. Because

Denzel is a certifiable man's man, and women know he wasn't hatched, there must be more perfect men. And they believe they can have their own Denzel Washington. Or give their man a Denzel makeover. Maybe come up with an Instant Denzel Kit: Denzel-in-a-Box, complete with wife-beater T-shirt, a blinding smile, hot and cold running machismo. Suits, leather jackets, and uniforms would be extra. If someone could figure out a way to do it, they would.

Now of course, it's not Denzel's fault he's so gott-damn lovable. He is the product of a Hollywood hype-machine that manufactures luminaries by selling a certain image and building on their enigmatic qualities to create modern mythology. But try telling that to a woman who decides she wants nothing more from a man than everything. She compares you to her vision of perfection and you spin your wheels trying to play to her every whim and emotion, which can change by the hour. She expects nothing less than perfection, yet insists that you be yourself.

Bullshit!

This realization led me to explore some ideas about that thesis: what do black women want?

I went to a bookstore and was astounded by the number of books advocating the rebuilding and remaking of black men. The shelves are teeming with information about reconstructing the black man:

> . . . make him less feminine, make him more feminine, make him a leader, make him a follower, make him rich! Make that lazy black man work harder! Make him into your new gay girlfriend whether he's actually homosexual or not and if he isn't, remake, rebuild, rethink, and reduce the black man . . .

Now, high expectations aren't just a black thing. White women seem to look to entertainers and rock stars as objects of affection. They are lifted to icon status, even. White women don't seem so intent on remaking their men into a fantasy character. They seem content to take men as they are. White women and black women are dissimilar in so many ways, but I don't know how we attribute this disparate difference in worldviews. Sure—there are "queer eye" makeover shows and the like, but you won't find books lamenting the state of white men, postulating about formulas and methodologies in an attempt to ostensibly refurbish and reform an entire race of men. Those books would not sell, you see, because the thesis—that a race of men are inherently flawed—is preposterous. But black women eat these books up.

According to these same books, black men are impossible brutes but black women are ethereal, queenly figures, divine in every way. The biggest flaw in the black woman, according to the books, is the black man. There is only one universal truth in the world: black men are fucked up. No other man on earth is required to measure up to the standards of others like black men are. No other men are even *asked*: they are accepted, warts and all. Thank God there are rare exceptions and the black man, as fucked up as he is, may not yet be beyond redemption.

Naturally, this is bullshit.

Still, bubble-headed talk-show hosts, cuckolded brothers, and advice columnists with multiple letters behind their names disseminate the false notion of a rare, excellently reconstructed black male all lesser men should aspire to and all women should relentlessly pursue. This ideal gives black women false hope that they will find the perfect man, as seen on TV.

You know who they want, right?

They are looking for Denzel Washington: D-Dub. The Dizzle. Just give her time, and the sister will try to figure out the best way to bring out the Dizzle in *you*. You know: the inner Dizzle you secretly want to be. Or she'll go out for drinks with her girlfriends and come home drunk on the Dizzle, berating you like a child. Why can't you be more like Denzel? Because being you simply won't do.

Black women like to pretend that a knock to one kind of sister is a knock to all black womankind. It isn't. Black men don't do our women the way they do us. When I break it down the way I'm breaking it, the brothers out there know *exactly* who I'm talking about. I'm talking about the women whining about not being able to find a "good black man." The truth? They have been so thoroughly brainwashed, that black women don't know what a "good black man" even looks like.

Now, every time you turn around, sisters say they just want a "good" black man, but being good is never enough. If it was, there would be no complaining, because there are good black men everywhere. There would have to be, right? We can't all be in jail, on crack, trudging through natural-disaster areas with plasma TVs strapped to our backs raping newborns two at a time, sick with the "DL," jungle fever, or otherwise afflicted.

This book is all about my life, sifting through unreasonable expectations from certain kinds of women. If you are a man looking for justification for your bad behavior and mistreatment of women, I gotta say right off-rip: this book is probably not for you. And while there are specific examples, they are pertinent only to my experience, so obviously, I am not writing about all women, black or white—certainly not in the dismissive, all-inclusive way women write about men. You should only take it personally if it sounds like I'm talking about you.

This is a personal journey I'm putting out there in hopes that women will read my experience and maybe it will help them find themselves, wake up, and find one of the good brothers, who are far less the exception than the rule. And the good guys out there will know that they are not alone. You can recognize them because, as unfashionable as it is, they are empowered to remain unbent, unbroken, and under no obligation to conform to trendy mores. This book is all about me, but will hopefully help women recognize the good in other men and covet those relationships, because we don't need a lot of people trying to change us into better people. Names were changed to protect the innocent, the guilty, and all the bystanders in between.

Truly great men just need good women by our side to be better.

The Denzel Principle

People talk shit, but numbers don't lie. According to smart white folks who know, two-thirds of all black marriages end in divorce, creating whole neighborhoods of single-parent families, usually headed by single mothers. This statistic really reflects less on black men and more on black women and their inability to make good choices. And it also precipitates the reason why many black women are looking for a man to be the father they never knew. They don't know him well or have never met him, yet expect their prospective mate to be everything the little girl in them imagines him to be. No man alive can measure up to those expectations. It's hard enough just being a stand-up cat in a world where nice guys finish last and assholes get all the pussy. But it doesn't really matter, because women will make a good brother go bad. Because when they meet a good man, they don't really know how to treat him.

See, a lot of sisters had no father growing up; they've spent their lives listening to their mothers argue with their fathers, talking down on that "no-good nigga," disrespecting anyone with a penis and simultaneously running boyfriends with expensive cars through her bedroom like she's a top barber giving half-price cuts. Consequently, years down the road, the daughter wonders why, after all the loud talking, acting out, and bad-mouthing, she can't keep a man in her unkempt house. Fuck it, she says. Her moms laid the groundwork for her daughter's life of unhappiness simply by being a bad role model. Common sense suggests you treat people how you want to be treated, but it's too easy for women to be like their mothers: angry and single.

Many of them have money of their own, but would rather use their pussy like a credit-card swiper to pay the bills. Not that they're gold diggers, but they are motivated by money. This may sound a lot like just choosing a mate with superior qualifications, but in practical terms, it's as if some women's affection and time can be bought. Most brothers can read that game from the curb, and they know how to play it on the cheap. They run the chick to the Waffle House, the motel, and leave her cab fare on the dresser. Then she's sitting there, talking about "that's cold." It's the man's fault he didn't hang out long enough for her to cash in. She turns to her girlfriends asking for advice, and they tell her to hold out for the gold-plated Mandingo pulling up in a Bentley with a trunk of Godiva chocolate to sweep her off on holiday to the Poconos. On her deathbed, she'll still be waiting.

Black women say they have trouble finding the right guy, but the truth is some of them manage to find a new one every night, and word gets around. Or they find great guys—legitimately good brothers with jobs, benefits, and all their own teeth—and stay happy for about fifteen minutes. Then they wear them out emotionally (rarely sexually), get bored, step out of the relationship, and throw the proverbial dice in hopes of an upgrade. This becomes routine, and they end up spending their golden years with

50 cats and 150 ceramic collectables, trying to lure the mailman inside with a plate of food.

Now, men get a lot of the blame for destroying the black family because conventional wisdom suggests they spend all their time beating up women, shooting dice late into the night, stealing watermelon from Ofay the Farmer and being generally useless and unmarriageable. And let's be honest: there are a lot of brothers out there fucking up, but not nearly as many as you think. Normally, those brothers wear their crazy on their sleeves. You can see—and oftentimes smell them—from the curb. Women tend to mask their crazy with lipstick, perfume, Apple Bottoms jeans, and such. Men aren't as smart as women about these kinds of things, and often don't know what they're getting into.

That said, the thing is I know brothers aren't responsible for the high divorce rate because we aren't that particular. Men are not complicated creatures and don't ask for much. All we want is a woman to work, cook, clean, and maybe give up a lil anal on our birthday. Sisters *think* they aren't asking for the world by just looking for a man to meet their minimum standards. But their minimum is either the bare minimum or over the top. I know, because I see it all the time: black women jumping from knucklehead to knucklehead, chump to chump, hoping to get it right next time by consistently choosing from the bottom. They are in the Internet chat rooms, wearing tight dresses to Big Butt Nite at Da Club, and outside penitentiary gates on parole day waiting to pounce on anything with a pulse.

THIS JUST IN:

There is a movement building on the Internet just for women who like to date incarcerated and fresh-out-the-joint-type brothers.

Women meet these guys, trying to help the penal system rehabilitate them, hoping to rebuild a man from the ground up. Not
that convicts aren't viable mates, but you can't meet anyone at the
coffee house, so you start trolling the prisons for husband material? What the hairy hot fuck is *that* about? Oh. Probably just a
hairy, hot fuck. Jesus Christ on a saltine, that's fucking stupid.
But some women are so desperate for a man they can mold and
control, it's come to that. Holy shit.

Then there is the other extreme: sisters going out in search of
Mr. Moneybags, who is most often an asshole. They try to lure
men with spoiled bait and complain about the quality of men
they attract. You know you can tell who they are, because they
want to know what kind of car you drive just after they tell you
to buy them a drink. They have an agenda, and they wear it like
fake Louis Vuitton: garish and proud. But this is a good thing for
Brother Paid N. Full. Because he can afford to shamelessly keep a
stable of hoodrats and wannabe chicken heads eager to be mistreated in exchange for a seafood dinner. And the women? Well,
they are more than happy to stand in line.

Strange, that.

Black women's unrealistic standards are probably borne of bed-
time stories about handsome, rich men on majestic horses rescuing
damsels in distress. Girlfriends often tell similar apocryphal tales
about the friend of a friend who nabbed a rich, hung sugar daddy
who saved them from a life of dishpan hands and lower-middle-
class drudgery. Through the influence of popular media and the
misguided advice they give each other, sisters combine these images and presumptions to draw a composite of a perfect black man.
No way he could exist, but far be it for something like common
sense to stop the average woman from looking. Her friends meet

men who are so close—so close, girl! With just one fatal flaw, like he snores or doesn't get DIRECTV. But girl, she was so close! So as a tribe, they all just keep looking, telling themselves that accepting anything less than perfection would be "settling," because they've been convinced that the perfect man exists. This goes on until this perfect black man becomes like Bigfoot or the Loch Ness Monster, with cults of nutjobs trading information, hunting tips, and fish stories about the one that got away, their lives committed to hunting and capturing a creature who could not possibly exist. But wait!—just like Sasquatch and Nessie, Mr. Right is on the cover of every magazine, the star of many movies, and the next guest on *The Oprah Winfrey Show* . . . right?

Of course he is.

This delusion is called the Denzel Principle, or the Dizzle for short. The Dizzle causes **black women's standards to be so high as to cause them to be disaffected, disappointed, or deceived.** It's an affliction most commonly spread in beauty salons and hen sessions. Many of the infected women will likely only find the kind of love that needs batteries.

In the rapture of what could only be groupthink or mass hypnosis, black people seem particularly easy to seduce with fabricated role models and messianic figures. It probably started with slaves' indoctrination into Christianity and the story of the mortal son of God performing miraculous things while in human form: promising—and delivering—all things to true believers. Slave women probably turned to their men in disgust, wondering why they were not brave enough or holy enough to protect them from slave masters. They began envisioning a messianic black man who would stand against the white man and protect his women and children and uplift his race.

25

Men like Frederick Douglass, Booker T. Washington, W. E. B. DuBois, and Marcus Garvey were wise men with strong ideas who were elevated to icon status merely by feeling free enough to speak up and be counted. In an age when the wrong look or intonation could get a black man killed, these men appeared nearly supernatural. They were either fortified by large constituents of influential blacks or cosigned by important whites: they were average men with above-average cachet. They became role models not just because they were iconoclasts intent on flouting the rules of conventional thinking. They were lauded largely because they set a nearly unattainable bar for their time. They had mastered the art of the "double consciousness," enabling them to navigate the worlds of whites and blacks without missing a step in either. Being loved and admired by all was an enviable talent.

Years later, with the advent of vaudeville and popular cinema, the minstrel and his various "coon" incarnations came into vogue. D. W. Griffith's silent film *Birth of a Nation* (adapted from Thomas Dixon's novel *The Clansman* and his play of the same title which glorified the exploits of the Ku Klux Klan) famously introduces the audience to Gus—a newly freed slave and evil black stud intent on raping and/or marrying white women—as well as a host of other black male criminal types. This is how most of America meets black men.

Birth of a Nation is one of the highest-grossing silent films of all time, but because its black male antagonist validated the worst fears of white audiences and typified the personification of evil and everything wrong about Reconstruction-era America, it was criticized in its time by blacks for stirring up hate and provoking white audiences to commit hate crimes (i.e. lynching). The National Association for the Advancement of Colored People (NAACP) protested the film, and the furor embarrassed the filmmakers. The NAACP would go on to discourage, but not eliminate, films and other media that blithely demonized black people.

Five common caricatures of black Americans emerged on-screen, having evolved from literature and radio plays:

- Uncle Tom (from Harriet Beecher Stowe's 1852 novel *Uncle Tom's Cabin*: male, loyal, hard-working, and deferential)
- Mammy (female, hard-working, sassy, and wise)
- The Mulatto (mostly female, tragic, and confused)
- The Coon (male, goofy, shiftless, and/or lazy)
- The Buck (male, brutish, and wanton)

The black buck (or brute) is the character that excites and titillates moviegoers and aside from Zip Coon the clown (Dewey "Pigmeat" Markham and Stepin Fetchit come to mind as Zip Coon–type comedic talents who rose to some prominence years later) is the character most often seen in early films like *House-Rent Party*, Walt Disney's *Song of the South*, and television shows like *Amos 'n' Andy*. Tap dancer Bill "Bojangles" Robinson (who co-stars with white child star Shirley Temple in a number of films) is a good example of the singing, dancing, grinning comedic Zip Coon that became popular. But Buck was the coon loved and feared by Hollywood as the perfect villain who got to the root of pre-integrated America's fears about widespread crime and race-mixing.

The NAACP cast themselves as the arbiters of race, the keeper of the black image. They encouraged all black Americans to put the best face on the race, and Stepin Fetchit, "Pigmeat" Markham, and Bill "Bojangles" Robinson were not helping the cause. But asking any one person to carry all the baggage of his people and undo the prejudices of ignorant people is not a reasonable expectation. During this time is when we see the emergence of what some would call the paradigmatic negro façade: the deferential, well-appointed black man for all seasons who was just black enough, but not so you'd notice.

Enter actor Sidney Poitier. He fit the bill exactly.

He was neither shuck and jiver nor highfalutin: he was a black man who knew his place in America, and he chose parts that reflected it. Poitier's various turns as the dignified assimilated black man in films like *A Patch of Blue* and *Guess Who's Coming to Dinner* seemed to sate both audiences. Poitier became an icon by making it more socially acceptable for black men to be occasionally assertive (as bulldog detective Virgil Tibbs in *In the Heat of the Night*), but mostly deferential (*Guess Who's . . .*), defeated (*A Raisin in the Sun*), docile (*A Patch of Blue*), and eager to help (*To Sir, With Love*). He was new, exotic . . . and acceptable. In the face of America's hostile Jim Crow politics and general inequitable treatment of blacks, his affability trumped his blackness so much so that most of black America rejected him (reading him as an "Uncle Tom" in the midst of a social revolution), much to the bewilderment of whites: why can't black Americans be more like Sidney Poitier? His Bahamian patois mellifluously masked any hint of post-colonial bitterness or the Angry American Black Man–ism, with all his demands and aggressive resistance to assimilation. He didn't wear dark glasses under a poltical hairstyle. He became white America's best black friend, and the measure to which all other black men were compared. His evident employability and role as the Next Evolution in black Masculinity made women of all colors swoon. But there was no way any black man could afford to be that cool and apolitical in those times. Still, everyone wanted to know . . . why can't you be more like Sidney?

Every few years, the public latches onto some poor brother who seems to exude all things warm, wise, and wonderful and he becomes the perceived model black man. These brothers are most often sports figures, ideologues, or micro-pundits. Athletes seem particularly ripe for canonization: Paul Robeson, Jack Johnson, and Muhammad Ali were at one time all portraits of black manhood. But they were dealt with similarly.

Paul Robeson was a renaissance man: an athlete and scholar with a brilliant bass voice and distinguished demeanor that endeared him to the mainstream. He was lauded as a great man and credit to his race. He walked, talked, and behaved like no other brother in his time, and white folks loved him. This was a black man they could trust. Of course, when he began voicing his political thoughts and raising consciousness about racial discrimination, he was vilified. He died an outcast.

Jack Johnson was the boxer whites loved to hate. His style and finesse in the ring made him a star: his swagger and refusal to play by anyone else's rules made him a pariah, even among black people. He embodied everything America loved and hated about black men: he was brutish and unrepentant, flaunting and stunting in his wealth and fame. He dated white women. He thumbed his nose at Booker T. Washington and the black leadership of his time, instead being man enough to be a man on his own terms. But it all came at a price, as he was harassed and eventually beaten down. His excesses were his downfall and America reveled in the demise of this once great black man who took his freedom and proudly thought for himself.

Muhammad Ali was also much a man like Johnson, daring

to defy the government by refusing to be drafted and declaring himself "The Greatest." Famously called "The Mouth" by sportscaster Howard Cosell, he was well-respected but not well liked. But once his crusade became his undoing as the beatings he gave and the beatings he took disintegrated his mental capacity—and quieted his voice—then, he became a national treasure.

So, examining the lives of these three men, considered by some to be important black male role models, the take-home lesson seems to be that if you dare to step outside of conventional thinking, dare to exercise your freedom in a way that offends conservative sensibilities, you will be destroyed by one means or another. White America only cosigns docile, wounded black men for hero status. True iconoclasts must be quashed. Middle-class black Americans share this sentiment.

In post–civil rights America, it seems like everyone wanted black men to be Martin Luther King Jr. Not the womanizing, chain-smoking party boy he was in real life, but the nonviolent, well-spoken vessel for change. The messianic Martin is a legacy far too luminous to contend with. He is worshipped by whites and blacks as the second coming of Jesus himself. Blacks and whites alike quote his speeches and cast him as a superhero, never acknowledging the inherent unfairness of casting a dead man as a viable role model, and his "dream" as an attainable goal, only to fortify the folktale by commercializing it. Young black men for years (and some still today) grew up with pictures of Jesus and Martin in the living room on the mantel. The message being: Dad is obviously too human to be a role model, son. So strive to live up to the impossible. Again, white America cosigns a wounded leader. Later, they would annoint two others with the mantle of leadership.

Jesse Jackson and Al Sharpton were once effective agents for change, but today are toothless, as they exist on the brink of self-parody. Media rainmakers, yes, sometimes they are on-message, but more often than not they subsist mainly by shaking loot from the white guilt tree at prescribed intervals. Jesse can't fight the power without some kind of bad rhetorical rap. And ever since Al's talk show antics with show host Wally George and fellow niggerati Roy Ennes, cameras follows them both everywhere, eager to catch their antics.

What the ideologues and the athletes have in common is the way they were created, nurtured, and summarily undone by the white mainstream. They were media-created apparitions set in place to serve as examples or object lessons: stay in line, or we will destroy you too. The only viable leadership for black America—necessarily cosigned by white America—is dead leadership. Celebrity athletes can be made and unmade, and this is the kind of paradigmatic black man the mainstream prefers: one who can be built and destroyed in short order, his message and appeal easily controlled.

The paradoxically effeminate man rose up in the disco era as the new paradigm of manhood. The women's movement rejected the tough guy/war hero/cowboy of the fifties and sixties in favor of men who embraced their feminine side . . . aggressively. The Stonewall riots and the gay rights movement it started also made androgyny commonplace, acceptable, and in some circles, preferred. White men began to wear bouffant hairdos and in the black community the conk—the smoothed-bank straightening that became fashionable for men in the early days of the rhythm & blues era—came back with flamboyant suits, hip-huggers, and platform shoes. John Shaft's black and proud Afro was rejected in favor of Youngblood Priest's flowing locks and manicured beard. So grown men sat in beauty shops everywhere with their hair in curlers getting their beards shaped up. Billy Dee Williams was the vanguard of the new black "it" man: super cool, not too dark, not too light, with a "no-lye" relaxer in his hair, he was just tough enough to open a can of Colt 45, but too soft to be taken seriously. And he wasn't: later, this image would become the sight-joke to many skits. He was probably a pretty down-ass dude, but Williams appeared on film to be the kind of guy who got sexed up in the discotheque but beat up in the street for switching like a girl. He was the chocolate John Travolta, minus the machismo. While the bald Telly Savalas, lollipop in hand (WTF?) asked a generation of women "Who loves ya, baby?" Billy Dee got over with an entire generation of black women who refused to date any man who could not be mistaken for a woman.

This continued on into the eighties, when men who looked like women got truckloads of pussy. Women wanted slight, effeminate men with long dripping curls and perms. Androgyny became a coveted quality in a man. I guess this explains how Jesse "Side Action" Jackson and the Rev. Al Sharpton, with their Jheri curls and permed-out hair could ever be taken seriously in the black community. Brothers like El DeBarge, Michael Jackson, Prince, and Rick James were everything every man should be back in the day. All those men, coincidently, looked and acted like women in some way. They were slightly built, with a coy, feminine affectation. Even Full Force, a talented group of weight-lifting singer/producers who wore a lot of lip gloss, mascara, eyeliner, and baby hair looked like a gang of jailhouse gorilla queers. Take a look back at rappers like Ice T, Dr. Dre, and Grandmaster Flash and the Furious Five and it's clear these brothers weren't shopping in the men's department. But that's what ladies were looking for. No surprise, then, that Michael Jackson would be the megastar of this era; a racially ambiguous, sexually ambiguous, singing and dancing black man sounds like a marketing executive's wet dream. I even fell into that bag in junior high school.

When I got to school, I borrowed eyeliner and (brown) lipstick from my girlfriend, trying to be sexy, and it worked. I got a few handjobs between classes and even got invited to group-sex parties after school. Thank God Run DMC came along. Before them, a lot of hip-hoppers—including myself—were sizing themselves up for lace gloves and elf boots. 'Twas the only way you could get any pussy. Small wonder that today's hip-hop is soaked in testosterone and prone, half-naked women. It's a natural attempt to balance black women's need to emasculate black men. Because they don't really know what masculinity looks like, they've been writing their own playbook. Hip-hop culture came along, unapologetically macho, and alienated the mainstream until corporate America refined the narrative down to a message—sex, drugs, and violence—that could be easily consumed and disposed of.

In the era of Eddie Murphy rose a black man who could be taken seriously. Undeniably, he owned the eighties, but with his leather pants, donkey-toothed smile, and laugh to match, Murphy was that goofy black guy who loves to make you laugh and you love to call your friend, but not the one you'd invite to dinner. Denzel Washington stepped up and made his mark in the eighties. The Dizzle picked up where Sidney Poitier left off, adding sexuality to the mix in a passive-aggressive, nonthreatening way. Murphy was funny, but too horny and pseudo-political to rise as a role model. Michael Jackson and Prince were too close to being women. Denzel was hard on the outside, but soft in the middle: he chose roles with depth. With an easy smile and a slight overbite, Denzel distinguished himself from the cast of TV's *St. Elsewhere* as the prototype of the American dream: an assimilated black man—a doctor!—devoid of anger or resentment, fully invested in the system and free of any radical politics or overt sexuality that might get him arrested.

Denzel seemed to choose roles early in his career that gave him wide appeal. In a career spent playing iconic characters (*Malcolm X*, *Cry Freedom*), flawed, talented men with the best of intentions (*Mo' Better Blues*, *The Hurricane*), streetwise detectives (*The Mighty Quinn*, *Devil in a Blue Dress*), lovesick dreamers (*Mississippi Masala*), and ordinary men in extraordinary circumstances (*Ricochet*, *Inside Man*), it is as if he never passes up a chance to play a hero. Onscreen, he's always delivering someone from great peril (*Man on Fire*), or experiencing a spiritual transformation that uplifts his soul . . . just before he gets killed (*Glory*). An exceptional actor, the Best Actor Oscar alluded him for many years. After years of being nominated, the Dizzle finally won for playing a character familiar and comfortable to the mainstream audience: Alonzo Harris. It's not hard to surmise why he didn't get an Academy Award until he played a villain. Up to this point, I think we assumed he was cast to type. In the mind of the movie-going public, Denzel is a hero. Sure, he says in interviews that he doesn't like being seen as a role model or the face of the race. But his humility and resistant ascent is part of what has lifted him there. Every rumor of infidelity is met with unequivocal denial as he underlines his undying love for his wife for life, Pauletta. He has managed to dodge scandal and become a success on his own terms.

He says in interviews that he doesn't choose bigger-than-life characters, that he is just attracted to good scripts. Maybe it's coincidence that he gets such damn good scripts. It bodes well for the Dizzle that in a world where black male stars have to don a dress to find movie blockbuster success (Martin Lawrence, Eddie Murphy, and Wesley Snipes come to mind), Denzel has never been punked by a role: he's never played a chump. Or a villain. So playing the corrupt cop in *Training Day* seemed like his most dramatic stretch to date. Small wonder he won an Oscar. He's the only black actor with two Oscars on his dresser (he won Supporting Actor honors for his turn as escaped slavebuck-turned-patriot in the Civil War drama *Glory*) and there was a lot of Oscar talk about his turn as Frank Lucas, Harlem drug dealer and anti-hero, in *American Gangster*. Honestly, if the Dizzle did an Allstate insurance commercial ("Are *you* in good hands . . . baby?") there would be Oscar talk. But a nomination and win wouldn't surprise me.

What's most interesting about his movies is that all that prevents Denzel's films from stepping into the realm of blaxploitation is so often just his dignity coupled with the latent politics. Think about it: *Carbon Copy* notwithstanding (we all make mistakes), without the Dizzle, *Virtuosity, Ricochet,* and *Training Day* would have been impossibly campy. Mainstream audiences prefer to see the badass nigger narrative as opposed to a layered portrayal that requires them to question their presumptions about black men. But Denzel brings his smile, his forthrightness, and that innate Dizzle quality that makes the ladies swoon and the men cheer him on. He's black, in the best possible way.

The other piece of Denzel's appeal—in the black community, for sure—is his tacit loyalty to black women. The film where he came closest to this line, *Mississippi Masala*, was a sleeper art-house film that flew underneath the radar of most of his fans. This film that traced the interracial cultural mash-up of a newly divorced black carpet cleaner and the daughter of an Indian hotel owner wasn't well received. Spike Lee's *He Got Game*, where Denzel is paired in a love scene with Milla Jovovich, also underperformed at the box office. Like that turd of a film *The Mighty Quinn*, most of his fans have not seen it. White women respect his racial solidarity, and black women have come to expect it. This is the brand of true-blue blackness they want in their men.

Even while rejecting it wholesale, he maintains the veneer of being the whole package, and black women claim him, and demand that their men rise to that standard, much to their dismay. This would all be bad enough, but as it turns out Denzel Washington is the perfect specimen of man. Seriously.

According to a *Newsweek* article, beauty is a biological trait attributable to the way your nose, eyes, and mouth lay on your face. Something deep in our subconscious is inexplicably drawn in. That's why some people are found to be so profoundly attractive. As it happens, Denzel's face is faultless and symmetrical, and therefore almost universally beautiful. It's not bad enough that black women want black men to be perfect, but they want us to aspire to be like someone who is genetically predisposed to exude perfection. How can you compete with the Dizzle? Shit, what happened to the eighties, when it was easy—all you needed was a Jheri curl to get some pussy? Now, you have to be the Dizzle to get any holla. I know, I know: you probably think you do okay, pussy-wise. You're wrong.

Every black man has been confronted by the Denzel Principle, in one way or another.

Black women are looking at black actors, entertainers, sports heroes, and public figures as post-modern archetypes to measure the worthiness of prospective mates. The problem is while every black man on TV fits a PR-crafted, camera-ready image, every ordinary Moe will struggle to imitate that and inevitably fall short, leaving black women disappointed, angry, and bitter. Brothers run around trying to be hard but not too much, rich but earthy, handsome but not pretty, doting but not docile, polite but nondeferential, tough but vulnerable, political but not radical, passionate but not hysterical, ambitious but not overbearing, evil but not beyond redemption, well-read but not nerdy, streetwise but not thuggish-ruggish, thug certified but not criminal minded, accessible but not transparent, mannish but not macho, gentle but not feminine, black but not militant, conscious but not pedantic, intuitive but not overly philosophical, sexy but not solicitous, flirtatious but particular . . . all these things on cue and in proper measure.

Now.

This is the portrait of the Ideal Black Man—Mr. Right—and black women won't accept anything else. Even the Dizzle rejects the idea. He tires of being seen as the pin-up perfect leading man and sex symbol, as he recounts in an interview for *Essence* magazine. "You wouldn't believe some of the things women say they want to do to me," he says. "I tell them, 'You may not really want to do that, so you need to think about what you're saying.'" But the Dizzle is not about who Denzel is. It's about who black women *think* he is.

Sisters decry the shortage of good men and say there is no way they are settling for less than a good black man. Not just a good one, but the *best* one: the Dizzle. She, of course, has no idea what that means, what she wants, or what a good black man truly looks like. That doesn't stop sisters from looking. But they aren't looking hard enough. Or they are, as Eddie Murphy's "Buckwheat" once sang, wookin' p'nub in all the wrong places.

I remember how I got caught up in the Denzel Principle: it started at a young age.

When I was about ten years old I can remember my mother being very excited that a show called *St. Elsewhere* was adding a young black actor to the cast. It was a news item on black radio, and everyone seemed to be noting his handsome face and tacit sex appeal. None of that registered with me. What I saw was a brother with a gap-tooth overbite and a slow eye in a doctor's suit. He was good on the show. But I couldn't figure out what the big deal was.

Some years later, he got good notices from his turn in *A Soldier's Story*. I was fourteen and all about trying to convince my mom to take me to see *Beat Street* or *Breakin'*. But as an avid young reader of newspapers and magazines, it became very apparent to me that Denzel Washington's appeal was slowly picking up steam and crossing over into mainstream America. So much so that his name was spoken with reverence until people just stopped using his last name. He was just Denzel now. Still, I didn't put much on that. It was just that Hollywood star power, right? No, no. The years would pass and he'd do movies like *Mo' Betta Blues, Malcolm X,* and *The Pelican Brief,* and in the thorough darkness of the theater, I'd get up to go to the john and look up at a sea of female faces of every age and color. And they were riveted. Enraptured. Swooning. All of them.

After the movies, brothers would spend more time in the restroom mirror than usual grooming themselves, giving that Denzel look, asking themselves, *Do I got it? Do I got that Dizzle appeal?* Most brothers, but not me. I just took a leak, washed my hands, and left. Maybe I should have preened in the mirror a little while longer. It would have turned me into a punk but it might have saved my marriages. They both wanted to turn me into some-thing I wasn't.

When I got married, I retired my player's card twice, and with it my Hustler Vision, which would have allowed me to peep game from the curb. And as sisters are wont to do, each got me twisted up in her game: loudly punking me in public, beating me up in arguments, and using tears to manipulate me into compli-ance. If I loved her, she said, I would go along with all of this, because a better man would understand the pain of a black woman. A man like Denzel. I was trying to be a good man. But being a good man was not good enough.

Oscar-winning actor Denzel Washington has become the post-modern paradigm who personifies the perfect man, and any-thing less would be unacceptable. Actor Terrence Howard may not be too long behind him.

Howard has made a name for himself in the hip-hop opus *Hustle & Flow*, but before that he played the light-skinned punk brothers love to hate in movies like *Dead Presidents* and *The Play-ers Club*. Even though his acting chops seem kinda light, he gets a lot of screen time, and there is talk in the beauty salon that he's bringing light-skinned brothers back as an object of virility and male sexuality. "I work to pay the bills, not to listen to the hype," he is quoted as saying. "I've been the next big thing in this busi-ness for a few years. It's funny to me when I hear it now, because I know the way it works. I'm not confused." Thou dost protest . . . just like The Dizzle, methinks. So brothers better get their hair texturizer kits and green contact lenses on sale, before the rush. The Tizzle could soon have the women in a tizzy, and black men will have to play the game all over again. Of course, now that Barack Obama has been elected president of the United States, the Dizzle has been shifted a little, but not by much, and I'll tell you why.

Obama isn't the new Denzel, he's the anti-Dizzle: not conventionally handsome, his story isn't conventional, and he didn't become president of the United States in a conventional way. Sisters envy his wife, Michelle, but since he was a broke community activist early in the game with a hole on the passenger side of his car, chances are good, no matter where he was educated, not many sisters would have given Obama any holla, and to let her tell the tale, it took Michelle awhile to be reeled in. Obama was subjected to the Dizzle too: you can believe no matter how good his policies, if Obama had a "Becky," he'd still be living in Chicago.

Barack Obama managed to short-circuit the Dizzle in much the same way a lot of good men do. Obama is man enough to have his own dreams and aspirations and make his own way, and that's the kind of black man who becomes successful, but not always the kind of black man women find attractive. Typically, men like that find it hard to get a woman until they are actually successful—then, women line up to get on. Obama lucked out and got a woman who was down to ride along, no matter what. It took a woman like Michelle Robinson, who grew up with a father and knew the frailties and foibles of men, to hear Obama's dream, see inside the heart of the man, stand beside him, and make it happen. Obama was the product of a single mother, driven to succeed by the abandonment of his father, wedded to an ambitious woman from a nuclear family. No one could have written a story like his: with all his drive and ability, the truth is, he lucked out. Even so, he will never be good enough. We have set him up for failure. He will be called upon to heal all of America's wounds like the Magic

Negro of cinema infamy: held to an impossible standard, he will fall woefully short in the minds of those expecting him to be all things to all people.

Sadly, more than the new Denzel, Obama becomes a God of sorts, much too great and unlikely to be mirrored, but just human enough to be admired. Black women can't hunt for another Obama because the elements that made him into who he is today are so random and pedestrian. Obama may be the first black president ever elected, but he can only fail to meet the messianic expectations we've put on his shoulders. He will never be all we expect him to be. So he gets the Dizzle coming and going: God-damn America.

As popular and loved as they are, I wouldn't be Denzel Washington, Terrence Howard, or Barack Obama on a bet. They all seem to carry the weight with great aplomb and humility. For many, they represent all that black men have to offer, and it's a wonder they can even pee straight with a weight like that on their shoulders. They are everything every woman thinks she wants in a man. To find a man like Denzel Washington, women have to allow men to feel free to be themselves and not live up to impossible standards. Once men stop struggling to be something we are not, we will emerge better men. Good men. Worthy men.

Demonizing Black Machismo

Call me a romantic, but I'm not looking for Superwoman. You can't reasonably ask for more than a gainfully employed woman with all her own hair who knows her way around a nuttsack. If she can cook and keep a decent house? You've lucked out, you're living the high life: it's Miller Time, and drinks are on *you.* Men are simple, stupid creatures; women complicate everything. Instead of doing the smart thing and just looking for someone who will tolerate their idiosyncratic behavior, women are looking for a "real man" and if you can't handle that, maybe you aren't "man enough" for them. This, of course, is bullshit. Because they don't know what a real man is, and nine times out of ten, you don't either, and it becomes a sore spot as she tests you, and you assert yourself. She's trying to change you into somebody you aren't and could never be, and you're trying to toe society's line: be the man everyone else expects you to be, and that changes from year to year.

Women want to change the role of men in the house and no one gets asked to change more than black men. There is more ink spilled and talk in the ether about changing black men instead of accepting us the way we come. White folks, black folks, *The Washington Post*, and *Time* magazine either celebrate our victories, prophesize our demise, or formulate our evolution from the bowels of despair and everybody has their own ideas. Everyone has a vote about how to be a black man . . . except black men.

And the few black men who step up to be heard, like Bill Cosby, approach the subject like wizards from the sainted order of Jack and Jill and The Right Side of the Tracks. Then it comes out in the wash that people like Cosby—Dr. Dope 'n' Grope himself—are just as fucked up as Willie Numnum from off the block. Cosby and his ilk are paper tigers, pastime revolutionaries and armchair anthropologists who get their ideas about black people from cable television. Cosby's trying to tell you how to act, raise your kids, and get your mind right, but in the meantime there are questions about how he gets along with his own kids, taking paternity tests, and paying off a sexual assault accuser. We know Cosby doesn't know what he's talking about, because if he did he'd sit down and shut the fuck up, best intentions be damned. Cosby famously jumped off a lecture stage and confronted a wheelchair-bound detractor, which wasn't my first clue he was out of pocket. When you start snapping on people's mama and kids in the name of social re-engineering, Dr. Cosby, you've crossed a line. You need more people. It's easy and sexy ink to decry the evil of black men, no matter who you are. That's not what manhood is about. At least, not for me.

These days, it's tough just being a man without someone telling you how to be. One year, it's cool to be black and macho, the next year, Oprah is fitting black men for bras. All the arbiters, it seems, are women. I've made my own path as a man, but it hasn't been easy. As an adult I can admit I had some difficulty mapping out my manhood but as a kid, it was clear what kind of man I was going to be.

Back in the day, it wasn't uncommon for some kids to put pictures of Jimmie Walker, Rodney Allen Rippy, or Reggie Jackson on their walls. Those were their heroes, the men they wanted to grow up to be. My walls were bare. I didn't look up to those nobodies. There was no question who I'd grow up to be.

I'd grow up to be my dad. He was my hero, and that's the way it should be.

My dad was a workingman, up at the crack of dawn for his gig at Bobbie Brooks, a seventies-era garment maker based in Cleveland. He hopped up, shit, shaved and showered, ate breakfast, and cleaned the plate in the sink. Left his wife and son at home with a kiss, hopped in his four-door Matador, and handled his business with no complaints. Quitting time, he never came home empty-handed—always had a bit of candy or a box of Cracker Jack for his son, and a hug and a kiss for his wife.

My father was a mountain of a man—a tall, thin man who walked with his chin parallel to the ground, eyes straight ahead, moving with great authority and steps so sure and imperceptible, he floated. Blow-out Afro, gray leather jacket with gray loafer-kicks and apple hat to match, he was genuine badass: he didn't need a gun or a gang—this, back when it was still cool to be a man. He demanded respect. He never spoke to anyone first and never said "Excuse me" to make his way by—the sidewalks split when he walked his way, collecting nods. He was a man all his own. He was a square with a hustler's mentality, a player who hadn't turned in all his cards: true to the game. He traveled light, but I was the lucky one.

In the summertime, it wasn't unusual for me and my dad to

go riding the streets of East Cleveland like we owned them. Everywhere he was, I was tagging behind, echoing his cocksure and unforgiving swagger, much to my mother's dismay. She loved my father, but didn't cotton to his ways. I didn't get that: my dad was the same guy she married. No point in trying to change a tiger's stripes. Not a tiger like my dad. To be fair, my father was not a conventional dad, but he taught me the lessons I'd need to know in an unconventional world.

He let me drive and take a sip of beer on rare occasions, and I can still remember him hustling guys for money on the basketball court while I sat and watched: I could smell the sweat, hear the cuss words bouncing and the Chucks squeaking off the floor. A job was one thing. But everything was about the hustle: the passion for the dollar to feed the passion for life. This struck me as the fuel for his engine, his dominant ethos and prime objective: to live life with passion and honor. Own your footsteps. Be all things to everyone, and a man, most of all.

This lesson stuck with me. So fuck Reggie Jackson, Batman, Superman, and the whole Justice League. Dad was my superhero. And I was his son and trusted apprentice in the Game.

We can argue about how appropriate it may have been, but it wasn't irregular to see me everywhere with him: the pool hall, corner bar, his girlfriend's house. R-rated movies, with titties swinging everywhere. Dad didn't shield me from much. Yeah, I know. I glossed over the whole "girlfriend" thing. It's true: he was a good dad, a great provider, but fidelity wasn't his strong suit. He liked the ladies and he lacked discretion. I learned the importance of doing your dirt and keeping your house right. Sometimes we'd pull into an unfamiliar driveway, get out, and end up in a plush, foreign apartment. And I'd pretend to watch

TV as he talked that talk to strange and beautiful women, and he looked at me and winked: it was our secret. Just a confidence between men. He respected me like that. This is not the kind of secret a boy should keep or a man-child should learn, but the hard fact is that I was going to learn it sooner or later. Better from my father than the streets, right?

It's important to note that while I idolize and romanticize my father, I don't try to make out like he was a *Cosby* father or husband, although, from what we know now about the good doctor, perhaps he was. My dad's was a listless soul, wild for women and the nightlife. It was hard for one home to contain him. I was a kid, and I didn't care about the rest of his life, as long as when he was ready to ride, he scooped me up. We made a helluva team: the two bulls. Fuck Cosby. I was "Lil Steve" and the streets called him "G-Man." But he was just Dad to me. Not just my father, but the man I would grow up to be. But not in every way.

So when, after a day of the bulls running particularly hard and reckless, we sat down in front of Sammy Davis Jr. on *The Tonight Show* with my favorite cookies and a hot dog and he told me he was leaving, leaving, small wonder the world stopped spinning and I couldn't hear anything but my heartbeat and the sound of his voice, telling me not to cry, that it wasn't my fault. That he and Mommy just couldn't live together, and he might be back one day. Or he might not. And he stood, to hold me, and I held onto his legs as if my life depended on it. "Please," I said. "Please. I'll be good. I promise. I promise. I promise."

My mother made it home just at this moment. "Don't let Daddy go!" I said. "I'll be good!" I was crying hard and loudly. She blinked her tears away and went into their bedroom and closed the door.

My father picked up a shopping bag full of clothes sitting by the door, looked down at me. "Shhh," he said, and I went quiet. Quiet. He bent down to hold me close, held me, pulled back, and looked me straight in the eyes.

"You're the man of the house now," he said. With that, he was gone.

I stood in the doorway, trying hard not to cry, not to scream, not to feel a thing. Because I had to get up in the morning and find a job. I had to buy myself a car. I had to be about my hustle. My mom was in the bedroom sobbing, and she didn't need a little boy. She needed a man, and to be a man like my father, I had some work to do. Seems unfair to ask a six-year-old to step up like that, but he did ask, with the same confidence he did everything else, and damned if I would be the one to disappoint him. If he was bold enough to ask me, I was bold enough to be that. I guess. Overnight, I became the only man-child on my side of the block without a dad. It was a hard way to grow up. Him acting this way, I shouldn't have been surprised my parents divorced. But I couldn't know that my father wasn't right. All I knew was that he was Dad, the head of our family, and in our home, everything was right. You never really know how your people get along, about who did what to whom. There are two sides to every story, and that includes stories about divorce. As strong as he was, I wish my father had been a better man. But he was the best man he knew how to be. And it sadly just wasn't enough. And now, it was up to me.

Being a man at six years old is difficult when you've lost the pathfinder and you have no footprints to follow. And it was rough going, not completely unrelated to the fact that I was raised by a single mother, and women don't know how to raise a man. Not by themselves.

My mother was grooming me to be her friend, not to be a man. She wanted to teach me how to dance, how to sew, how to cook. These were things I would need to know, but they shouldn't be the rudimentary lessons of a young man. Sorry. I don't think what she was doing was intentional and I'm not knocking my moms, it just is what it is. She did the best she could. But as a rule, a woman can't make a man. Not by herself—it will take an army of uncles and grandfathers to shape his character. It's easy to teach a young man to be a gentleman—he needs his mother for that bit of polish. But young black men grow into a world that examines them critically and suspiciously, and women don't have any idea how to prepare a young man to meet that challenge. They deal with something different, equally as troubling, which is why young black girls need their mothers. When you're young, black, and male, you really have to stand tall at an early age and account for yourself in ways others don't. Not because you want to, but because the world puts you to a decision: either you take the world on your terms, or the world takes you on. Neither way is acceptable, but there are only two choices. Every young black man has to figure out which way to go, and choosing isn't always a peaceful process. I never got in any trouble worth recounting, but I made some choices that I should not have made, that I probably would not have made if my dad were around to show me the way.

My mother discouraged me from looking up to my father, and I never understood it. I imagine it was because he was the way that he was with women and the streets: she didn't want me to grow up to be a womanizer, a street nigga. She'd diss him openly, but it didn't matter. I knew what kind of man I wanted to be, exactly how much of my dad I should become. I think what happened between my parents prepared me for a world where rings and vows don't mean anything to anyone—male or female—and to get my head around the idea that if I am going to love a woman, any woman, unless she has wings on her back, she is as human and fallible as anyone, and to know early on that what we have could sustain something as (relatively) petty as infidelity. And vice versa. Maybe unlike my father, I also sincerely wanted the opportunity to be faithful to the right woman, whatever that meant. I was never angry with my father for his misbehavior, because I don't know for a fact what all broke my parents up. What I know is that my father's imperfection is what drew me into his shadow: I wanted to be a man like him, but I wanted to be a better man than he was. My mother would have no part of any of it.

As a kid, it was cool for me to be her best friend and tag-along: it was just she and I against the world. I helped out around the house, helped her get ready for work, gave her back massages. I consoled her when the loneliness bore in on her. "I'll never leave you," I said. We hand-danced in the living room and watched Mae West movies together. I gave her beauty advice, even. She dissuaded me from sports and more toward the creative arts. Nothing wrong with reading and writing, but roughhousing is an important part of growing into manhood. She tried to steer me from that. And me? Well, I'd had a few school-yard altercations, and I liked to fight. So much, that I thought maybe I'd be a boxer. Or a fireman. But I got in trouble when I fought, no matter if it was on principle or for sport. She rejected my father's input and discouraged me from looking up to him, instead presenting her father—my sweet, docile, pliant granddaddy—as a viable role model. Granddad—a jolly plug with an easy smile—was a lovely, wonderful man but he held the hem of my grandma's apron like a lifeline. An honorable, hardworking provider and loving father, Granddaddy was a great man, but he wasn't necessarily the kind of man I wanted to be.

When I hit my teens, something in me naturally rejected the role of my mother's girlfriend and valet. She even wanted me to model, and convinced me that I should. But that demeanor—what, with the pensive sexy poses and effeminate affect—wasn't a good fit for me, not that I necessarily knew what was. My dad, by virtue of some of his own fuck-ups (Mom's explanation) and the games that get played with children in these types of situations (his version) was not allowed to have me at his place, and he wasn't allowed to visit. Because my primary male role model was not in the house, I had to make it up as I went along, like a lot of young men of my generation. I looked to cues from pop culture to see what women admired: Prince, Rick James. The Bee Gees. Billy Dee Williams. None of them seemed particularly manly or masculine. Of those, Rick James was my choice and when my mother wasn't around, I took to wearing a suit jacket and bow tie with no shirt, à la Rick James on the cover of "Street Songs," much to the confusion of my peers. See, they mostly took their cues from each other or an older brother. I think one of the reasons my mother started attending the Kingdom Hall—church for Jehovah's Witnesses—was at least partially in an effort to establish a role model for me.

Elders (deacons, essentially) are supposed to be role models at the Kingdom Hall of Jehovah's Witnesses. It normally helps if you can connect with a role model on some level. But in my congregation, elders were these old-school cats who'd long ago pawned their player cards for Jehovah, wearing seventies-era double-knits, talking about Jesus this, Jesus that. They talked at me, not to me, and treated me like they were trying to exorcise free thought from my body and mind, and turn me into somebody devoid of blackness, maleness, or any individuality to speak of. I couldn't relate to these cats. They weren't men, as far as I was concerned. Not men like my father.

Growing up was hard on my relationship with my mom—I was noncompliant and hard to control. I had a lot of my father's moxie, but not a lot of his sense, to the point where I left to go live with my paternal grands when I was fifteen. My father had remarried years before, and wasn't financially able to take me in. Living with my father's people, it makes sense that my grandfather (whom I respectfully called "Buddy") became my central role model, for better or worse. I adopted much of his righteous fury and hubris, being a man on his own terms and no other. And that's who I am today. A man of my own making: all of my mom's sensitivities and charitable compassion, my dad's hustler instincts, and Buddy's immovable spirit. Yeah. I am that dude. I don't need anyone to tell me if I'm a man or not. I'm man enough, and that's all you need to know. But people have questioned my manhood, as people are wont to do. Like when I started working in a gay bar, for instance.

When I started deejaying in the early nineties, it wasn't just for love of the music. I wanted some kind of vocation that wasn't a lot like work and could get me a lot of pussy. Next to male modeling, deejaying is that kinda gig. It's like being a rock star, complete with groupies, but without the overhead. This was the age of the super deejays like Frankie Knuckles and Todd Terry, and I wanted to play records for anyone who was gonna pay me. I thought I would segue a career as a deejay into record production, and this would be my road to fame and fortune. It may have been, if I lived in a place like New York. But not in Cleveland. That didn't stop me from trying. I was caught post disco, post new wave, smack in the middle of house music and the new jack swing, and my eclectic taste made it tough to get a gig in Cleveland. Most of the bars were segregated by color and sexual preference. Me? I didn't care about how people got down in the bedroom.

The gig, by and large, was a lot of fun, but for a long time I stayed locked in my booth trying to stay away from the gay community, as if whatever they had was contagious. I didn't know how to communicate with these folks, and I didn't want to learn—what was the point? I was there to make money. Well, it occurred to me that that was a small, immature way to deal with the situation. I was a guest here, in their environment, on their turf, and being a deejay is a people business. I couldn't be a good deejay if I didn't know the people I was playing for. I had to grow up a little. So, as often as I could, I came down from the booth and introduced myself to patrons, took their requests, and got to know them. Over time, I got to know everyone by name, and found out that they were just regular people with the same problems as other people: outsiders, desperately trying to belong somewhere. This was their place, and these were their people. And I could dig it. Little by little, I got over my homophobia. I manned-up and realized I had an obligation to be a gracious guest. But it wasn't always easy.

The worst thing about working in a gay bar or being around other gay men is that there is some feeling, real or imagined, that they will try to recruit you. That's the biggest problem, because of the action itself and what it implies—that somehow, my masculinity may be lacking because you think I am, in fact, recruitable. It's an insult and a compliment most men aren't entirely sure how to deal with. The first instinct is violence, yes. I don't know why that is. But I never got violent: I had to learn to be gracious and creative. After all, I was working in their bar, so I guess in their minds, that made me fair game. But no means no means no.

Anton was a marvelous drag queen—as Deception, he could pass for Janet Jackson. We had become good friends, so imagine my surprise when he came up to the booth to make a request and grabbed my package on his way back out. Well, this put me in a weird spot, having to yoke a man dressed like a woman. But yoke I did into a naked choke hold and as he struggled I whispered gently into his ear: "If you and I are gonna stay friends, Anton, you are gonna have to keep your hands to yourself." And from that moment on, we had no more problems. He was clear on the depth of our relationship. He was man enough to dress up in drag and be who he wanted to be, and I was man enough to affirm his right to do so—as long as it didn't impede on my rights to my personal space. And that's the delicate balance. Sometimes it seems as if the gay community wants straight folks to affirm and cosign them in an interactive way. That's not a fair expectation. I affirm my gay friends, but I don't have to be complicit. I think there needs to be more bridge building between blacks—gays and straight—so politicians can't divide black folks over the issue of sexuality like in the 2004 election. Me? I'll go to the weddings, buy gifts, deejay the reception. But I won't be in the wedding, and neither will my kids. That's not homophobic. It's hard enough getting any pussy being black and male, facing all kinds of accusations, without being mistaken for a homosexual. Accusing black men of being gay has become the last, best way to insult them: gay men are "funny" because, certainly in pop culture, they aren't taken seriously. By attacking black men—who struggle to be taken seriously—in the one place they are universally respected, valued, and empowered in a way that can't be proved or disproved, you neuter their psyche and rob them of their essence and dignity.

While I was deejay at Numbers, I got on well with the community and I flouted convention and challenged conventional ideas. I mean, would you catch Denzel Washington spinning records in a gay bar? Not bloody likely. I was the token straight guy, and I was alright with that. I don't pretend to understand human sexuality, and frankly that isn't my concern. But I learned a lot about manhood working in a gay bar—naw, naw, not like *that*. It takes real chutzpah to live your life out loud, the way you want, and be fearless in the face of criticism and violent resistance. The gay friends I made—men and women—were more man than many of my straight friends. They are man enough to *be*, and man enough to *let me be*, and that's how we got along.

So, naturally, in a move to assert my manhood, I wear a sarong from time to time.

Let me explain.

When I was in high school and becoming image conscious, I asked my father if it was true that clothes make the man. "You're a man on two feet," he said, disgusted, rolling his eyes a bit. "Man makes the man." Back then I wore WilliWear, by black designer WilliSmith—I had an eye for style, I guess. Twenty-odd years later, fashion sheep will be loyal to any tag with a name on it, but I am still the urban style iconoclast. During the summer, I'm known to rock a sarong now and again.

It was the fall–winter-ish of 2000 when I first thought seriously about sporting a wrap. I was going to see soul-singer D'Angelo and I wanted to sport a different look. See, just like in your town, dudes be wearing any type of Sunday suit hookups or Technicolor ensemble to the spot, and I had to separate myself from the suckers. Besides, I'm ashamed to say that at the time, I didn't own a decent suit. Of course a sarong seems like a logical alternative to consider.

I wore it to the concert and caught snickers from the derby and doo-rag crowd. None of them had heart enough to say anything stupid—after all, I'm kind of a big guy. I saw one of my dudes at the spot and he ran up to me, mouth agape. "That is just the phatest shit," he said. "I wish I was man enough to play a wrap—are the sisters checkin' for it?" Were they ever. My then-girl really dug the look on me, and so did everybody else's girl—all eyes and heavy sighs whenever I passed by. Afterward I retired the wrap, just breaking it out occasionally. But I vowed I would find a way to play that style every day.

So, flash forward a summer or two, and, I decided I was gonna wear wraps in place of shorts—shorts make my boys sweaty and give me heat rash—and with the heat in the nineties on the regular, this seemed like the time to set it off. So most days you'd find me on the streets of Cleveland, downtown no less, in a skirt. To be honest, there was little to no reaction in my hometown—nobody even blinked. I don't know if it's because I'm a somewhat well-known writer there, and people assume anybody who writes for a living must be crazy anyway. Or maybe between the two feet of hair and the floor-length sarong, their circuits are just completely overloaded. Whatever the reason, I walk the streets unmolested, save for the women who stop midstride and fall out of car windows trying to check my steez.

"You are the sexiest thing I have seen today," said somebody else's woman, staring a hole through the front of my gray-and-black wrap.

"How would you know?" I responded. "It's still early." What can I say? Chicks dug the skirt.

I even wore it to work. Dat's right—and I worked for the white man, just like you. I worked at the global headquarters of the United Church of Christ, and there was nothing in the dress code that says I couldn't wear a sarong to work. The first time, there were second looks and a strange inquiry. ("What do you have up under your skirt?" asked one of my female coworkers. My response? "How badly do you want to know?") But my bosses are mellow—they accept my wrap as an extension of my Afrocentricity, and that bodes well for their progressive thinking and commitment to diversity. I'm a long time from that gig, and I doubt if you'd catch me at a day job with a sarong on, but not only because of their dress code.

See, the wrap has come to symbolize my refusal to be reconstructed by whatever people's assumptions are. It's the ultimate assertion of manhood for me: it speaks to my roots, my warrior status, my fearless nature in a way that fake dashikis don't. I mean, it's like there's an "S" on my chest or something. I have never felt more masculine, not ever, than when I don the wrap. Why? Well, maybe because it is so not a question of sexual preference or identity. I don't have any gay friends with balls enough to wear a sarong. Besides, it's unisex, stupid—if all it takes to make you question your sexual identity is a garment, you've got some issues, RuPaul.

See, the thing about wearing a sarong is that, as a man, you have to have a certain confidence, a certain arrogance. You must be absolutely secure in your manhood—flat out—or it won't come off well. You'll look like a man in a skirt: clumsy, misplaced, and utterly ridiculous. In a wrap, whatever wherewithal you have as a man is up for scrutiny: you've created an artificial vulnerability that requires strength to secure. Plainly speaking, a man in a sarong projects an audacity and demands a respect that khakis don't. Fact is, you might not be man enough to pull it off. This isn't a fashion guide, but you know what? If you think you're ready, I got a few tips for you.

Finding a wrap is more than a notion—it's not like Laura Ashley makes a men's skirt line. The trick for me was to find something masculine—a tough skirt, if you will. I couldn't find what I was looking for at first, and the cultural shops in my town wanted too much bread for some of the stuff they had. So I improvised: I went to my local head shop and got a few of those groovy, thin cotton throw-rug joints for twenty clams each.

Choose earth tones when picking out a wrap. Browns, blacks, greens, burnt oranges, and yellows are preferable—bright colors denote femininity. Only traditional or tribal patterns—no tie-dyes or flowers, Nancy. Wear fitted T-shirts or short-sleeved shirts on top: let them guns blaze. Footwear is player's choice—blunted toes for winter and sandals for the summertime look best. If you're hot like that, take a bold leap and play a three-button jacket with an open flare-collar shirt. Mudcloth is an okay material for winter, but roll with a light to heavy cotton in the hotter months. Wear linen pants up under in the wintertime; in the summer, anything goes. I'm pretty sure this style won't catch on, but maybe it should. Dad was right: clothes don't make the man. A man can stand on two feet—sarong and all. It was my way of challenging the status quo. This was my very public way of putting the shoe on Denzel, metaphorically—because he might kick my ass otherwise. Wearing a sarong sometimes is me showing the world I am my own man.

I hate the constant discourse about black manhood. Too many people make a living discussing, arbitrating, and moderating it. One cat, in particular, rubs me wrong. His name is Kevin Powell. Never heard of him? Sure you have.

Kevin Powell was the first in a series of what would come to be known as the Angry Black Guys of reality television. His stint on MTV's *The Real World: New York* is legendary, as he alienates everyone onscreen with his brooding anger and angry brooding. I think his appearance resonated with MTV's audience because he was a portrait of the new black nationalist that appeared shortly after the L.A. Riots: a well-read, half-educated, and unfocused bus-pass revolutionary with a lot of talk but not enough people. He got people when the show was over, as he captured a zeitgeist in the minds of some, and was subsequently hired to write at *Vibe*. After he stomped out of there in an angry fit sometime in 1996, he began a college lecture tour on—what else?—The State of Black Manhood.

I found it troubling that he would pick this subject because I don't think anyone under the age of fifty—including me—is qualified to speak about manhood, in an abstract. You can talk about what manhood means to you, how you live your life as a man. But you can't pretend to lay out the paradigm as some kind of expert. I also reject the notion of some people—friends and colleagues even like Mark Anthony Neal, who wrote *New Black Man*—trying to recalibrate it. Most disturbing is you rarely see any books rapping about white men, or white manhood. It's all about changing black men, and changing black manhood, which presumes there was something wrong with it in the first place. I think a man can make his money any way he chooses, but I tell you what: anytime you get up on stage purporting to know enough about manhood to discuss it with authority, you're gonna need more people. Dr. Michael Eric Dyson has Kevin's back, but still—more people, dog. And I'm gonna tell you why.

Now would be a good time to mention that Kevin wrote an article in *Essence* magazine where he details his physical abuse of women. It took a real man to write that joint, to stand up and make that admission. I can give that freely. He even wrote an interesting follow-up essay in *Ebony* magazine, where he calls on all men to speak out against domestic violence. But, it feels to me that he's used his psychosis as a kind of vulgar credential or pickup line, like, "Yeah, I used to beat up chicks, can I buy you a drink?" Aside from his stint on *The Real World* and in *Vibe* magazine, woman-beating has become part and parcel of his whole rap. I think any man who beats on women should be shot and killed. Seriously. Women are a gift from God, so I can't rightly forgive him for that. I saw my father hit my mother once, and we don't talk about it, because I haven't forgiven him. The problem for me isn't the mea culpa, more like, that it's nothing to pimp on: being a former woman beater is not the hustle to be going from town to town lecturing about. That said, it's hard to knock a guy coming out so hard against D.V.—we need more black male voices in that dialogue to facilitate a truce and lead a healing dialogue. He's right that more men need to be out front talking about domestic violence, but I'm just not sure he's the guy. The problem is it seems as if Kevin has multiple hustles going on at any given time: he's a writer, a lecturer, an activist, an aspiring politician, a hip-hop historian, some sort of vanguard in the movement to recalibrate manhood, and a domestic violence counselor. He was even hocking a mix CD at one point, to raise funds for his campaign. While his credentials for punkdom are flush and well documented, his qualifications to discuss manhood in anything but an abstract are madd light. If Kevin would focus on one thing— like domestic violence—he could really be a force for change. As much I would like to believe in him, it all reads like The Hustle of the Week.

If you beat on women and haven't been put in jail, then count your blessings, sit down, and shut the fuck up. Write a dissertation and explore the psychosis. But I just get the impression that his cathartic diatribes about manhood and being a reformed misogynist are all part of a self-serving, Keith Sweat–type hustle, and I ain't down with that.

When Powell was in Cleveland working with the Rock and Roll Hall of Fame and Museum during their hip-hop exhibit, after he gave a lecture, I heard him take questions afterward and invite a young lady back to his hotel room, supposedly to continue "building." What the fuck are you building at a hotel—you gonna put the tables together and make a clubhouse or have serious conversation? I wasn't mad at his swagger, but I wished he'd just call it what it is. I felt like his invitation was grossly inappropriate, like he was pimpin'. It was as if his lecture wasn't about the message of hip-hop or the history of it. Like, it was all about this moment he chose to hit on this chick from the stage. Stories came back to me unsolicited about Dude trying to pick up other dudes' girlfriends while they stood right there, watching. He spent a good deal of his time onstage talking about manhood in hip-hop culture, and I was kinda like, what the fuck is this guy talking about? Exactly what kind of manhood is he on? That's not the kind of man I'm trying to be, nor the kind of man who can build a nation. But you know what? You take people how they come, and as I watched him ascend and build his brand into kind of an Al Sharpton–lite affect, I never held any serious ill will against him. We just have two vastly different worldviews. In his world, he's some authority on black manhood. In my world, I say "get the fuck outta here with that shit."

Years later, he ends up in a Page Six item biting some guy on the ankle. I blogged about it, and just aired it out: here is Kevin, up to the same old shit again. Next thing you know I get an e-mail from the man himself: call me up, Jimi. And I do. And we have it out, man. Man talk. I'm not down for the hype, but he tried to put me in his shoes, this incident he would describe to me as an effort to protect his lady-friend. All of this strikes me strange because, me, I'm thinking about the least manly thing you can do in this life is get caught biting some guy on the ankle. It's not the kind of man I am.

I live my life with a lot of confidence and authority, but that hasn't always been the case. Young in the game, I was kind of a nerd: withdrawn and shy, because those were the type of men women were attracted to. After my first marriage, I just snapped out of it. I'd bent over backward to be the kind of man that she, her mom, her mom's friend, and all the church gossips would like, and we still ended up divorced, and I still got the stink end of the stick. When you're a man, people presume when you get a divorce, it's obviously something you did or didn't do. You didn't meet expectations, some kind of way. After we divorced Frances bad-mouthed me and Cleveland is such a small place that it doesn't take much for word like that to get around. I didn't know exactly what her beef was, or why she felt it was necessary to tell tales. She was telling people she thought she had an apology coming of some sorts. I did the best I could to stay above the fray, until it became clear there was some kind of black male apology movement afoot, as evidenced by an assignment to review a video making the rounds at the time called *Sister, I'm Sorry.*

Sister was a docudrama starring a lot of pretty-boy black actors like Blair Underwood, Tommy Ford, and Michael Beach reciting bad Keith Sweat poetry, intercut with teary testimonials where one by one, women sit in front of a camera to tell about how badly some black man has done them wrong. The idea was to guilt black men into genuflecting—perpetual apology—and start a movement that would catch fire and go from coast to coast, kinda like lace-front wigs or the Electric Slide, ostensibly in the name of healing black women. *Sister* was an emotional carjacking that used mass-hypnosis and browbeating to bully black men into some manner of artificial contrition.

The finale featured the Rev. Donald Bell sermonizing in a packed church, reaching out his hand to ask the men assembled to personally apologize to every woman present for . . . just being men, I guess. Amid all the testimony and waterworks, the men are dutiful and penitent. Afterward, they look spent and confused as they take their seats, as if to say, "I'm glad that shit is over." The Right Rev then invites any woman not satisfied with her apology to stand up and get another. Naturally, every woman in the place stands up, and the men lurch forth again to grovel, with the preacher in the back preaching, "It's Daddy Time!" What the fuck is that shit?

My thing was that some of those women had been real victims of real trauma, and it was heartbreaking. Others? Not so much. Like the one teary-eyed sister who talked about "the charmer" who broke a late-night "no ejaculation" contract in midstroke, leaving her high, dry, and nine-months fat. The Rev never got to issues of bad judgment or personal accountability with these women: everything was a black man's fault. It emboldened women to feel entitled to an apology from black men—any and every black man—regardless of whether they had one coming or not. Casting black men as bad, apologetic little boys on one hand and as some kind of "daddy" on the other creates a pathology that is emasculating and unnatural. I've apologized to the women I've wronged. Like, both of them. And I stood with 999,999 other men during the Million Man March day of atonement and made amends in front of God, country, and CNN. I've been used, abused, and refused but I haven't gotten a card, flowers, or a sympathetic plate of food from the ladies, and I don't expect to. Who the fuck am I, John Coffey, here to absorb the sins of black men and fix the white man's kidney stones? No sir. Sister, I'm sorry . . . only one apology per customer.

I don't need anyone telling me what makes me a man. There are too many cooks in that kitchen as it is. The conversation about black maleness, for me, tracks back to feminism, when men and women were re-imagining their roles. The Pill gave women a freedom they didn't have before, and with the advent of the sexual revolution, there was conversation around that seemed to suggest it was time for everybody to throw out all the rules and start over. The problem with feminism is that it was largely conceived to make women equal to men, but black men were struggling just to be seen as men.

The women's rights movement piggybacked right on civil rights, and women had their props, but the black men weren't part of the equation. The call for women to mobilize independently presupposes that your community can still thrive when married people are cleaved and alienated from one another in the name of popular mores, without once considering how a dogma like that could further damage and marginalize poor people and people of color, already at war with the system. Feminism gave men an excuse to opt out and gave women an excuse to kick them if they were too much man, or not enough, whichever way the wind blows on any given day. This is where the movement started, and that's largely where it remains: feminism mandated that women kick their good-for-nothing men to the curb and raise their children by themselves and created a generation of black men with more questions than answers. Am I man enough? Who's the man? Who's the paradigm? Who knows?

I know.

I'm my own man. I know about the lines, about where they are and when to cross them. About what's important to me, about wearing my worldview with pride and without apology. This is who I am, and I am always evolving. I will change, as all things do, but on my terms, by rules that fit my liking. I'm not afraid to be myself, and that kind of freedom intimidates some people. Freedom, yes. I don't feel beholden to the opinion of others, and being a man of my own making is liberating. But it's not easy being me.

When you stand up while others live on their knees, it makes you a target, and I've caught my share of knocks. When I was in high school, I wore my favorite pair of fashionably holey jeans and a teacher had me suspended for sexually harassing her, because if you strained your neck a lil' bit, you could probably see my junk. When I got to be an adult, at my first magazine gig the boss told me the other staffers were scared to critique my work, for fear I would beat them up. A woman once complained to management because she thought I was looking at her too hard. Some would look upon my black maleness and my unabashed determination to be recognized as something to be feared and reviled. The independent black man is suspicious, but the independent woman? Well, she's another story. I don't have a problem with the people talking about black manhood, so much as their conclusions. Black men are dangerous, and black women should free themselves from us by any means necessary.

Now, I want an educated woman too, but just because a sister has graduated from college doesn't necessarily recommend her as a mate.

Often, I've found that these sisters spend a lot of time and money acquiring degrees and simultaneously adopt the "independent woman," quasi-feminist ideal that has no practical value for black women at all. Being independent is one thing, but even liberated women should know how important it is to get a man and keep him, if you are intent on having a family. Women nowadays want kids, but they don't want a man, thinking they can do it right by themselves. They are wrong.

I've dated a few feminists, so I can say this without fear: feminism holds no practical value whatsoever. Black feminism equals frustration plus aggression minus family values, accountability, and common sense, divided by economics. Feminism isn't a philosophy based on any family values. It's an "-ism" designed to pull men and women apart: it just gives black women another reason to feel entitled to browbeat black men for not being good enough. Feminism clouds judgment with slogans and common sense ideology. I mean, you treat all people with a modicum of respect and this includes women, right? If women meet a man who won't respect them they shouldn't try to change him—they should move on and let that simple motherfucker live his life: easy. A lot of "black feminist" sisters say they can't find a man. Odd, that. What they really mean is that they can't find a man who's willing to get punked.

Feminism killed the black family, and left a space to create a mythology of the Denzel Principle: the strong black man who will work, play, fuck, cook, clean, paint toenails, *and leave*, on cue. Black women want men more like their girlfriends: semi-tough, just masculine enough to take the garbage out. It's become unfashionable to be too much of man, so black women make sport of capturing and neutering any man who exhibits masculine qualities, discarding him once he becomes too soft, and summarily declare a "shortage." I think all the real men are living in underground cities where only the women with sense can find us. I just bought a backhoe; I'm digging my way down there right now, where me and other real men can wait. All signs suggest it could be a long, lonely wait, because sisters are looking for Mr. Right in all the wrong places.

The Denzel Principle props up the fantasy of the perfect man, but doesn't allow men to realize their inner Denzel—their own unabashed manhood. When women allow men to be men and not boys or women, they will get the man they have always dreamed of: A man who loves them genuinely, passionately, and completely.

The Exhale Years

My first wife said she'd leave me if I wrote anything bad about author Terry McMillan's movies. I did. And she did. Why was she so invested in McMillan's story? She had the Dizzle.

McMillan filed for divorce from Jonathan Plummer, her husband of six years, some time ago. McMillan famously documented the magic of their whirlwind love affair in her novel *How Stella Got Her Groove Back* and a subsequent film in 1998. McMillan was a woman in love, and wanted the world to know about it. She wasn't just smitten, she was bitten, emboldened, aglow, a-flitter, a-flutter, gloating about her prize: a man. Not just a man. Not a run-of-the-mill black American. *The man.* She found herself a prize— a man she could own in the last place she would expect to find him: Jamaica. For a minute, it looked as if she'd become a travel agent and organized sex cruises down there. She became a one-woman travel brochure, and her sojourn became a big part of her promotional book tour, as she tried her damndest to convince legions of women to troll the islands of Jamaica looking for a younger man to pop that pussy. Go to the island and hunt down the Lil Prince Charming of the Caribbean, she said.

This, you see, would be the ideal arrangement: the exotic, beautiful yard boy, hypnotized and beguiled by the worldly ways of an American dick-troll, would agree to be flown from his savage environs to the wilds of the States, where he would become the pliant, diminutive arm piece and woo you all night with the genteel motion of his Nuttsack Voodoo. Like her Jon Jon. T'yeah, well this kind of presumption can only ever go wrong—it's karma, right? Karma gets to your intentions, and whenever you intend to keep or cage another human being for your amusement, you are asking for trouble. Nothing good will come of that. Pictures of them out on the town showed her all aglow, handcuffed to her man . . . but we'd all be looking, like . . . hmmmm . . . Jon Plummer? Something ain't right with that boy. You know you were like that. Don't front.

Not surprisingly, a few years down the road, it became apparent that all was not well in McMillan land, when an astonishing revelation came to light: McMillan's groove thang liked to get his groove on with *other men*, and she was the last to know. A nation of black women, packing their best bikinis, high-heeled sneakers, and Victoria's Secret, clutched their pearls, and travel agents everywhere were deflated. It was the end of an era.

Yeah. That's a shame.

Divorce hurts, but I can't feel sorry for McMillan. Not even a little. She knew he was gay, man. Hell, Stevie Wonder could see that boy was gay. Aside from that, her novel and subsequent film ushered in the Exhale Years, some of the hardest times for American black men in the history of this country. Maybe. Certainly, as it involves finding a wife and/or getting some. You see, all that energy she spent churning ill will toward black men came back to find her in a way she hadn't expected. Truth to tell, she got off cheap.

The Exhale Years started in 1995, when *Waiting to Exhale*, the big-screen adaptation of her well-received book, hit theaters everywhere. During this time, black film was experiencing a resurgence of sorts, and audiences were hungry for more. Director Spike Lee had challenged commonly held notions about black female sexuality in his film *She's Gotta Have It* a couple of years earlier, but films that colored outside the lines were few and far between. Lee's films dared to expand the black film palette while John Singleton's coming-of-age drama, *Boyz n the Hood* satiated the need for gritty urban fare and initiated a new kind of message film, but there weren't films that explored the relationships between black men and women the way Lee touched on. *She's Gotta Have It*, with its sex-positive portrayal of a promiscuous professional black woman wasn't one that could be easily embraced by black women. Lee was adept at capturing the dichotomy and modernity of Nola Darling's balance of the blithe indifference to conventional mores governing the behavior of "good girls" with a seemingly overpowering, conflicted need to be loved. Tracy Camilla Johns gave a riveting performance. Still, this was the reimagining of black female empowerment from a man's perspective. Lee's writing is surprising in its complexity and ability to nuance inner conflict. There was room where the film could have been all about the men, but Lee avoids this pitfall. In the end this was a film about sex, not romance. It answered some questions about female sexuality, but left a huge gap in the conversation about whether black men and women could learn to love each other on mutually agreeable terms. Could a black man love a woman independently of society's conventions and let her enjoy freedom in a shameless, nameless way? *Exhale* tried to answer those questions, and it did fill that gap for some. In the meantime, black men were waiting for a film with characters that looked more like them. Black men wanted a film that treated them as emotionally complex people as well, I think.

Now, I've often said that cinema isn't a reliable public relations vehicle and should not be depended on to cure society's ills or change its perceptions. But I've also said that cinema is the way a lot of people integrate their circle, and the way white folks know blacks best. I tire of watching black actors play absentee dads, disposable sidekicks, rapists, or unlikely, magical beings. *Baby Boy, Lethal Weapon, Just Cause*, and *Eve's Bayou* come to mind. Seen this way, black men longing for a three-dimensional portrayal on film isn't so unreasonable, if only in the interest of widening the dramatic palette. It's not that all the film roles have to be redemptive, but it would be nice to see black characters that weren't always the abusers (*The Color Purple*), womanizers (*Boomerang*), and no-goodniks (*New Jack City*) that fill the roles of modern cinema. With Forest Whitaker in the director's chair, there was some hope. Instead, *Exhale* was populated by male characters drawn from every negative stereotype ever projected on black men. I think Forest went out of his way to give the film a realistic, unvarnished depiction of the battle of the sexes in the black community. Mission accomplished.

McMillan, a former journalist turned author (imagine that) is no screenwriter. Her scenes are crammed with the worst stock characters of minstrel shows and romance fiction waxing poetic in reams of inauthentic dialogue to give the script an illusion of buoyancy and momentum: to make the story feel as if there is something happening, when there is, in fact, nothing happening. All the female characters sit high atop a dichotomous, entitled faux morality that excuses—and even encourages—bad behavior, in a world where they are victims and completely unaccountable. Everything is someone else's fault, having nothing to do with bad motivations or hastily made choices. In this world, every black man and white person is an enemy, but every sister is a true-blue comrade in the struggle for truth, justice, and a steady fuck. The story begins and ends in the same place: four desperate women, alone on New Year's Eve. They are all different parts of the worst in themselves and seem unwilling to grow beyond that. It's like *Sex and the City*, just blacker and bitter, with a big girl added to the mix. The characters don't grow or evolve in any measurable way, but we learn a bit about them in the between time.

Bernie's (the main character) douchebag husband John—who vaguely resembles Billy Dee Williams with a smart haircut—leaves her on New Year's Eve—for a white woman! He is rich and successful, and clearly cares little for the welfare of his children, because he left their mother—for a white woman! According to Bernie, her husband isn't man enough or black enough to be a good role model for his kids, therefore she put limits on when and how he can see his children. And if he takes her around the white woman, boy, will there be hell to pay. We don't know what she has done or what role she plays in the downfall of her marriage. We only know she is a victim to be pitied and her husband is a sociopath, a point she makes while unloading his closet into a BMW and setting it all ablaze in front of her home. She later cuts her hair and has affairs with married men. But once she has sued John—repped by a sista-girl lawyer, no less—for half of his assets, all is forgiven. Finally, she can exhale. T'yeah.

Her friend Robin is involved with Russell, the smiling cock-smith who woos her with promises of leaving his wife. She's aborted one of his babies, but hopes he'll leave his wife so they can have lots more. She also keeps Troy, a drunk with some apparent drug issues that she's trying to rehab, on standby. Never mind that everyone knows you can't redo a dope fiend. In between, she beds Michael, a chubby coworker who is just happy to have sex with a woman. He's got a fat paycheck and teary, pathetic desperation for her affection that makes her moist. "What do you want from a man?" he asks her in the breathless afterglow of the world's shortest love scene. "Everything," she replies thoughtfully. He nods affirmatively as he winds up for round two, and his silent IOU suddenly makes the sex oh-so-much better, once he agrees to suit up for a trick bag. Truth to tell, her men are a parade of tricks and micro-pimps with nary a backbone betwixt them, and she's virtually unmarriable: a hoe-bag to end all hoe-bags who can't figure out why no man wants to take her as his wife. Obviously, it's them, not her.

Oh, the humanity.

Gloria, the porky homegirl with her own hair salon, has an asshole son named Tarik she is fighting in an attempt to keep him under her thumb. She catches dude getting head—from a white girl!—and threatens to send him off to live with his newly outed father David, gaunt, wearing a thirsty-looking drugstore Jheri curl, who apparently had been on the DL since the disco years. Truth to tell, he could only look gayer in drag. Dejected, Gloria's aching for some dick—any dick—so she seduces the single guy across the street with a plate of food as he confides while looking at her ample rumpage: "I like a girl with meat on her bones." Right. She'd snap him like a Slim Jim.

Savannah, the woman who describes herself as "single, desperate, with no morals"—surprise!—just wants a good lay. She hops in the sack with Lionel, a broke pretty boy weed-head with no income and fake vegetarian ways who—strangely—uses her toothbrush. Her heart really belongs to Kenneth (DIZZLE ALERT), a tall, dark, handsome brother in the medical profession . . . who is the epitome of everything right about black men . . . except for the fact that he is cheating on his wife and daughter. Clutch the pearls.

Every male character is useless—except for Joseph, the gay hairdresser fully engulfed in flames, and James, the brother caring for his sick wife—a white woman! Even as sex objects, all the male characters are earnest but inept. The women suffer through these motherfuckers making animal sounds—GRRR!—wearing here-I-cum faces two minutes in, as the ladies lay there confused and helpless: a woman's work is never done. You know, when a black man can't even use his dick right, he's of no use at all.

These women are victims whose only empowerment is their right—nay, duty—to blame all their problems on black men—and white women! They derive pleasure and affirmation from sleeping with married men, hunting and bedding lesser men, and wondering why no "good man" will have them until they finally decide that—you know what? As much as they want a man, they don't need a man. Deep sigh, The End. Oh yeah, did I mention that white women, along with the lazy, good-for-nothing black man, catch an "L" in this film? Seems like I should.

The film was the impetus of the Exhale Years, and it was a rough time for brothers: if you had ever dated a white woman or been unemployed or didn't spend more than half an hour eating pussy, you were indicted on sight. Before you could say "hello." Unless you were a milquetoast or insanely rich, you had a hard time getting any pussy at all. All sisters wanted to do was exhale. *Exhale* seemed to start a new black women's movement of its own, separate from the conventions of feminism, one that was personified at the 1997 Million Woman March in Philly, which I attended. I went as a reporter and—I can admit it—it seemed like it might be a good place to pick up chicks. Boy, did I get that one wrong.

It was more like a lesbian recruiting rally than any call to the spirit resembling the Million Man March. Speakers railed against men, all things masculine, and the traditional family, encouraging the crowd of angry women to kick their men out of the house, hire a sitter, go to college, and run for Congress. Noted adultress Winnie Mandela gave the keynote speech, but don't ask anyone who was there what it was about. Because even though organizers encouraged women not to spend any money in Philly as a show of economic solidarity, marchers fanned out through Philly and besieged every mall, boutique, wig shop, haberdashery, and chocolatier for miles, much to the delight of Philadelphia officials. The negative, anti-male energy was palpable: if there had been a chance any of them would have put down their shopping bags, I was sure I'd be killed. Thank God for Godiva.

What I took away from that event was a T-shirt, a few phone numbers, and an impression of how hard it is to be compassionate to someone who nags you about your failings as well as their own. They seemingly bear no culpability for their own shortcomings. I mean, hell, I want to be a better man as long as it doesn't involve my unquestioned genuflection and repentance for the sins of all men, for all times since Adam. That's bullshit. Black women hold their men responsible for all the world's ills, whether it was their fault or not, causing them to be combative and adversarial. No men on earth are scrutinized and judged like black men. By everyone. This thesis seemed to crystalize during this period. Black women authors and voodoo gurus rose up to profit from the Exhale Years, thinking it was time to fix you and your man, and for them to make a profit. Iyanla Vanzant was one of them.

Vanzant created a following based largely upon her appearances on radio and television, most notably on *The Oprah Winfrey Show*. She traded her job as a lawyer for a more lucrative position as an oracle of wisdom, penning a number of books, establishing the Inner Visions Spiritual Life Maintenance Center and Bookstore in Silver Spring, Maryland, and producing a CD, *In the Meantime*. The "meantime," as she explains on her CD and in her book of the same title, is the time spent between relationships in your life: the intermission between setting your goal and realizing it.

This, of course, is some bootleg, New Age bullshit. I have never heard of anything so ridiculous.

You'd think at some point, the public would tire of being Oprah-fied to death, captivated by the myth of "mammy," the all-knowing, all-loving, all-cooking heavy-bosomed negress sage. Since the days of *Gone with the Wind*, seems like people are always seeking out the counsel of overweight black women, as if they know something special, or those boobs give them some kind of mystical, magical knowledge. You'd think that, in this day and age, people would have grown past that. You'd think that, but you'd be wrong.

At the front end of the Exhale Years, Vanzant had a "girlfriend chat" in Cleveland as a preamble to her *In the Meantime* tour. I wanted to see Vanzant and hey, I can admit it: I wanted to hear what girlfriends chat about. It piqued my journalistic curiosity. I should have known better, but I was a hungry freelance writer in Cleveland trying to brand a byline: *hard but fair, down for whatever*. I was stupid. I didn't see the danger of stepping into a roomful of angry, dejected black women, and it probably would not have mattered if I did. I live for this shit. So I made my way out.

The meet and greet was being held in the grand room of an upper-tier restaurant downtown, and I hopped in line and waited for the doors to open. There were a lot of women in line—many with fully groomed facial hair—and they stank of the stench of all bitter women: cheap, drugstore perfume. After they sized me up, some of them sneered. I stood my place in line like a soldier. When I finally reached the door and tried to enter the venue, I was promptly pulled aside by a P.R. flack from an agency overseeing public relations and marketing details for the tour. Working the light-skinned independent woman look, she was a cutie.

"I'm sorry, sir," she said. "This event is for the ladies."

Well, after I presented some makeshift press credentials, she changed her tune a bit. She looked impressed, as well she should. Didn't she know who I was? I had, like, three clips, two with *no typos at all*. She better recognize.

"Wait here," she said with a girlish grin. "I have something for you." Obviously, she got the message, right? I hate having to pull my balls out for inspection, but you know like I know sometimes, that's what it takes to get your props. She peeped my steez, then realized she was out of pocket. And I waited patiently, thinking she'd return with a plate of appetizers from the buffet table, a drink, or a perhaps a promotional T-shirt. Instead, she escorted me to a special VIP seat—in the back of the hall. Not just the back row, but the table farthest from the stage, where the help was folding napkins. I was so close to the kitchen, I damn near needed an apron. 'Twas a good spread, but I could only smell it from where I was seated as the women sucked it up.

Where's my drink? Where's my T-shirt? Where the fuck is my shrimp? Something in the mix, I said to myself, has gone awry.

"The talk has got a little heated in other cities," the flack explained, "and we wouldn't want you to get hurt, would we?" What d'fuck? Again, with the not knowing who I was.

But I took a look around the room, and for the first time in a long time . . . I was scared, man. Think about it: the only thing worse than an angry black woman is 250 angry black women locked into a room with only one exit. Talking about everything that pisses them off—and there you are, the lone black man. That's a recipe for an ass-kicking, and I was shook. But in case of an estrogen riot, I had a Baby Ruth in my breast pocket, and you know like I do that the crowd was filled with the usual suspects— desperate fat chicks guzzling three diet sodas at a time, eating fudge-dipped ladyfingers by the handfuls. So if things got hairy, I'd lob the chocolate into the crowd and escape in the ensuing melee. Nothing like the impending wrath of the black woman to bring out the MacGyver in a brother.

"Ain't nobody gon' hurt me, guh," I said, as I slumped into my seat. She told me I was the first man ever allowed to witness a "girlfriend chat." And it's true—except for the help—all men, serving refreshments—I was the only one there. But this isn't to say men didn't try to get in. Girlfriend chats, ladies' nights, and lingerie parties will almost always attract a brother looking to benefit from having a lot of single, bitter/drunk/horny women in one place. The problem is you can never know which emotion will be dominant. But if you're a man, it seems like even the off-chance that you might happen upon some pussy is always worth a shot.

Brothers came trouping up to the door ready for admission, but were handily rebuffed by the flack and the crowd. You've never seen anything quite like it, I promise. They'd swagger up to the doorway to be met with a corps of would-be bulldykes physically twisting them around and pushing them back out. They formed a phalanx Leonides would envy. Somehow, a man did manage to sneak through the gauntlet, an athletic-looking brother in attendance with his white wife. He walked with a pimp's gait, eye on his wife's butt. After a buzz rose up from the gathering, my man got gaffled and pushed toward the door in a rush, face screwed up, mumbling profanities. His wife was encouraged to stay and she did, sheepishly. But her man was two-times wrong, let one sister tell it: "Agitate the gravel, O. J."

When the chat began, I was anticipating Vanzant's arrival and it seemed everyone else was too. What they got was a flunkie rolling out a TV/VCR combo presenting Iyanla, in all her ethereal wisdom and beauty—on tape—inviting her girlfriends to talk amongst themselves, purchase copies of her publications, and buy $40 tickets to her *In the Meantime* tour. After hours waiting in line, this invitation was not immediately well-received. "I could see Luther and all the Isley Brothers for that kinda money," one woman commented. Damn right. This sister would later be at the head of the line to buy tickets for herself and all of her church group.

The "chat," led by said flunkie, consisted of self-improvement rhetoric between admonitions to do as Iyanla teaches and "trust the process." There was lot of bullshit talk about this "process." Thankfully, men and relationships were mentioned only in passing and then there were normal expletives and profanities— "lazy, no-good, muthafuckin' niggas!"—but no violence. They began discussing ways to find and keep a "good man."

Now.

Ask me why a room of 250 women with only two and a half men between them would turn to each other for dating advice, and I'd draw a blank. I'm all for flouting conventional thinking, but that idea is just plain fucking stupid. Two heads are better than one, only if one of the heads knows what the fuck it is talking about: if the other head is in a different (read: better) bag. When it comes to these hen sessions, black women are often their own worst enemies. But I guess word around the candy shop is Vanzant has all the answers, 'cause she can keep a man—her third time at the altar—and sisters wanted to know how, as tickets for this event sold out quickly. I sat, listened, and snuck out of the venue as soon as I could. Before leaving, I secured my premium seats for the *In the Meantime* event later in the week, where she was actually going to show up—in person. Not that I had any longing to see *her*, but the spectacle of it? Yeah . . . this I had to see.

The following Tuesday, I sat in the second row of Cleveland's sold-out Palace Theater. The crowd consisted mainly of black women, with a smattering of couples and white women throughout. The lobby was occupied by an Oldsmobile information booth on one side and an *In the Meantime* merchandise booth on the other, both with long lines for buying T-shirts, incense, and other useless bullshit. The lights flickered and this meant it was showtime.

The nearly four-hour extravaganza consisted of Vanzant's monologues and music drawn almost completely from her *In the Meantime* CD. Vanzant and her band performed on a set that looked as though it was borrowed from Janet Jackson's last tour as she chanted "Trust the process, sistuhs!" and "Today is the time!" and other heady counsel you could probably glean from any bumper sticker. There was dramatic lighting, smoke and fog, interpretive dancers, and three costume changes to boot. Part brain-jacking, part liturgical break-dance demonstration, the crowd, inexplicably, ate it up. During a break in the vomitorium, she even encouraged impromptu testimonials from the audience. Against the odds, a man stood up. He was too broke and ashy to be a plant. No, he read like a Clevelander.

Vanzant brought the older black gentleman—looking like the kind of old-school club rat who stops women going into and coming out of the washroom—up from the audience to bare his soul and take us into the innermost depths of his most personal struggles. Tearfully, in a suit he obviously borrowed from Cab Calloway, he spoke of his conflicted need to walk with God while coming to terms with his crack addiction.

A noble struggle indeed, best shared with his pastor or his God in the solitude and sanctity of a prayerful moment, but certainly not as a segue in a quasi-religious hootenanny . . . sponsored by a car company no less. It read fake, even if it was real. The event ended with a solo dance number by Iyanla, equal parts Fosse, Tina Turner, David Koresh, and Gator the Dancing Crack-fiend. People chanted her name in jubilation as Vanzant exited the stage. It was the only free thought she allowed the audience the entire evening.

How could this woman stand in front of anybody and purport to be some kind of spiritual leader? Oldsmobile using this gathering "in the name of the spirit" to prey on the professional black female demographic bordered on sacrilege. It reminded me a lot of malt liquor companies that sponsor black history calendars and black bourgeoisie social events. What a crock.

Years later, Vanzant got a TV show that received some of the worst ratings in television history for a talk show. She ended up on some "reality" show as the life coach/voice of reason, and that's about where she belongs: with the rest of the nuts clamoring for their fifteen minutes of fame. Recently divorced, clearly Vanzant doesn't have the answers, and never did. Vanzant used the Exhale Years to peddle horse sense and bootleg psychotherapy to black women already spiritually, emotionally, and economically fragile. She built a cottage industry telling people things they already know. True, some people don't have common sense—they smoked it up or something. Those folks ain't got no business watching Iyanla, buying $40 tickets, or listening to self-help CDs anyway. But during the Exhale Years, self-help crap was flying off the shelves, and sisters were rushing to see *How Stella Got Her Groove Back* for McMillan's tips on how to find the perfect man.

Yeah, well. Notsomuch. We see how McMillan crapped out.

Y'know, as I see it, the only way McMillan's fairy tale romance could have possibly ended was in divorce. That was the *best*-case scenario. The idea of vacationing in Jamaica and picking up a husband like a souvenir shot glass is ludicrous. Let's keep it gulley: she was past forty when she met him—why wasn't she a little smarter in the game than that? Because—if you ask me—she was horny, that's why. McMillan was a predator and an opportunist— he was broke and she took advantage of him. In Plummer, McMillan met a guy she could groom as a personal manservant. She didn't want a man—she wanted a girlfriend. A pet. McMillan filed a lawsuit claiming deception by fraud. Now, I don't know whether or not he knew he was gay going into the relationship (sexuality is complicated, but certainly his preference for man-on-man pornography merited a talk with the man in the mirror . . . who was probably jerking off) but I reject the idea that he targeted her because of her wealth and fame. Plummer couldn't know Terry McMillan from any other tourist booty bumping down the beaches of Jamaica: she's pretty average looking, except for the scary Grinch-that-Stole-Christmas face she's prone to make lately when talking about her divorce. Back in the day, she could've been anyone—how would he have recognized her? Dude doesn't look like the kind of guy who reads a lot of romance novels.

Oh snap!

As it turns out, that's exactly the kind of guy he is.

To the extent there is such a thing, my gaydar isn't flawless—I've tried to pick up women only to find out that they were lesbians. At least, they told me they were. But all those days ago, when I saw those early press pictures of McMillan and Plummer together on the red carpet, I said to my then-wife: "Dude looks a little light in the loafers."

Yeah, I know—Bad Jimi.

But Plummer looked like the third-place winner in a Hairdresser of the Year contest. Not that there is anything wrong with hairdressing—but dude definitely looked gay: slightly built, slightly effeminate, slightly too well-dressed and groomed. The kind of guy who probably does a mean updo but can't take out the trash without breaking a nail. Not that there's anything wrong with that. Taking out the trash is overrated.

Now, I hate to go here, but Plummer asked McMillan to set him up with a dog grooming business to keep him busy, and I gotta say this offers something of a clue. Most men are talking about getting a pit bull farm going to train them for fighting and breed them for sale. That's the kind of dumb hustles real men think up. What kind of man wants to be set up in a dog grooming business? The kind who doesn't like women.

Now, I'm a writer, and I get accused of all kinds of faggotry, so I know—it isn't fair to judge a man by the job he takes, because there isn't really a "gay vocation" of any sort. But some shit is definitely gay-ish. "Dog groomer" is right up there on the list with "bathhouse attendant" as suspect. Look, your man doesn't have to be a blacksmith or run a strip bar, but c'mon. He wants to be a dog groomer? Let's be serious. According to reports, Plummer and McMillan had restraining orders against each other, and she ran around calling him all kinds of faggots and sissies. It'll be interesting to see what kind of cross talk her flamethrowing will provoke in the black gay community.

Which brings to mind another thing: the "Down Low."

The term "down low" is shorthand. It used to mean any relationship you had that people didn't know about, like, for instance, the fact that your wife is fucking the pastor is (mostly) on the down low, but as a result of the media predilection to pathologize the behavior of black men, it's become the buzz term for the alleged phenomenon of "straight" men sleeping with other men in secret. Of course, this has been going on since Ham fantasized about his father Noah in Genesis (yeah, I know) and Roman soldiers went out on those long missions . . . alone. But now that the media thinks they have discovered a curious new negro trend—like break-dancing, for instance—we have to stop the presses, as if scientists have isolated a new black flu or sickle cell—an unstoppable pandemic decimating African American nightclubs, poetry readings, and barbecues from coast to coast. I never bought it. Not because men don't sleep with other men on the side—I guess they do. But I don't think it's a behavior any more or less common in the black community than any other.

JL King, author of *On the Down Low*, when in town for a book signing, is also hosting a "women only" conversation at a Cleveland nightclub, as a stop on his *Love on a Two-Way Street* Tour, not entirely unrelated to the fact that he has a novel of the same name being released soon, and a DVD to follow. His flier trumpets this as a "must-attend workshop for single women, married women, and mothers with daughters." I skip the signing and make plans to attend the "conversation," as I'm curious about what women think they can learn about their men from a bisexual man. It reads to me as rather counterintuitive. Granted I'm just one person, and a skeptic to boot. I'm sure the masses disagree.

About ten minutes before the event, the nightclub where the event is being held is empty, except for a few people milling about. Tammy, a slight, brown woman sits at the bar, marking time. She's here helping a friend who is setting up, doesn't even know about what's going down. When she finds out who and what is going on, she's circumspect. "I used to be cool with this guy who was gay, know what I'm saying? And he used to talk to me as if he was a woman, but he really wasn't a woman . . . and from being a man, he already had the point of view of a man, and can relate to what I'm going through with my man because he's just a man, who wants to be a woman. I can relate to what he's going through and he can relate to what I'm going through." I can see from the stoic look on her face that she's not kidding. The idea of gay guys lending advice to straight women makes a lot of sense, she says. "After all, a gay man and a woman are always going to have something in common." Gay or bisexual men, she adds, may give better relationship advice to women than a biological man.

"How is that possible?" Robert, a plump young brother who resembles a black Chef Boyardee, says as he sets up the catering.

"Anything, anything, *anything* that's done in confusion is not going to help anyone—you gotta know which way you're going first, you can't go this way today, and this way tomorrow. You not focused." He sits behind his setup of vegetarian fare, flummoxed. "So, how you gonna sit up and focus on a group of ladies that's already hurting because they been mistreated . . . you gonna come up here with your confusion and try to tell them something?" He shrugs. "I don't see it." His friend Mike sees it differently.

"I think it's possible," he says. "Who's to say a man can't give a woman advice on another man, because each individual is different. You can only ever give your perspective, as far as what you've dealt with, when giving advice—I don't know that sexuality comes into play. I don't know if it's good or bad—it's open to interpretation." He sits back as we all look toward the front door: no patrons yet. "Personally speaking? I think it's a racket. All of a sudden you come up with a term, 'down low' and it becomes a cottage industry?" He rolls his eyes and snickers. "To me, that's a racket." He has a healthy bit of cynicism, wouldn't you say?

Hillary is also here working—volunteering to work the door and manage the expected crowd of women hungry for knowledge. Like most of the people I'll talk to, she hasn't read the book. She's willing to give him the benefit of the doubt, but thinks the "DL" alarm could all be a scam to sell books. I ask her why we don't hear more about women on the down low. "Society accepts that a lot more—it's the truth," she says with a grin. "If I hug this woman, nobody would even bat an eye. Females expect something different from men. Besides, the idea of black men on the DL is a bigger moneymaker." How's that?

"I'm gonna be honest," she says. "In the black community,

homosexuality is more taboo. Being that it is a taboo, and when the light is drawn to the situation, it draws more of an audience." She doesn't need anyone to tell her how to deal with her man or tell if he's gay—she says she's very intuitive about men and women on the down low. Her girlfriend—a delicious dark-skinned dom dressed in black leather—concurs.

King tells me he loves women and men equally, and he sounds sincere enough. He says that while he acknowledges his role as Mr. Down Low, he hasn't fanned the flames of this invented pandemic for fun and profit. He gets four or five marriage proposals on the road from women who would just be happy to know what their husband is up to, even if that means he is up in another man. He says bisexual is the new black, with a lot of famous black women getting involved with gay men just for some stability and companionship. He takes me to task when I make him to be a gay guy who just dabbles in pussy, saying that God not only ordained him to spread the gospel of bisexual men, but he endowed him with a magnificent stroke. "I'm so good in bed," he says, "I could probably outfuck YOU."

OK.

Let's say this first: he's a nice enough guy, but it's difficult to believe that his wife ever thought he was straight. Like, ever. King oozes deception from the bottom of his faux reptile shoes to this impossible suit he wears when we meet: navy blue with plum stripes, and a leaf-green shirt. He's flamboyant, in an effeminate way—his brand of garish fashion faux pas is the kind you only see on street pimps or drag queens, the kind of people whose stock in trade, essentially, is to sell lies. King doesn't identify as gay, and won't be identified as gay—just a man who's knows what he likes—which is pretty much everybody.

"I didn't write a book about men that cheat on women with other men," he starts, as we sit down before he is to meet with his horde of curious fans. "I just told my story, and people took my story and related it to their story and stories they knew. There are many men out there that could have told the same story. I just happen to be the one God chose to tell my story, and it took off from there." He's right—the book is deeply introspective. Still, unsophisticated readers, like most of us, will read the use of statistics and the various scenarios he paints to infer illness upon the whole: black men are constantly being biopsied and diagnosed. It's not hard to see that his tome—complete with a nifty shorthand, just like mine!—could set off a panic about this largely mysterious breed we call the black American negro male. Color me unconvinced: I think that JL King cooked up his book knowing the fervor it would ignite, and he's been cashing checks from a nation of paranoid sisters ever since. The black man is like some mysterious, lazy, good-for-nothing Sasquatch only modern science—and JL King—can help us figure out. He rejects the notion that he's exploiting the down low phenomenon. He gets himself together, as the clock strikes the magic hour, and he's got a chance to tell hundreds of women exactly what's wrong with their man. "So, it's like whenever you have a conversation about that DL, my name comes up. It's kind of taken on a life of its own. I think it was wrong, but I can't control what people say and think. I can't control the media. I can only control what I do."

What he does is release a commercial for his DVD that is rigged to scare the bejesus out of women. Called "Top 10 Signs of "Down Low" Behavior and More . . ." it's supposed to be a PSA for women to be able to spot a closeted bisexual man on sight.

Part health-class propaganda, part B-movie horror, it is supposed to be a must-have purchase for black women everywhere to stave off the pandemic of black men lying about having sex with men. This, from the guy who would know, the self-proclaimed "relationship expert." Jesus Christ, it's a good hustle.

Heaven, a hot African bartender bursting out of her shirt and the back of her pants (!) doesn't need anyone to tell her if her guy is a closet fruit. If she's with a guy who decides he wants to stick it in her butt, Yahtzee! He's obviously got a problem, and probably having sex with men. "Look, an ass is an ass," she figures. "If you fuck a girl in the ass, you can fuck a guy as well." This, of course, doesn't jibe. What about cunnilingus? An animal will eat a pussy, properly motivated. "I don't like all that licky-licky," she confides. "Honestly. I prefer the full-grown *dick*." I make a note.

Now, I'm on record as an ass man and I've been known to stick The Business in a honey's hideaway from time to time, and I gotta tell you . . . that's HOT. Heaven sets me straight.

"When you a buttman, you do backshots," she says indignantly. "You don't be havin' to stick it in the *hole*." Well sometimes, I explain to her, you like to have your cake and eat it too. She rolls her eyes. "That ain't no muthafuckin' cake," she says.

Well. No, I guess it isn't.

Heaven doesn't need King to tell her how to spot a guy on the DL. She's got her own list.

Heaven's Five Ways to Tell if Your Man Is on the Down Low:

1. Too many guy friends—"What, is he fucking his homeboys?"

2. Likes anal—"I'm definitely going to stop the proceedings and ask him what his problem is."
3. Vain—"Like, if he's always in the mirror, lotioning up a little too much."
4. Criticizing another man—"Like, if he's a hater."
5. Prefers other activities over sex—"Like, if he would rather play Xbox than fuck."

I tell her that nothing on this list would be a reliable indicator: it's all fairly arbitrary. She admits that, unless she catches a man in the act, there's no way to tell if a man is bisexual. She's not sure if a bisexual man could offer her any relationship advice, and as it turns out, she's not in the minority. King's "conversation" ends up being more of a monologue, just him wrangling together the volunteers and two other people that wander in. They talk about men, music. Fashion and such. Stuff a gay (down low or whatever) man might actually know something about.

As far as I know, I don't have anybody in my crew on the down low: I don't want any phoney niggas down with me. All my gay guy-friends and chick buddies (none in my crew—sorry) are on the "up high," and it's the thing I respect about them the most. It's okay to lie to yourself, but not to people you care about. Best to be open about your sexuality to all parties involved, I say. I don't respect cats who can't come clear about how they get down—again, to the extent it's even relevant. Mostly, I've evolved past the point of giving a fuck, but informationally, it might be a nice note to have. Like, if I'm headed to the strip club and looking to posse up? Maybe I should count you "out." But when I'm clothes shopping? I dunno. Having one of my gay friends around could save me from a fashion embarrassment, like wearing spats over sneakers, for instance. By and large, I don't care how the next man gets down. If you are taking it up the tucchus, be a man about it, for Christ's sake. Don't fake the funk on my account.

In the meantime, bisexuality, irrespective of race, is not a new phenomenon. Some say that in the age of AIDS, screening brothers' sexuality has become more urgent. Maybe. But I'm not convinced that the increase of AIDS cases among black women reflects an increase in homosexual activity among black men so much as it suggests an increase in irresponsible sexual behavior by black women. Like *ladies going on vacation to pick up Jamaican cabana boys*, for instance.

That seems like a far more likely scenario than brothers walking around with their tongues out talking about "I jus' gotta get me some 'DL.'" Gimme a break. It feeds the idea that black men are always trying to victimize black women somehow. The easiest way to dismiss, besmirch, or insult a black man is by questioning his sexuality—something that cannot be proven or disproven with any degree of accuracy—because it puts that man in a spot where he has to prove himself. Always, ad infinitum. And if you are a woman and a man isn't attracted to you, it couldn't just be that *you* are too fat: it has to be that *he* is on the "low." Whatever. It doesn't seem like you need an excuse to accuse and abuse black men.

Black men of any age are presumed to be dangerous, inferior animals in need of reformation or incarceration. Black men have no advocates, no apologists (or really, really lame ones), just pathologists eager to dissect and diagnose them. I won't drink the Kool-Aid. I don't think we need apologists—they may be the problem, in fact. I think everyone has to be accountable. It's hard, but it's fair.

I have a problem with the double standard: as a race of people, we have to elevate the discourse from that of victimhood. We have to rise up as a community and figure out how to deal—not necessarily coddle—our problem children, regardless of their gender. We have to learn how to include our LGBTs in our conversations in constructive ways. We have to be willing to defend the honor of our men and our women.

Me? I think a lot of it begins and ends with the presumption that men are either useful or useless, and in need of reprogramming in either case. I am not anti-woman so much as pro-male, a stance we don't see often, or often enough. I've been branded a lot worst than misogynist. But the feminists among us can't embrace a faux sense of independence on one hand and cower as victims on the other. That isn't intellectually honest, as I see it. Empowerment comes with a set of boots, cape, cowl but no Kleenex, and no excuses. We are all victims of something. Let us move forward. And that includes my sisters. You can't have your cake and eat it too. But black women do.

And until black women come to terms with that—the fact black women need, really need black men, be they fathers, lovers, husbands, or brothers—we will always be offbeat. Our steps will never mesh. We will always have the higher divorce rates. You will always be raising children alone or with rotating men. Our communities will suffer. And Oprah will always have a job.

The bookshelves are overrun with crazy books vilifying black men—anything that emasculates, demonizes, and denigrates black men will become a best-seller. Black men are some kind of mystery monster, and people cash in on our backs by trying to tag and identify us as if we are some kind of wild species. I'm waiting for the book celebrating the rest of us: the hardworking, bone-straight brothers who can't find a decent black woman. Maybe

Terry McMillan will write one. But I suspect she is too busy chastising Plummer. She was looking for love and settled for sex: I don't know how she could blame anyone else but herself for that. But she continues to recriminate Plummer for being gay, and not asking herself how she fell for the okey-doke. I know how she fell for it: high on the Denzel Principle, she was convinced she could make herself a Denzel of her own. She was wrong, and all the women who bought her books and others like that should do themselves a favor and hold a book-burning party, or give them away to the homeless—people for whom companionship is no longer a priority. McMillan helped give the Dizzle credence. So maybe now that her fantasy has failed her, she'll write a book about the reality of finding a good—straight—black man.

Maybe.

But I won't hold my breath.

Pimpology

There are many definitions of the word "pimp," and most are fucking antiquated and imprecise. *Webster's New Twentieth Century Dictionary* cites it as both a noun and a verb, and traces the etymological origins of the term back to the French word *pimper* which means to "entice (especially by dressing smartly)." *The Oxford Dictionary of Slang* concurs. My favorite definition is certainly from Geneva Smitherman's *Black Talk*, which includes five different explanations of the word: a man who lives off the earnings of a prostitute, a man who lives off the favors of women, a man who has a lot of women. Verb: to exploit someone or something, to dominate one's competition in sports. It's thought that the word was first printed in English in 1605 in a book called *Your Five Gallants*, a Jacobean-era comedy about five ne'er-do-wells: a whoremonger, a pickpocket, a pawnbroker, a cheat, and a pimp. This might surprise you but brothers are all over William Shakespeare, though not so much Jacobean-era farce. So I don't know how the word got from the book to the bar stool, but I know the word has many meanings, all varied and contextual. For our purposes, these are the most popular ways the word turns up:

Pimp (*n*) The Man, the HNIC, The Boss, Ladies' Man. (*v*) e.g. to pimp: to adorn with fine clothes, electronics, or accessories. To upgrade or be upgraded. To use or to misuse. To manipulate or be manipulated. (*adj*) abnormal, idiomatic usage, highly irregular compounding with another adjective, i.e., pimp-tight, pimp-strong, pimp-hard.

These are the most common ways the word turns up in the streets. There are two types of pimping: vocational and situational. The difference is that vocational pimps are in the business of procuring women for the purposes of prostitution. That guy is a bastard. Situational pimps master the art of rhetoric to manipulate women and others to do their will. To some degree we're all pimps: husbands pimp wives to clean the house and watch the kids, wives pimp husbands to keep them living in a certain fashion, kids pimp parents to test their boundaries. Pimping keeps the world in motion. Like it or not.

In recent years, the mythology of the vocational pimp has come off the corner and into the American lexicon: the mythology has a certain kind of middle-American kitsch appeal. For something we know very little about—the history of pimps and pimping is apocryphal, at best—it gets brought up a lot. While there are reams of books and primers from Iceberg Slim's *Pimp* to Alfred "Bilbo" Gholson's *The Pimp's Bible* that offer different literary and brutal explanations of the nuts and bolts of the occupation of pimping, it's hard not to read it as bullshit. If you ask a pimp he may say that pimps aren't made, they are born to coerce, protect, and enable women into the underworld of prostitution. Said that way, it sounds almost like some bootleg Sir Walter Raleigh–type chivalry, and this offers some hints as to the pimp's appeal. Not so much the man as what we perceive to be his life-style, his demeanor, and his worldview: a maverick living by his own rules who owns all he surveys and does not give a fuck about the laws of God or man. Read any book about pimping—and I have read quite a few—and you'll learn that this is the essence of the pimp. He is a man of leisure without shame or much ambition beyond acquiring money and material wealth. He is not without motivation: he wants to master his domain, to be king of all he surveys: to own his footsteps. This is the pimp as noun, the guy you warn your daughters about, and the one some young men say they want to be. He is the last purveyor of righteous swagger in an age when men are still admonished to sit up straight and eat their veggies. You can bet pimps don't eat their fucking asparagus. Not unless they want to, Bitch.

Pimp, as verb, is the power to make people—but specifically women—do things that they may regret later. It's smooth talking, like when former president Bill Clinton got a blowjob from the intern, lied about it under oath, and kept his job and his wife. Now, if that isn't pimping, I don't know what is. There's probably an argument to be made that Clinton brought pimping back into vogue. I dunno.

What I do know is, yes, the pimp has always been around, and even if the names change, the game remains the same. Somewhere in the latter part of the twentieth century, pimping got a face-lift, so to speak. There are even Halloween costumes where your kid can dress like a pimp: feather boa, large-brimmed hat, high-heeled boots and all. So now your kid can choose: will he be Spider-Man, Superman . . . or Willie Dynamite? How did the pimp become a superhero?

Black men were not the first men to prostitute women, but

between our presumptions about the devilish ways of the under-educated black man and his oversexed women, the portrait of the pimp is always drawn with darker colors. Men like Hugh Hefner and Larry Flynt don't exude the same evil or menace, so it makes more sense to call them something like pornographers, a term that suggests they are fringe artists of the erotic instead of what they actually are: men who profit from the exploitation of women.

I want to be clear: that's not the kind of pimping I'm writing about. My mom is a woman, and my daughter will be a woman one day too, so I can't cosign that kind of behavior. I'm writing about pimpin' in the more colloquial sense, that is, as a science, two parts psychology and three parts rhetorical gift. It is the art of a rich palate, the sweet tongue that propagates promises, a lure with every lie, always finding a willing ear, a warm embrace, and a brand new place to make until morning breaks. I'm talking about the kind of pimping that got your mother's panties off.

Come on, don't front. Pimping is just game: mastery of the hustle, whatever the hustle may be. Sometimes, the hustle is love. Women know that better than most.

Sisters don't like the connotations of the word, yet they find themselves doin' the pimping more times than not. Women are writing books of poetry and prose about how to be better pimps. Women mask gorilla-pimp tactics in quasi-feminist bullshit so that brothers will feel less progressive if they don't go along with the hype: just put the bra on and shut the fuck up, nigga, like good a hoe's s'posed to. Let me put it down this way for you.

Men are instructed to do right by their women. From the womb, men are counseled by their single-parent mothers that a good, Christian, responsible man will dote on and defer to every need of his mate. It's the duty he inherited with his testicles, especially if there is no dad in the house. Someone has to be the man of the house, and the practical responsibilities that we attach to that role—like taking out the garbage for example—fall to the man-child. It's not an unreasonable request to ask a young man to step in and do things an older man would do if he was there. This makes young men feel special growing up, and moms appreciate the help.

Later, some women exploit this training by convincing men that responsibility equates to debt—you owe women a certain amount of servitude. And you don't stop serving until they tell you to. Some women believe that men need to cart them around in the fanciest cars, and owe them fancy nights out at the priciest restaurants wearing the most expensive jewelry their money could buy. Some men put aside their manhood and bend to the whims of their women, even if it means being subjected to abuse of every description. By virtue of manhood, brother, you have incurred debt. And because of your background as the product of a single-parent home, you hardly know the difference. This is as clear a brand of pimping if ever there was one. The "perpetual debt" hustle invented by them old street pimps who helped wayward women find their way back in the day has been innovated and passed on from mother to daughter and sister to sister. This is a hard hustle, a key part of pimpology. But there's more to the way some black women pimp on black men.

Conventional wisdom says that yes, brothers, we owe sisters something for those hundreds of years she supported her families and carried us on her back. Back during the time when black men allowed their women to be raped and killed, those decades of odd jobs, spousal abuse, and endless public and private humiliations for the "black nation" entitle her to an eternal ass kissing.

Me? I'm not buying it. Men have suffered twice as much, watching our women be taken and mated like animals, breaking their backs and spirits on our behalf, rendered helpless by the lynching noose, Jim Crow, and modern forms of hiring discrimination. His notion that black men were just shuffling around drinking moonshine, shooting dice, slack jawed, scratching our heads while black women donned the cape and cowl to save the world is ludicrous. Black women have had no franchise on pain and indignity and the suggestion that they have is offensive. I don't want a woman who can save the world—I'd settle for a woman who knew how to butter toast. I don't know the secret bar where all these superwomen hang out, because half the sisters spouting this New Age trash can barely cook or clean, much less have carried the burden of a nation. Beyond commiseration and compassion, nobody has anything coming. I don't know any brothers waiting on their women for a handout. But I know plenty of sisters trying to finagle rent, jewels, or a free meal from whomever will pay for it in exchange for some imaginary punani the man may never even smell, let alone penetrate. So who's pimping who? Looks like black women have mastered the psychological pimp hand, and trust me, that pimp hand is *strong*.

I've had sisters approach me with a laundry list of entitlement. Dinner is one thing, but I've been hit with shit you wouldn't believe. Sisters have tried to hit me up for credit card bills. Boob lifts. Bunion removal. Clit/navel/nipple piercings. Tattoos. Rolling papers. Tattoo removals. Tuition. Venture capital. Car note. House note. Moustache removal. Pest control. Bail. Car wash. Ammunition. Tampons. Baby food. Abortion (for kids that weren't mine). Attorney retainer. Car repair. Manolo Blahniks. Benihana. Weed. Parking tickets. Dry-cleaning. Ass implants. Gym membership.

Tarot card sessions. Military-strength douchebags. Weight-loss surgery. Bikini wax. Oil change. Cigarettes. Diaphragms. Strangely, when I inquired about my due I was met with strange, empty stares or the classic "WHUTchu TALKin' 'BOUT WILLIS?!" double take. Sometimes I'll get an angry blowjob but most times, not even that. Women I've met seemed well-versed on what they are "due" but are clueless about what it takes to get and maintain a man. And it's not all about sex.

Sexual conquest has become insignificant and irrelevant. Nowadays, brothers are looking for wife material. Some sisters want you to spend some bread to earn the illusive "free-ass pass" that gives you rights to her goodies. What the fuck is that? A woman whose devotion is predicated on material gain is certainly not wife material. She's a prostitute. I know—that's impolite to say out loud. Better to speak plainly, I say, than have you guess at the point I'm trying to make. It would be easy to call me a "misogynist," except that I don't hate women at all. I love them enough to call a spade a spade and tell the truth. If a man has to take you to dinner for you to consider having sex with him you are trading sex for money. It's prostitution. That's what it's called in the dictionary, but you can call it what you want. Thinking brothers know that material women are flighty and untrustworthy. They bounce from wallet to wallet, each benefactor bustin' that ass more than the last, trying to get his money's worth. She's having fun spending his money, and he's having fun using her as his personal spooge-catcher. No one loses, right?

Not exactly.

After years of this—many, many, many, men down the road— this woman will want to be someone's wife. She's been flown everywhere, copped all the diamonds, ate all the shrimp, and had all her bills paid so now she's ready to settle down and act like a lady. But the problem is women cannot run from their reputations. No, ma'am. Doesn't matter where you go, brothers know how you get down. And nobody is trying to wife a hoe. Sorry. Promiscuous women might change their ways, but the world keeps on spinning around them, and most often, men don't want a flagrant, loose woman on their arm, because it makes them look bad. People can't tell if you are her hubby or just the trick of the week, and it's humiliating. In a world where eligible men outnumber women, it doesn't make sense to gamble on a reformed pimptress. It's easier to shoot the dice and stay single. So of course, this sister will try to find a husband, only to have them turn her away time and time again. Next thing you know, you'll find this sister on *Oprah*, crying, or pouring her heart out to Iyanla Vanzant because she can't find a good man, never realizing that no "good man" wants a promiscuous woman whose favors can be bought with an Extra Value Meal. Sisters don't realize that comeuppance by virtue of a big butt and a smile is no come-up at all. None of this explains the newfound popularity of the Pimp. But take heart, ladies, because Iyanla can't keep a man, and Oprah can't seem to close the deal either. Not judging. Just saying. Sometimes, the player gets caught up by the game.

To really get a grasp on the new pimp appeal, you don't have to look any further than *Flavor of Love*, a show that ran on VH1 for a few years. Now, if you've never seen it, just close your eyes and imagine Stepin Fetchit in silk pajamas chasing Playboy Bunny rejects around the Playboy Mansion. How's that for a visual?

When I watched the show for the first time back in the day, I kept reaching to turn the channel, but I was drawn in by one nagging question: "Is this for real?" Could twenty ordinary women really be fighting each other, spitting on one another, and losing control of their bowels for a chance to be alone with a grown man who walks around with a clock around his neck screaming "Yeah Boyee!" All these years I've been walking around—clockless—with my hat turned the right way. Maybe I had it all wrong. I dunno. Why would any woman put herself in a stable for a forty-eight-year-old man in a Viking hat to choose from? And then it hit me: *Flavor of Love* is the product of the New Feminism. Women burned bras and changed their names to "Ms." so that the Flavorettes could choose to sell their souls for a shot at reality-show fame.

The women chosen as contestants say they sincerely wanted a chance to share a life with Flavor Flav. But they mostly turned out to be hoochies looking to parlay their screen time into a payday. They lined themselves up on the off chance that they might get pimped on national television. I think these young ladies saw how easy it was for Omarosa Stallworth to turn her stereotypical angry black woman schtick into a career and said to themselves, "Hey, I'm crazy too!" It's not ditchdigging, but it's honest work nonetheless. Reality shows have become the new hustle for female hustlers: an easy way for strippers and stripper wannabes to increase their marketability. Nothing wrong with that, per se.

But let's not forget that Flavor Flav started out life as a member of Public Enemy, that militant rap group espousing self-empowerment. I think *Flavor of Love* shows how easy it is to sell out and cash in by pimping on the aspirations of young ladies who will do anything to be famous. No one remembers Flavor Flav, the revolutionary; he has successfully scuttled that legacy and any relevance it may have had. Flavor Flav's been reduced to a caricature of Bobo the Sambo Pimp, an embarrassment to pimps and sambos everywhere. But we can go back even further to see how pimps went primetime.

When Bishop Don Juan appeared on Geraldo Rivera's talk show with diamond rings, alligator shoes, and a gold and green suit ("green for the money and gold for the honeys," he'll say, if asked), he brought a taboo into safe-space mainstream America, one they could feel free to embrace as a caricature, without fear. Bishop Don "Magic" Juan, the pimp-turned-clergyman, makes a good side-hustle acting as "spiritual advisor" to stars like Britney Spears and Snoop Dogg, who is considered to be something of a pimp (probably situational, as we know he is married) in his own right. The Bishop represents something missing from American manhood: he's equal parts showman, throwback, media spectacle . . . and American dream.

That's right.

Here was a guy living on the edge of society, flouting its rules and conventions in favor of life on the edge in black America's criminal underworld. Somewhere in the rubble of his life, he claimed to have found "the lawd" and started a church to serve other pimps, players, hustlers, and prostitutes looking for answers. Somewhere—probably between Geraldo and MTV—the limelight seems to have dimmed on his mission to save the sinful. But that didn't change the public's perception of him: he piques the interests as an American success story: a criminal reborn, defanged, reformed, and commodified. He sold out—nothing is more American than that.

His profile fit neatly into a colonial stereotype, and he was welcomed into the public space with open arms. Hell, if anyone could decode his street-corner patois, I bet he could have been a guest on *Hollywood Squares*. The good Bishop brought something that is, in reality, very secretive, insidious, and dangerous out from the shadows and into the lap of middle-American housewives. His sugar-sweet rhetorical rap was repackaged and changed the image of pimps as animals of opportunity and turned him into another revolving talk-show mess making the rounds and cashing in on the American fascination with all things dark and mysterious. Because let's face it: as far as narratives go, it doesn't get more dark or mysterious then being a black pimp in America.

This mystery lay at the base of pimp mythology and the science of pimpology: the mastery of carnal desires and the art of inequitable exchange. Spider-Man can throw webs from his hands, and Superman can leap over tall buildings in a single bound. A pimp can convince a woman to buy him a drink—how's *that* for superfly?

By looking at Bishop Don Juan, I don't mean to imply that this is a new development, or that America's fascination and conversation about pimping started with him—on the contrary, long before cinema immortalized and demonized him in films like *Willie Dynamite* and *The Mack*—the pimp has been a ghetto celebrity and folk hero. Kids wanted to grow up and be pimps—it was a street-grown vocation, a cottage industry that just required moxie, nerves of steel, and the quiet, cool ability to disconnect your conscience from the thing in all of us that can't be party to the suffering or exploitation of another human being. The high-minded, well-heeled among us can't relate to the plight of some in the business of prostitution or drug dealing. And you have to know, growing up, none of the pimps or prostitutes could either, no matter what they may say. Given options, no kid wants to be a part of that life. I've known (vocational) pimps and prostitutes, and talked with them at length. It's the kind of life that sucks you in before you know it. For some, it's about eating and feeding children. Others—the pimps, mainly—just want the American dream, and they see no other way to get it than to exploit the flesh of another.

The system failed them or they failed the system, and they didn't invest in education or the dream it can sometimes afford. But the School Of Hard Knocks gives out plenty of degrees in hustling. And hustling is more natural and makes more sense: in the end, it's the same thing everybody does every day. We are all just trying to survive in the worst of circumstances the best way we know how. Not to romanticize the plight of the pimp, but pimps are people not unlike the rest of us. If your list of options shrank to nothing, who knows what you'd do just so you could taste the dream. I've seen these men pimp out their wives and sisters with cold indifference. It's hard to know what kind of monster you'd become to survive. How does a monster become a role model and anti-hero? We forgive the monster and consider the man. We defang him: the image we've come to know of a jive-talking, lilt-walking, will-o-the-wisp in the age of mass media easily captures our imagination, like all good legends do. We don't think about what he does for money, because the truth is we don't exactly know. Or at least, we pretend like we don't. He's kinda become like Johnny Appleseed in platform shoes: someone we are reasonably sure existed, someone living their lives a little left of center without apology, and in our heart of hearts we wish we could emulate them. And when I say "we," I mean men.

The seventies were dominated by Peter Frampton, Adrian Zmed, the Bee Gees, the Solid Gold Dancers, and other men wearing perms and tight pants. The Village People replaced Charles

Bronson as the new portrait of the macho man. Of course, they couldn't really be taken seriously, and that was part of the problem: the world is an unforgiving place for men, specifically black men, who cannot be—above all else—taken seriously.

Like Dirty Harry, John Shaft, and Mike Hammer, I believe the pimp entered the zeitgeist through films as a natural push back to a wave of political correctness that sought to affirm and prop up the new women's movement and the burgeoning gay rights movement by devaluing traditional ideas about masculinity and removing what was seen as over-the-top masculine tropes and replacing them with more ambiguous role models and personalities for a new era imagined to be enlightened and progressive. I can't prove causation, but I suggest some correlation with the women's liberation movement. Because as divorce lost its stigma, rates of divorce skyrocketed and in a world where increasingly more men were being raised by women, there was a sudden turn when America became infected with a brand of pop-culture androgyny. In retrospect, it looks like a concerted effort to quash manhood as something not quite feminine but less than masculine. Men were disappearing from the landscape, and there was no longer any need for masculinity. Now, there was no more man of the house paying the cost to be the boss: any rights and privileges that had been previously associated with the roles of men or masculinity were out. Men, in many ways, had lost control of their own lives. Women no longer needed men. Enter the Pimp.

Looked at this way, it makes sense that killers, detectives, drug dealers, and pimps would populate and dominate the cinema in the seventies: there was a battle of the sexes, after all. Women were fighting for their rights and identity, and men were struggling to find their place within the new construct. There was a contingent of male America who felt besieged and put upon by what was clearly an attempt to regulate masculinity by celebrating sexual ambiguity. They needed a hero who could not be rebuilt or influenced by the ways of women. The Pimp is such a man. The pimp—noun—is a man in control of his passions who manipulates simple people into relationships based on inequitable exchange, where both parties are satisfied with their portion. Pimping—verb—is living life with the kind of confidence that emboldens you to use natural charisma or manufactured influence to control your life and the lives of those around you.

Early on, I was the kind of guy to pick flowers, buy chocolates, and send "Do you like me? Check yes or no" love notes and all that corny shit all boys do in elementary school. I understood my physical attraction to women, but had no idea how to create a union. I was a fool for puppy love and I went broke buying a lot of sweets, let me say, before I figured out I wasn't getting anything in return: they toyed with my affections and moved on quickly. Not like I was supposed to meet my soul mate in sixth-grade gym class, but trying to prove my affection, I got my heart broken a lot. I was pursuing women who had several men pursuing them, and I was just another trick in the rotation. The only way to neutralize it was to sling hard dick and bubble gum, but I was always short on bubble gum.

There's always some explicit entitlement on the table: not just layaway and credit card debt, but some kinda karmic duty I must pay, for the last guy that wronged 'em. And as it turns out, it's a long list, and it usually starts with Dad. So there I am, trying to make up for some girl's daddy. Impossible. *Right*. That's women, flipping the game. You owe something you can never repay, so they keep you trying to pay it. Like a gambling debt or a payday loan. And your manhood is contingent on your ability to step in and step up. Like, a *real man* would come in here and be a father to my eight kids while their eight daddys are in jail. And a *real man* would pay off my credit card debt so I can run it up again, and ruin his credit too. A *real man* would be the father I had. Well, a real man would run and hide from a trick bag like that, but see? If you opt out, then you're not a "real man." So they got you coming and going. That's a real trick bag for you. That's some serious pimping.

You also run into a lot of women who want to know how much money you make, in the name of judging whether or not you are a suitable mate. If you don't make long paper, or you're not driving a late-model car, you can forget it. She isn't really looking for a mate, because a mate is someone who makes you happy. She's looking for a meal ticket. Some of the true players of this game are our single mothers. It's tough to say, but ask around: brothers are getting broke off. Now a lot of people are reading this book, thinking, "Wow, jimi, you sure are hard on black women." Maybe. I think, like a lot of the women you see commiserating in *Essence* magazine, I am being true to my experience. I can't rightly say anything that applies to a whole race of women, but I can definitely tell you what my experience has been. These are my experiences, yes, but also the travails of a generation of young black men. The stuff I'm writing about? You could hear at any bar, barbershop, card game, strip joint, or any other place men come together to commiserate and talk shit. The truth of the matter is I'm hard, but I'm fair and I'm hard on everyone. The conversation about black men and black women has been largely a one-sided conversation. I'm just here to add balance.

But I digress.

There's a lot of talk, massaged by statistics, that there are so few eligible black men around—as in gainfully employed, college educated, and straight—that black women have no choice but to go find themselves a white boy. Things are so bad out there, that sisters just have to flip it up, because black men aren't earners, so naturally black women have to get themselves a white boy, who are more accessible now that the workplace is more diverse. I didn't buy that back in the eighties, when black men were saying something similar about dating white women—that the playing field had been expanded, and black women weren't good enough for the new successful black man—and I don't buy it here, on the other side. To be sure, economics should play into choosing a life mate, but if that is the primary consideration, you probably aren't looking for love: you're looking for an insurance policy. Or a pimp.

I'm on record: I don't have a big beef with interracial dating. I did it. I do it. My thing is, as long as you aren't fetishing your partner. As long as you aren't with them simply because they are the other. That's bad juju. What happened to the idea that love, in the raw, is colorless? Of course we know, that's bullshit. That film *Something New* should have been marketed as science fiction because there is no sister on earth who would marry the lawn boy prima facie, not knowing if he was the owner of the business or just pushing the mower. But too many sisters complaining about being single aren't looking for love: they are looking for a meal ticket. Someone to help them raise someone else's kids. Not to knock successful women or women with kids—because I got a few kids myself—but I think if you are gonna start and continue a conversation about da poor black woman who can't find a good black man without insulting everyone's intelligence, you have to have all the cards out, and be honest about what's happening. You have to look at who's pimping who.

The idea that brothers aren't making bank is ludicrous, I don't care what it says on paper. I can introduce you to six single cats in my crew, right now, who have made or currently make six figures—legally. The problem they run into is that they got too many women into their wallet and not enough trying to get into them. In my experience, white women don't behave that way. Not that the wallet isn't important, but "can you buy me a drink" is not the first question on the application. When women ask this question before they even say hello, are they looking for a mate, are they looking for love, or looking for money? Real pimp-ologists know the deal.

Pimps have become heroes because they are not controlled by women. They are the last unreconstructed men on earth, for good or bad. The fact that they cannot be controlled makes them enviable to most men.

Pimping is a science and an art form. Like boxing, it's subtle, almost genteel. Sure it catches a bad rap, but still and all, every-body pimps. Doctors, lawyers, politicians, and preachers. Every-one uses the art of rhetoric and the science of persuasion to create alliances, form business relationships, and engender compliance. And I think everyone plays the role of pimp, hoe, or trick—or all three at once—at some point. I don't recall when I first encoun-tered the Pimp. I'm from the ghetto, and despite what you've read, pimps aren't like mailmen, moving through the houses, drop-ping love and game at every door. It was a poor neighborhood, but there was no open prostitution or hoe strolls. No, I don't even recall when the word became part of my vocabulary, but I can vividly recall how I came to know what a "hoe" was.

My mom moved us to Shaker Heights when I was about nine or ten. Until then, I lived in East Cleveland and went to school at Chambers Elementary, a fire-engine-red brick school just a few blocks away. It was a good neighborhood school, as these things go, and this was back when you could still walk to school without getting shot. It was the tail of the Carter era. People were poor, but things were still good in the hood.

When I was in fourth grade, me and this dude I walked to school with came up with this scheme, whereby we stole money from our mothers, bought bags of popcorn from Lester's Convenience/Candy/Liquor Store for ten cents, and sold them to kids at school for fifteen cents. We dealt in other snacks and candy at a similar markup, but popcorn was the thing that moved for us. We would turn around and eat the profits in candy or just walk to school with that unmistakable jingle of money making music in our pockets all day. The truth is, kids could have bought it themselves on the way to school, if they wanted to. But they didn't. And in school, as the day wore on, they became like dope fiends, feenin' for those Now and Laters, Boston Baked Beans, Lemonheads, or that buttery popcorn goodness. And then, they came to see us. Me and my manz ran the playground: we had that shit for cheap. This is how I learned to be always living with an eye to maximize opportunity for monetary gain, as long as no one gets hurt. In the streets, they call that "hustling." In college Econ, they call that "capitalism."

One day after particularly brisk sales, my dude came at me with a long face: he was broke. But how could that be? We should have cleared about six dollars apiece. "I spent it up in kisses," he said. I looked at him with a nine-year-old's indignation: I didn't know what the fuck he was talking about.

Seems that the night before, there had been an episode of *Happy Days* where Joanie Cunningham got the bright idea to open up a kissing booth to fund some kind of bullshit, white bread, middle-American fantasy plotline, and some girls from my school became inspired. Not so much to do any fund-raising, but to start selling kisses for profit. There were three of them as I remember it, the three prettiest girls in the fourth grade, which means they had all their front teeth and didn't pee on themselves. They were down for a good game of grab-ass too. This, being the days before it fell out of fashion and became "sexual imposition." So these young ladies were forward thinking and sex positive long before their time. They put on the tightest jeans they owned and at recess, they sold their wares.

They'd stand against the fence in a line, hands on hips, giving the boys happy eyes and a coy little jingle to go with it:

"Kisses for saaaaaale, we'll give you *time* fo' a *dime*! Give *us* some *muun-eee huun-ee*."

Where were the monitors? I dunno—who can know? What I know is that three girls selling kisses and a feel for a dime had the kind of reaction you'd expect in an elementary school environment. Word spread quick, business went apeshit, and three seven-year-old girls broke half the school off for ten dollars in dimes. My partner was one of the victims. Or patrons. I dunno what to call him. He got broke for his loot, but it seems so wrong to call him a trick. But a trick, he was.

The girls were ecstatic, sitting in the schoolyard all smiles and happiness, imagining all the dolls and candy they could buy. Big John, who'd been left back a few grades, burst their bubble.

"Y'all ain't nuthin' but a bunch of hoes," he said. "How much for some coochie?"

All the boys howled with laughter. The girls? Well, their faces froze and cracked.

They cried, and wailed, not sure what they'd been called, but sure it was nothing nice. Mrs. Peterson, all peach-faced, round, and kindly came over to see what was what, and when it was explained by all parties, she was mortified. But to her credit she put together a very special, very uncomfortable classroom meeting.

"Whutza POSS'daTOOT?" one of the boys queried.

If you think teaching is an easy job, try explaining prostitution to a class of fourth graders.

"A woman who sells love for money," Mrs. Peterson said.

"What's so wrong with that?" one of the girls asked.

Someone turned to the girls.

"Ya'll wudn't selling no love," he said. "Y'all was sellin' PUSSY!" and as the whole class erupted in laughter, the girls cried so hard they were removed from class.

After the school secretary came and got them, Mrs. Peterson, red-faced and spent, turned to the class and said that if anyone ever brought this incident up again, they would be sent to the principal's office. Back then, that meant swats with a paddle. And days went on. And the girls came back to class and we never spoke of it again. But you have to know, the girls were changed forever. They didn't raise their heads and laugh out loud anymore. Not in the same way. Everyone learned what a hoe was, whether we wanted to know or not.

I know what you're thinking, and no, none of us lost any innocence that day. When you're poor and black in this country you grow up quick. Sex education, substance abuse, and methods on navigating and propagating an underground economy? That's just another day on the corner. The only difference this time was we learned something about the streets in the class-room. And even if we didn't exactly understand the mechanics, we understood the underlying implications of a girl selling her body, and we were bound to learn the ins and outs about hoes sooner or later. Granted, that's not the kind of education you spend your tax dollars paying for. But in a lot of ways, it was just as important, just as vital. Better to learn on the inside, where it's safe, than wait 'til the wrong cat with the wrong rap made the right offer and turned one of the moffets out.

Harsh? Yeah. Life can be like that. But I'm getting ahead of myself.

I don't think of myself as a pimp, or a pimp-type: I don't ex-ploit women. I got game—or so I've been told, and there's evi-dence to suggest that's true—and game is a critical element of pimpology. I have a talent for meeting women and getting what I want. So much so, that people have accused me of being a predator, preying upon weak-minded women. Which, of course, is bullshit. I don't date weak-minded women: they don't interest me. Once we meet, she buys me a drink, and she's cooking me eggs, what are we gonna talk about over breakfast? I've been mar-ried and divorced twice, so obviously my game isn't that tight. I'm not anything like a pimp, because if I was, I wouldn't have gotten tricked out the way I did. Women are the masters of pimping and by far better pimps.

I first learned how to manipulate women from my dealings with my mother. I don't mean sexual seduction, obviously. What I mean is that I learned how to relate to women and get into their thoughts by dealing with my moms. I peeped game early, and milked my only-child status for whatever I could: toys here, cook-ies there. TV time—when we had a TV—in between. By school-age it became apparent I had a liking for the ladies, with the ability to incur their wrath and desire in the same space—not a whole lot different than the life I live today. Some girls would let you share their lunch, squeeze their butt, or kiss their cheek if you said the right thing. I had a little charm, and I worked it. Over time, I learned to apply the same techniques with grown women. Different target, different aim, same principle.

Little boys are so adorable, and we all know how far you can get on that "waah waah, I'm a baby" hustle. I got too old for that bit, and in my situation, it was just me and my moms coming up: no father to lay down the law or enforce it. You'd think I'd want to be the obedient kid for my moms, and sure, that's the first inclination. Women do raise boys to be men alone, but they shouldn't. My mom was no different, but it's not like I was a bad kid. I was a mama's boy without being all milk-sopped and pliant. But please believe that I got over on her, when I could. Kids don't necessarily know any better. Or maybe they do. Me and my moms went through periods of push-pull, just like most young men go through with their moms. She won most of time. My victories had more of an impact.

My mom would let me get away with a lot if I flashed the right smile and said the right thing. I don't mean to imply that my mom was stupid or a simpleton. No, she just gave in to my boyish charm, I guess. My mother is hella smart and not the kind to fall for much, so I used sweet talk and a little doe-eyed faux innocence to cull her favor and trust, so that I could enjoy a little more freedom to goof off and run the streets. Like, when I was six or seven, my mother had the "streetlamp" rule: when the streetlamps came on, I had to come in. Well, that hardly ever happened. And I wasn't really allowed to go off the block, but I did anyway.

Waaaaaay off the block. And when she came looking for me, I gave her some line that was half-lie, half-true but all too sweet. All with the best intentions, and her best interests in mind. After all, she didn't really wanna beat my ass, right? It hurt her more than it hurt me, right? Sure—I didn't wanna put her through that pain. Not me. Of course, my mom is one of the smartest people I know, and sometimes, I got my ass beat anyway. But about a third of the time, I was able to talk my way out of a whopping and talk my way into situations like staying up late, more cookies, please? and the like. As a kid, I mastered the hustle and I thought it could carry me in my teen years. Well, you don't have to know my mother very well to know that my mom is nobody's sucker. She's not of the streets, but she wasn't born yesterday. She had game of her own, and was not one to play with. But that made it all the more challenging.

I developed a drinking habit in high school, and told all kinds of lies to conceal it. I stole a little money from her purse I didn't think she'd miss. It was real fucked up. But she was controlling my life, and if I could control her, I could, by extension, control my own destiny. She only kept tightening the grip as I got older, and that didn't work out so well, and I ended up at my grandparents' house. But the freedom they gave me allowed me to road test my rap.

One of the many drawbacks of growing up as the child of a single mother is that while she may be a soft touch, there's no one to tell you that in the wider world, women have game of their own. Of course, your mom could tell you, but she won't. Why? I don't know. Maybe because they'd have to show you their cards—the things they do to manipulate you—and I don't think most mothers would admit they have their own kind of pimpnosis. For me, a talk about the wiles of wild women from my moms would have been beneficial, because, coming up in the game, I thought I knew more about women than I did, and it made me an easy mark—a trick.

A "trick," in the streets, is a person—normally a man—who patronizes drug whores or prostitutes. That's his life, that's what he does, and he has no shame. He pays for it, and he likes paying for it. You can usually recognize a trick by the look of lovesick desperation constantly on his face. And he's always at the pay-day loan place . . . *every* payday. At the bar, that's him, the dude knocking other dudes over to buy women drinks. At the strip bar, he is the guy sitting right up front, center stage, sweating like July, flipping loot out of his wallet as the dancer—oblivious—bends down to put her anus right on the bridge of his nose as she mentally writes her grocery list, and he sits there, nose open, tongue wagging, fantasizing about what life will be like when he takes this woman off the pole and makes her his wife. Oh yes, what a grand life that'll be. He's a lovable loser, delusional in every way.

Another more (relatively) common kind of "trick" is a person— again, normally a man—who is easily separated from his money or culled into an inequitable situation by cunning, coercion, or compulsion. They are frequently smart people whose logical mind is disconnected from their emotions, softhearted and simple-minded folks who ignore the painful facts their logical mind and eyes may reveal in favor of following their heart. They are lured in by a good sob story or the "you-owe-me" hustle, and they stand ready, at-attention ready to be stripped clean of their money and dignity. Sometimes, they call themselves "sugar daddies" and wear nice suits and lots of jewelry to lure in wayward birds in need of shelter. The sugar daddy imagines himself in control and embraces his role. In his mind, he's a pimp of sorts: he holds the purse strings and he controls the women, who are basically at his beck and call. He pays for it, he knows it, and he loves it. He's in a trick bag, and we know this because he can't see his way in or out of it. Hell, he doesn't even know he's in it. He thinks he's living a charmed life. Everyone else knows better.

Rarely do you see women in a trick bag because women don't get in them—instead, they sit at home crocheting trick bags for men to hop into. Real talk. Men are easily manipulated by the promise of love, attention, and/or pussy. These men are idiots. Often, that idiot has been me.

That's right.

I've never hurt for the company of women or been terribly desperate, but there have been points in my life when I was willing to do almost anything for love, and there were women there to exploit me. Like every other guy, I've been rolled for free meals, concerts, clothes, tuition, cars, computers, stereos, and furniture. I helped a woman take care of her infant child—took care of him like he was my own. The truth? I wasn't excited about trying to play daddy to someone else's child. But better men than me have done it, and every child deserves a daddy.

So I ignored good advice and went all-in with my heart, paying medical bills, for groceries, riding lessons, and clothes—and trying to build a home and future for our family. The next thing you know, she broke camp to be with some ashy nigga with half a job. I really came up out my pockets, but all told, I got off cheap. The woman was disposable, but I couldn't believe that, after knowing this child for six years or better, that she would uproot him from the only father he knew or was likely to know in favor of starting over. She didn't start over, so much as opt for a new trick with someone more desperate for the affections of a woman and not terribly concerned about the impact on the child. I tried to keep my composure, but I couldn't. I raised that child, and when he was taken out of my life, I stopped eating. Lost forty pounds. The pain of the loss was unbearable, but I had no legal recourse. It's the kind of pain you learn to live with, but I wouldn't wish it on a goat. I hope once that child is older, he'll seek me out. But I'll have lost those years in between, and it won't be the same.

This is typically the way trick-type niggas crash and burn: they invest all their emotions, hopes, and dreams on someone Stevie Wonder could see is shady and ultimately crap out magnificently. When the dust cleared, and all the dead were counted, all I had left to rebuild my life with was three sweaters, a broken black-and-white solid state TV, a few pairs of jeans, and a box spring. I was walking around in musty clothes, broke as a muthafucka, shocked and awestruck: I'd seen niggas get twisted up and sprung, but I knew it could never happen to me. I was so traumatized, family and friends took pity and started coming around with food and advice.

My grandmother was very upset with me.

See, she tolerated the young lady, but she didn't like her. Didn't like her attitude, didn't like the way she carried herself, didn't like the way she never came around, and didn't like the way I'd tell her my whereabouts or call ahead if I was going to be late coming home. There's nothing right about a man calling a woman to give her his whys and wherefores, she said. I called it being considerate. "*Henpecked,* boy," she said. "She got you in her pocket." So when I told my grandmother my hen had flown the coop, she wasn't at all surprised. "You know where you went wrong?" she asked. "You worshipped her. Tried to feed her heart's desire. Treated her like *gold*. You can't treat a black woman like that, because she will run all over you." I was shocked to hear my grams suggest that mistreating a black woman was the only way to keep her. I didn't much like the sound of that, so I talked to my twenty-three-year-old baby cousin, Mary, who is, on some matters, wise beyond her years.

"You just need to stick to white girls, man," she said. "And I'm gonna tell you why I say that. Because you don't bring many bitches around the family anyway, right? But when you do what I notice is, the white girls? They be nice and shit, and they really seem to be into you. They treat your family with respect. Then you know, you bring these black chicks up in here who turn their noses up at us and act a fool, and it seems like they just try-ing to get over on you."

You'd think your people would be happy seeing you do right by a black woman, with all the guys beating up women or chop-ping them up for brisket. My people were not excited about the relationship: the woman thought too much of herself, they said. I was in love—more with the child than the woman—and I made a critical mistake: I stood by the woman in the name of doing the honorable thing. Never denied the child a thing, and gave in to every indulgence. Showered her with gifts and helped her find some peace of mind, so she could get her life together. I felt like I owed the child that much.

"Your first debt is to yourself," my father said from atop his stool at the Master Plan, a corner bar that has become something like the family stand. "You knew that bitch wudn't shit. I know you think I'm all ice cold and shit, but shit, I gotta tell you: you let that bitch play you, and you know better. I *know* you, so I know. You got caught up with the kid when you ain't owe that kid a damn thing." Men learn how to play women by looking how they were played, and turning the tables. The idea is that by studying women, you can nullify their pimp-hand.

The truth is that women are the smartest creatures on God's green earth, right above dolphins and chimps. Men are, like, distant fourth- or fifth-placers. The best you can ever do is just be able to see the game working and get out of the way, because the minute you think you're up in the game, women flip the script. So rather than note the game point for point, it's better to peep game to get some idea of how a certain kind of woman runs hers down. You study women like you'd study a prospective chess opponent looking for passive-aggression or strong, seemingly innocuous moves that could change the game further down the line. The way to play the game is to know how it's played. Then you become a true player: not necessarily a man who uses, abuses, and disposes of women, but a man who knows how to beat women at their own game. Just like men call conniving women "bitches," sometimes women call men who know how to play the game "dogs."

Go figure.

So it came to pass that I spent time really thinking about what women did to twist me up. I took the little bit I knew, picked up the rest of what I'd learned, and educated myself. I turned back to the world with no regrets and started my life anew. This isn't the point at which I was gonna turn into a pimp, because I believe using or manipulating women is wrong. But it was important to me to level the playing field. My father told me something when I was very young that I'd forgotten over the years: there are more men than women in the world, so why pick one?

Sage advice.

So I had fun. I kept women, lots of women, around me, vying

for my affection. Wrassling for a place in the pecking order, working to ingratiate themselves with me on the off-chance there could ever be one. Now, I know what you're thinking: "Jimi, that sounds like some player shit to me." Nah, it wasn't. Players don't tell the women they're playing. They play and play until it gets played out, and then people get hurt. Honesty was my policy. This is who I am, this is what/who I'm doing. You can get down or not. I'm not a player, but I'm not the marrying kind. I gave them enough information for them to make informed choices. That's hard, but it's fair. I kept this mind-set for a while, and it was exhausting. All the coming and going, demands on my attention, fending off hard sells for matrimony, it got to be a lot. Most women are out there trying to hunt down a husband, and even when you tell them it's not in the plans, they want to change your agenda. They think if they cook for you, clean your house, and put that thang on you, that you'll want to buy them a ring. Maybe some guys. Not me. Not anymore. So I learned the game, and I learned how, as they say, to "pimp by dick."

What's that mean?

Well, it means that I learned that if I put down some good dick, I could just about neutralize any woman's game and basically put her pussy in my pocket. It's not that I'm Casanova or any great lover, or that I dope chicks, or that I'm toting an eighteen-inch penis. I got the equipment, and I know how to use it. I'm not a novice or apprentice: I'm in the fucking union. Yeah, I know all this sounds egotistical and fucked up. I don't care—women do the same thing with men. They don't call it "pimping pussy" or being a "hoe," but when you use your sex to control people's minds, then that's all it is. Best to be real about it than try to gloss over the obvious.

More and more, black men are opting out of marriage. There

used to be a time when everybody—including men—imagined an idyllic life with green grass, a three-bedroom house with the doting wife, all babies and cream. I thought like that for a long time, and I wouldn't date a woman I didn't think was "wife material." But there isn't much in the way of "wife material" out there.

Now, the kind of thing that happened to me? Not unique at all. It happens every day. Men get caught up in relationships that turn out to be more like variations on the long con, whereby you just milk a mark by inches. The mark doesn't have to be rich—I sure wasn't. But I was a nice guy, eager to help, and those two things are all you need to run a scam on someone. Nice guys like me are getting tired of being played out and burnt up. So we soak up the game from women and turn the tables. It's the manipulation of their imagination. It's about turning the Denzel Principle against women, and pretending to give them something that is not there, and could never be there. So sometime, men work the Dizzle, f'r shizzle.

Pimpology ain't pretty, but it keeps the world spinning.

She Hate Me

Back in January of 2005, I got wind of something called the Take Back the Music (TBTM) campaign. Conceived by the editorial staff of *Essence* magazine, TBTM's stated purpose, according to their mission statement, was to:

- provide a platform for discussion about extreme images of black women in music;
- discuss the effects of hip-hop on young girls and boys;
- achieve balance in the hip-hop narrative;
- start a discussion about misogyny and hip-hop;
- promote positive artists; and
- discuss solutions.

Noble aims, all, I thought.

Essence magazine has a history of propping itself up as the black warrior princess of women's magazines, running through the jungle in Donna Karan and Manolo Blahniks spearing skinny white models with MAC eyeliner pencils and castrating black men with nail files, fresh hair weaves awash in the wind. Exceptional men—like Denzel Washington, for instance—are occasionally celebrated and deified, but within the pages of the magazine, men are mostly nagged and guilted into submission, until they are so sorrowful and emasculated they feel compelled to lock themselves in a basement and chew their balls off. Sistas celebrate over a glass of merlot. *Essence*'s demographic all look the same: moderately overweight single black women, often with children in tow, who can't figure out what they did to deserve their lives, or married black women who are trying to figure out how to upgrade. Guiding principle? "It's all his fault." Between makeup and hair-care tips, this has been the magazine's bread and butter since it started, and it's only changed by degrees over the years. It's about the black woman's esteem at the black man's expense.

This said at the top, I doubt you'll be surprised that when I heard about *Essence* magazine's campaign, I called "bullshit." I have to give that it was a brilliant idea: nothing like blaming the black man to get magazines flying off the newsstands. You'll never go broke putting black men on blast.

There's a reason why women have such a hard time finding a comfortable space in hip-hop culture. Female rappers struggle to bring a relevant message to the foreground that doesn't involve sex, money, or using sex to get money. And it's not hip-hop's fault either. Rap music graduated from the corner to coffee shop to the party. When rap music became a commercial venture in the late seventies, the lyrics were always about partying. The first ladies of hip-hop, The Sequence cast themselves as sassy ladies and fellow revelers. With hits like "Funk You Up," they asserted their feminity in a sex-positive way without sounding slutty, overly aggressive, or solicitous. Later women cast themselves as friendly adversaries and instigated lengthy beefs with their male counterparts in an attempt to expand the narrative, with uneven results. Super Nature (later known as Salt-n-Pepa) would follow years later with "The Show Stopper," probably the first answer rap song by a female rap group. Lyrically, they tore into Doug E. Fresh and the Get Fresh crew. Next up were the endless parade of Roxannes who stepped up to rebut U.T.F.O.'s "Roxanne, Roxanne" by attacking the rapper's manhood and asserting their own prowess as rappers and sexual beings.

Then there were female emcees rapping about independence and empowerment, who managed to be sexy with all their clothes on. They didn't need to attack men to establish themselves, but by that time the rules of the game were decided. I don't recall a lot of raunch in popular rap music of the eighties. Luther Campbell's 2 Live Crew was so regional and cartoonish that, on the cusp of the New Black Nationalism, his message didn't resonate until he went pop. It took Choice, the first lady of Rap-a-Lot Records, to take the female emcee to a new place: the bedroom.

Unlike Queen Latifah, MC Lyte, Monie Love, and other lady rappers who extolled the virtues of abstinence and safe sex, Choice chose to embrace the power of promiscuity and celebrate her sexual freedom. This would've been fine and sex-positive if the message had evolved. But it hasn't. Sure, you have your Jean Graes, Bahamadias, and Lauryn Hills, but by and large, female emcees haven't elevated the discourse in rap music to anything beyond boys vs. girls in a quest for sex and money.

Female emcees sell records, but not many—listening to any woman brag about the size and depth of her genitalia is only sexy for about ten seconds. Unless it's a wild night, I don't want to hear any woman cussing and carrying on about where to lick her. Not on the radio. I don't know if that means I'm getting old or that female rappers have become increasingly unladylike.

It's true: the references to women in rap music have devolved from "ladies" to "freaks," "honeys," and "sisters" to "skeezers," "bitches," and "hoes." That devolution parallels the economic politics of hip-hop culture, and the role women played. In the best of times, women were celebrated: they were dance partners, disco queens, and objects of desire. As the battle of the sexes heated up, women chose sides. In the hood, resources became scarce, so women decided that their men were only good for money: any man who could not provide a certain kind of lifestyle for them was disposable. That created a natural push back, and that's evident in the tone and timbre of the music today.

The truth is, from "I Got a Woman" to "In the Bush," women have always been sex objects in popular music. That doesn't make it right. What has changed in rap music is the bald antagonism of it: whereas lyrics in pop music had heretofore been relatively subtle in their documentation of the conflict, rap music is very clearly men vs. women. Male rappers take on the role of men with resources who expect women to behave like whores to get some, and female rappers take on the role of strippers eager to outsmart the men by exploiting their sexuality to acquire money and material wealth. Respect is a two-way street. I have run across more independent black women who have little or no self-esteem or self-respect and look to me for validation. Somewhere along the way, the "niggas ain't shit," "no money, no honey," and the "I don't need no man" model for intraracial relationships has fostered resentment on both sides, and rap music—among other media—documents this. The dismissive, disrespectful attitude some male rappers have toward women is being matched against the dismissive, disrespectful tone some black women have toward their men. It only makes sense. This message has crossover appeal because while white folks can't relate to the politics of what is often called "conscious" rap, everyone understands sex.

Yes, of course—they do this because sex sells. Male emcees are stuck in a rut too. But when they have the chance, why aren't female emcees changing the conversation? *Essence* doesn't talk about that.

Rap has always reflected an honest, raw sexuality—not unlike the blues—that young, white people rarely hear. The major record companies mainline the "money, cars and bitches" smack into the zeitgeist not because of some anti-woman agenda, but because big butts and skeet sells in Idaho. Black sexuality sells—since the days of Josephine Baker and the Cotton Club—and it always will. How do we combat it? Not by attacking rappers trying to make a living. We use what little we have in media clout to offer a counterbalance. But the fact is that those media entities are businesses and they profit from the objectification of women in hip-hop and everywhere else, so there is no motivation to change a profitable formula. Any boycott of the music industry would be met with indifference, because the companies are so diversified and omnipresent that we'd have no idea what products and services we'd have to give up. The entire culture has lost its way because black people allowed it to be mass-marketed and repackaged as a commodity. Everything about the face of hip-hop has changed with the demands of its primary consumers—young, white teenagers. This fact seems to get lost in the thick of this discussion, but that isn't the only problem with *Essence*'s referendum on hip-hop.

Essence magazine is the angry black woman's guide to hair, makeup, and ritual torture of the no-good black man. Between the articles about how to find the best pair of big-butt jeans, financial stability, and how to catch a white man, the black man sometimes appears in the Denzel-Washington, exception-to-the-rule archetype or on the pages of "His Say," where some poor asshole gets roped into crafting eight hundred words about how often he falls short, how long-suffering and benevolent his black woman has been—despite his unworthiness—and how he owes it all to black women. If black men ever forget about their infractions—real and imagined—then *Essence* magazine exists essentially to remind them. I generally dig the quality of the writing. But I don't need any reminders—I know how fucked up I am.

More than anything, like a lot of women's magazines, *Essence* functions to disseminate and propagate a feminist world-view: men, as change purse or oppressor. Between beauty tips, you get to vote on fifty mainly shirtless and suspect-looking "Do Right Men" one month, read about the winner of an $11 million dollar sexual harassment suit, discuss switching up to white men, and trying to give them "Four Smart Love Moves" the next. Nothing in between. The content approaches all matters from the workplace to home repair to fruit salad with the thesis always the same: everything is an us-against-the-world type proposition going in, and everyone and everything that is not dedicated to the uplifting of black women is an enemy-oppressor by default, and every true-blue black sista is a comrade in the rage against the machine, whoever the machine is this year, this month, this week, or in the latest issue. This is an oversimplification to be sure, but it is an honest assessment of how it reads to me and other men. Women start reading *Essence* and their attitude changes immediately: sweet women turn bitter and defiant, bitter women curdle and sour, and whenever you see a fresh issue of *Essence* on the kitchen table, black men can be sure of two things: no home cooking and no blowjob for a month or better. White men? Well, I'm sure they are just as confused.

Now, you might read into all this and think I'm not a progressive, or that I'm not a feminist, or I don't support women's rights. Well, I don't think anyone would mistake me for Alan Alda—I love the skin I'm living in, and I see the world from the perspective of a man. When I think of sexism, I think of people who use the implicit privilege of their gender to browbeat and persecute. Like some feminists I know. That's not me. I'm no feminist, but I'm not a caveman either. I find myself confused by ever-changing mores, where women want to be recognized as equal on the one hand, want to be recognized as women (read: beautiful, sexual, and sensual) on the other, and then want to manufacture some brand of guilt-based Amazonian authority over men. That's my problem. At least, that's one of them. I love and deeply respect all the women in my life. The most interesting thing about me and my relationships with women (as if) is that there is a mutual respect of gifts that has little to do with gender. I am decidedly pro-male, not anti-female, even though I don't think men and women can ever be equal.

Women are smarter than men, more intuitive than men, more complete thinkers than men. Women are wonderful political leaders and captains of industry. Women bring the miracle of life unto the world—how could we ever think that we are equals? In a lot of ways, women are better than men. The thing about a woman's gifts is that the things she's not good at, she's not good at at all. This is why there are men, and men have their own nature. I'm not opposed to the rights of women, but I don't believe the sexes are equal. Someone has to fix the toilet and take out the garbage and someone else has to cook dinner. Each one to their gifts, I say. What are my gifts? Making love and making money. Not in that order. Not that I'm a millionaire, but I got the skills to pay the bills, and I'm not afraid of work.

And—have I mentioned?—I do okay in the sack. Ask around.

I'm not particularly handy, but I haul Glad bags and call plumbers while you (woman) strip down, strap on a Williams-Sonoma apron and a pair of stilettos, and make with the dinner, already. Not because I can't cook. I can, and I do. But I don't look so good in stilettos. Men and women have gifts that make them ideal complements. When women try to adopt masculine qualities and insist that men become more feminine is when expectations change and problems arise. Women can't pick and choose the masculine characteristics they wish to usurp: this, among other things, is the fatal flaw of feminism.

Another flaw with feminism, as it relates to people of color, is the guiding principles. From what I understand, suffrage and the women's liberation movement were designed to create parity between men and women . . . specifically, within the burgeoning white middle class. Voting rights and fair wages, yes, and it was a necessary fight. But out of these changes grew calls to change attitudes and the social order that recognized men as men: there was an idea that women could be men too. They could function as captains of industry, government leaders, and heads of household. On these points, you'll get no argument from me. But as it regards the family unit, the women's movement seemed to advocate for gender roles that nullified conventional ideas in favor of a seemingly more cooperative approach. This idea looks great on paper. However, it doesn't work for two reasons.

One, because it defies the laws of nature: if you turn men into women, who will fix the dishwasher? Protect the family? Make the mortgage? Not that women can't do all that, but men are hardwired to protect and provide. Women nurture and caretake. Once you start tinkering with the wiring, that's where you end up with problems and a society of spineless wonders with no balls, no ambition, or ego but lots of knitting needles and designer cookware. There's nothing wrong with knitting, cooking, or the men that do it. It's just that at some point, someone will have to be the man of the house. In a world where the playing field is level, and women and men are equal, women have no reason to complain. You can't be a feminist complaining about the lazy black man's lack of earning power. Because if you want roles to be interchangeable, then you should have no problem with a man laying back on your check while you go out and make the bacon. Women should be man enough to do it and suck it up without bitching about it. But it isn't, and they do. When we have a social order where there is no manhood, we are in trouble. Feminism gave white women a leg up, but there was no model for feminism within the constraints of poverty or racial discrimination. This is why there is no black feminism, just a lot of bitter, angry, single black women driving expensive cars with the soundtrack to *Waiting to Exhale* in the CD player on repeat.

Dr. Bill Cosby once implored women to take the leadership role in their community.

Okay, a disclaimer of sorts: I used to be a Cosby fan, as someone who grew up on Cosby entertainment, and even today, I appreciate his talent as a comedian. He's funny, until he starts in with the amateur social engineering theory. He went from America's father to something like Chris Rock's drunken uncle with worse writers and no research staff. I think Coz is entitled to his opinion, and his opinion is that since most of the blacks graduating from college are women, then they should strap the future of the race on their backs and carry black folks, since black men are so inept. This thesis, it seems, lays at the heart of black feminism: picking up the slack for the good-for-nothing black man.

That would be all fine and dandy, except that black women in (nonpolitical) leadership roles within the black community is *precisely* the problem: it's an uncomfortable positioning of the family structure. There is one immutable fact that tells us why some black communities are in such a shithole: too many black women as heads of households who fuck up, and then blame black men, who are nowhere to be found. Too many black women as lawmakers and lawgivers, too many black women without any birth control making babies and pointing a crusty finger at the shiftless black man for being irresponsible, when they are at least as culpable for their lot. Too many black women who would rather be black men, and create a tribe of black men who would rather not be bothered. Too many liberated black women who suddenly forget that liberation comes with responsibility and culpability. Too many women calling any man that looks at their butt, raps, exudes any masculinity whatsoever, or dares to disagree with women on anything a misogynist, when too few black women even know what misogyny means. Too few brothers willing to snatch the reins back from black women and take control of our communities again, lest they be called something less than progressive. Too few black women who can't make the inextricable connection between feminism and the decline of the black family. Too many black feminists in the Thursday-night big butt contest, using their acceptance speech to talk about how hip-hop objectifies black women. Too many black women using their sexuality as a weapon wondering why men respond in kind. Too many brothers willing to opt out just to get a sniff instead of standing up. Too many brothers trying to be Booker, Martin, Malcolm, or Denzel. And too many black women pressuring them to be that way. Too many black women telling black men to "stand up and be a man" who have no idea what that even means. Too many black women who want men to be women. Too many brothers writing books that concur. Too many black women who will believe anything they read about black men, as long as it destroys his identity completely. Too many black women who don't know a good black man when they see one. Too many black women who can't cook, clean, or iron (and don't think they should have to), and think that having a pussy should be enough for you, Bootney. It's all the same old story, and it's too much like copping out, is what.

Month after month, the same types of stories run in *Essence* magazine: "How My Man Fucked Up and I Put Him in Check, Girl!"; "How Hip-Hop Demeans Black Women"; SPECIAL TO *ESSENCE*, IN DEPTH: "Shake it Fast: But Watch Yourself!"; "How to Rise Up the Corporate Ladder in These Fabulous Big-Butt Jeans!"; "Girl, Get Yourself a White Boy!"; and my personal favorite, "It's All Tyrone's Fault: The Complete Checklist." You know what? I probably made all these titles up. But I think *Essence* feeds a readership of too many black women waiting for an apology, and too few willing to give them. Too many trick-type brothers in lobster bibs begging women for a sniff, who think they are living the dream. Too few black women not willing to step up against their sisters and say "Hey, Lafonda! That man-hating, pseudo-feminist antagonism against the black man is some bullshit!"

When black women fuck up—whether it's her fault or not—everyone blames the black man. It's always sexy ink to blame the black man for the downfall of black people as a whole, and the black woman specifically. It'll always fill column inches, and you'll always stay king of the bar as long as you follow conventional thinking. People think that by offering a counterargument, it means that I'm crazy. As a writer and culture commentator, I call down that which you have taken to be true without question. I'm trying to convince you to think for yourself. That's my gig. You like it or you don't.

But how can someone's absence lend causation to a predicament? That's the money part of the hustle: it's your fault because *they say* it's your fault. And because you want some pussy, you concede. We always presume the worst about black men when we see single moms, when the story might be pretty complicated. How can something, logically, be anyone's fault completely, in absentia? How does that make sense to anyone? Let me break it down.

So you, as the absentee father, are not there, for reasons that could be very simple (you are promiscuous, young, and irresponsible, and so is she, or you are on crack, etc.) or very complicated (she lied about her age, you have no marketable skill, you are not vertically compatible, you are sober now, etc.). Lafonda has five kids by six daddys, and no man will live with her to help her support that brood? That somehow makes him less of a man? How about, no man is willing to embarrass himself trying to feed and clothe that tribe by shacking up with the neighborhood incubator. I have yet to hear of anyone step up and vociferously demand that women take responsibility for their own behavior. When I read the stories that blame black men for the proliferation of single mothers, that part seems to be edited out of the articles.

Also missing is the graph detailing the schematics of the solar-powered, remote-controlled leg-opener black men are given just after puberty that compels young ladies to spread their legs. C'mon, you know what I'm talking about. It's obviously equipped with a mental decapacitator that brainwashes girls so they can't find the "family planning" section of the local drugstore, where spermicidal lubricant and other birth control options for women are plentiful. I don't know how this part comes up missing time after time in these articles condemning the irresponsible black man. Maybe it's just bad editing, but I never read anything fresh about what role black single mothers play in their own lot. I know I'm getting long in the tooth—and I hope someone would tell me if things have changed—but last I checked, it takes two to tango. That is, the last time I was making babies, that's how it was going down. That fact alone suggests to me that the irresponsibility occurs on both ends. Big time. Both parties need to own up and face the music. Back when my grands were doing the do-nasty, women had an excuse for getting knocked up by more than one man or having multiple babies. They didn't have the Pill. Now, there are all kinds of birth control options for teenage girls and adult women that do not require prescriptions or any of that shit.

You have whole neighborhoods without a man because, let's face it, can you reasonably expect a man to get with you and your five kids by eight different daddys? I mean, love is grand, but kids are expensive. It's hard enough to get along with your woman, then you fuck around having to keep her baby-daddys in check. So with that drama, feeding them kids, when do you have time to sleep and wash your ass? You gonna add *your* kid to that collection? You a fool. Sure, it's noble to step in for the next man—who we presume is just fucked up. But the kids can't eat nobility.

The irresponsibility piece enters way before the kid is even born. It goes all the way back to Big Butt Nite at Club Drink N Fuck, when you, woman, spied Keith Sweat's brother Doug schvitzing out a $69 suit from the Steve Harvey Collection and let him buy you two half-price drinks. You saw he was rolling nice in his mother's '96 barf-green LeSabre sittin' on tinners and took that trip to the Mo-Mo, where y'all went half on a thirty-minute room. C'mon now. Next thing you know, one thing leads to the next and—surprise! He doesn't have a condom, but that's cool, because he just wants to nutt on yo' big-ass titties any muth-afuckin' way, bay-bee guhl! And of course, you like the freak in him. Thirty seconds later he's putting his shoes on and nobody knows where that nutt went. Nine months later, you can't find him, but you found out where that nutt went.

Or the dude ends up in the Boom Boom Room, balls deep in that cigarette girl, talking about "You on that pill, right?! You *sure* you won't get pregnant?" "Yes yes *yes!*" she says as you hose her cervix down with baby-batter. When she turns up nine months fat, it's clear that she wasn't. Everyone has to take responsibility for their own behavior. No matter how trifling. People make bad choices but women choose who they have sex with. Sexually active single women who are not on birth control are just lucky. With your luck, you'll get knocked up. Why leave it to chance when spermicidal lube is so damn cheap?

But, no, there's more.

The irresponsibility string actually starts way back, at the single mother's home where she was raised. I keep waiting to hear why these irresponsible black men chirp out as soon as the baby is born. Does it happen? Of course it does. But the way it's being reported, you'd think it was the rule. The numbers look interesting, but I have another perspective you haven't considered.

My mentor and friend Margaret Bernstein writes for the *Plain Dealer* in Cleveland, Ohio, and she cowrote a series in December of 2007 about the decline of Mount Pleasant, an inner-city neighborhood in Cleveland. She talks to a forty-four-year-old woman who got pregnant at eighteen, whose eighteen- and fifteen-year-olds turned up preggers (the eighteen-year-old, *twice*). They all live under her roof and as of this writing, there is no man in sight or on the horizon. You know why? "I think marriage is a good thing," she says. "You want that companionship. But I can't get with these men staying in the bathroom longer than I do, leaving the toilet seat up, and watching my every move. I'm just so particular. . . . My mother, she took out the garbage. She didn't need no help. She wasn't one of those people that needed a man to screw in a lightbulb or put up the Christmas tree. My mother educated herself." What she's suggesting is that it's a lot easier to be a "strong black woman" than be compatible with a man. They'd rather not be bothered: as long as he sends in checks to kick in on the rent and upkeep, they could do fine without him. Sure, she could use the help, but a man's help ain't the kinda help she needs. To hell with giving her kids a stable home environment and a balanced upbringing—doing it by yourself, she reasons, enables you to treat yourself to the little luxuries in life—like having the seat down and ready when you have to pee. Revolving lovers. Screwing in lightbulbs and taking out the garbage, evidently, provides a liberating sensation many of us could not imagine.

Now, she comes from a coven of these "strong black women"—women who, against all conventional wisdom—decided that it made more sense to try to parent a kid by themselves than compromise and, you know, be a woman and try to work it out with a man. And she passes this pathos down to her kids, who will no doubt pass it on to their kids, and so on. It wasn't subliminal, she wasn't hypnotized—she was modeling behavior. She made this choice of her own free will. She, her mama, and her mama's mama decided they would rather do it on their own than have some man tell them what to do. Women like this inevitably end up on public assistance or on *Oprah*, bemoaning the lack of good men. Or both.

Berznie also talked to another young lady who said that her single motherhood helped her put her life into perspective. "I was into partying, staying out all night at a very young age, driving my mom crazy," she said. "My kids, I feel that God put them on this earth to protect me because I wasn't doing the right thing." She needed another mouth to feed to keep her from kickin' it. Naturally, it's the black man's fault. There ain't no man trying to sell this smack. This bullshit is being passed down from mother to daughter. What needs to happen is women need to make better choices in men and stop teaching their daughters that single motherhood is an enviable vocation—because you don't need no good-for-nuthin' nigga telling *you* what to do any muthafuckin' way. That's that bathtub feminism that trickled down to the hood. Unless a dude is beating your ass, single motherhood is not preferable to marriage or partnering as parents.

Women are training their daughters to be the kind of men

who fight men. This idea is reinforced everywhere. In magazines, in books, reality shows, and music. For a dude, it becomes easier to chalk it up than to put up with the fighting. I've never laid a hand on a woman (except in self-defense), but had crazy bitches—literally—swinging at me, and I'm a big dude. Seriously, what are mothers teaching their daughters? Mothers should raise good, strong women but it is irresponsible to instill them with a hostility and prejudice that will make it hard for a prospective mate to stay the night.

My moms was a single mom. My dad and her were too young and too stupid, and then there were two. She was strong and all that shit, trying to raise a man-child. She made some mistakes, man. A lot of mistakes, to the point where I couldn't stay. I went and lived in my grandparents' *two-parent* household. And I didn't go thinking the living would be easy. My grams was kind of a soft touch, but my grandfather was no punk, homie. Real talk. Some of the most important life lessons I learned at their kitchen table. It took two. My moms did a decent job—but it broke her, in a lot of ways. Single motherhood is not what's poppin'. But mothers are encouraging this route for their daughters. To encourage single motherhood as an option over having a viable partner is irresponsible.

But then, some of these chicks have kids—madd young!!—because they are emotionally needy, and need something that will love them unconditionally. And more and more, babies have become the new hood hustle, the new welfare check in the age of welfare reform: women who are afraid to actually go forth in life to try and fail sometimes have a gang of kids so they don't have to engage society in a substantive way. They have multiple kids by multiple dads, go out and buy purses or be at the club with the money, and kids be home busting out of clothes, ashy as fuck. The kids are staggered in age to the point where they can all just suckle the system until it's time for SSI. The fathers either pay up, or go to jail, and may or may not get to see their kids. The woman has control—she can take the kids, but doesn't have to let the father see the kids. How do you step up in circumstances like that? You "L" up if you can afford it, but otherwise, you're ass out, and then you look like a fucked-up dad.

You think I'm making this shit up. This is the realest shit I ever spit. I been on all sides of the baby-daddy saga, and I can tell you without fear of contradiction: black women are *at least* as responsible for the upsurge in single-parent homes as men. They hold all the power, all the strings, at every turn. All the daddys are not in jail, on crack, or undereducated ne'er-do-wells. Women get the babies, and kick many of the men *out*. *They* make the decision to be single moms. And black women need to step up to the counter and tighten up their spermicidal lubricant/sponge game.

The problem with the argument about the absentee daddy is that in order to buy into it, you have to believe that black women are dumb as rocks, with no free will, self-control, or access to birth control and that the black supercock is a mystical one-eyed wonderweasel that mesmerizes and hypnotizes defenseless young black girls who have no choice but to lay prone and powerless to the power of the dick. I've heard I pack the Extra D, but I hope it's not that serious. Black men need to step up and claim their kids, *yes*. By any means necessary.

Singer R. Kelly helps make the best argument for the two-parent family. How so? Let me explain.

As you may recall, Kelly's trouble stemmed from a tape that leaked onto the Internet and then the streets of America where, among the many scenes where he has sex with several different women, he has sex with a girl alleged by authorities to have been underage at the time. Years ago, when the story broke, I viewed the tape in its entirety and reported on what I saw. When word came that singer R. Kelly was found not guilty on fourteen counts of child pornography in 2008, I wasn't surprised at all—but I was surprised at the legions of black female fans willing to take up for him. I was stunned by their lack of regard and compassion for the alleged victim, and caught by surprise when the truth behind the events finally sunk in.

Part of me is happy to live in a country where the legal system works. After all, the female principal denied it was her on the videotape, and her family denied it was her too. Then there was the parade of witnesses with shady histories and muddy motivations going head to head with a firebrand young lawyer making a name for himself. This, on top of the indisputable fact you cannot look at a piece of film and reliably determine age. Defense attorney Sam Adam Jr.'s job was to raise reasonable doubt, and there was reasonable doubt all over the place.

The other part of me—the father of a young daughter—couldn't help but wonder where the parents were: where's Daddy? Why was this young girl calling some man urinating on her "Daddy"? The verdict suggested to me that we've crossed a threshold and revealed an ugliness we didn't know was there: when daddys can't, don't, or won't protect their little girls, and the law can't either.

Reports of the verdict mentioned that jurors were concerned about the motives of those close to the young woman. Upon discovery of the tapes, the first call family members made was to a lawyer, not the authorities. I question their motives too. Friends say they didn't know of any relationship between Kelly and the alleged victim—I don't buy that. And the parents? What kind of parents allow their children to hang out with adults, unsupervised, Michael Jackson–stylee? Where were all the friends and family when the girl was allegedly getting down with Kelly? Instead of trying to cash in with a rent-a-lawyer, why didn't the family reach out to try and protect the young lady?

I don't know.

Another news story I read went down in Orange County, Florida, where twenty-two-year-old Morris Williams went to jail for having sex with thirteen-year-old Alisha Dean, which would be right on target, if not for the fact that Dean lied about her age on her MySpace page, and got another man, twenty-four-year-old Darwin Mills, sentenced to five years in prison. Seems like her thing is luring men in with her MySpace page and having sex with them. According to her parents (!) the young lady still keeps late nights, and only recently took her MySpace page down. What's happening here?

As a reporter, I've covered enough cases of people behaving badly to read them from the curb—I have an unnatural taste for hunting game where the answers are not clear, where there are no heroes or villains: just the truth, the process, and the scum it can leave behind. But the R. Kelly case was different—see, I have a little girl. And I have little girls in my charge. What struck me first, once the trial ended, exactly as I said it would, was that someone's little girl had to grow up too fast. Instead of her hanging out with her friends and talking on the phone, a grown man was offering her money to be his plaything. And that little girl is damaged. Forever.

And after all the cameras are gone, after all the (alleged) hush money is spent, that little girl, now a woman, will one day be left alone to wonder where her innocence went. She will ask her father to account for (allegedly) selling the soul of his daughter. What will he say?

What would I say?

I wouldn't say a word because I wouldn't be answering that question. I'd be pressing my hands against the Plexiglas window of a maximum-security prison, sad that I couldn't touch the face of my precious daughter, but knowing that I rose up to protect her where the law failed. Daddy needs to be in the mix. We have to figure out how to keep our family structure intact. Black women cannot do it alone.

I can admit real feminism has a lot of merit. But the "boys vs. the girls" part about supposedly not "needing" a man strictly speaking, trickled down unfiltered into the economic reality of black people as a whole—e.g., that people on the bottom rung of society can't afford to be divided by sex politics—thus effectively nullifying any practical use for feminism with black or poor people. They simply didn't have those options, if they were ever going to take a legitimate shot at it. The real-world functionality and practical application of feminism for women from communities that could not afford to be divided got lost in the wash. Seems like the "personal responsibility" piece of feminism got lost in the rinse. That's the Kool-Aid Oprah Winfrey and *Essence* are selling. Men are only useful as sponsors, sperm donors, and free labor. Oprah doesn't even have any use for her boyfriend Stedman that anyone can see, and she's the new black female role model. Her mantra is, you don't need a man to be successful, and it's true. You don't. But when you're a billionaire with no kids, you have more options than most. The rest of us may need a partner to bring their gifts to a progressive union that, in fact, might not even involve marriage. Seems like black women are looking for sparring partners, not life partners. And that's how it's been for as long as I can remember. This is how you turn neighborhoods into ghettos.

Let me explain.

NEWSFLASH: it's your body, and birth control, like spermicidal foam, is cheap and readily available. I mean, dating a woman with a few kids is noble and healthy. I've dated plenty of women with kids, some seriously. But when their dads start to multiply, sister, forget it. And you can't go on *Oprah* crying about why you can't find a good man. Evidently, you already found a few. But it's the evil black man's fault that you didn't protect yourself, right, and got pregnant by a nigga that could barely support himself, with no education, no ambition, and no prospects. T'yeah. Like all the rest of the girls on the block, until your enclave starts to look like the lost dark tribe of Amazonia. Nothing but pregnant women and kids. And niggas, running from the bus stop/car to the stoop to the bedrooms and back out again. When it gets dark, there is no man in sight, unless he is pulling a late-night snack and/or booty call. Like roaches.

And it's going to be hard for you to work, sister, what with a bunch of kids. So now, you're out of the game for a good eighteen years, so get on food stamps, HEAP, and all the freebies that come with being poor, black, and female. You might get a job off the books as a cashier at the Arab spot, where you can blow Abdul for groceries (and this is often how it goes down) and make some money to buy a drink on Big Butt Nite. After awhile, you become accustomed to the culture of the working poor, like all your girlfriends do. You buy Fendi and Coach purses, designer dresses. Then, the Section 8 house where you live starts to lean. Freda's boy starts to sell drugs to keep the lights on and buy new Jordans every week. Bullets fly to protect fertile drug selling grounds. Cops, Domino's Pizza, and the mailman refuse to come to your block. Then, a good brother *does* come along, and gets shackled with all the stress, emotional baggage, and credit card debt, and becomes the babysitter while you go out to Big Butt Nite looking for what? Then, scratch your weave and roll your eyes when he decides to chirp out. "Niggas ain't shit," you say.

You wake up and realize you have turned your hood into the ghetto. Congratulations.

Now, I'm sure you think it's a black man's fault for not being there. But how can it be his fault if he didn't raise those kids? If women were ever meant to parent alone, how come they can't get control of their neighborhoods? It's like comedian Chris Rock says: just because women *can* raise children by themselves, doesn't mean that's the way it's supposed to be done. And the proof is in the pudding. Somehow, some people would have you believe that all this maps back to rap music. Those people are wrong. Thinking about the Take Back the Music campaign, I was always curious about where they were taking the music back to. I think they miss the good old days, when you couldn't tell black men from black women.

Personally, I think we all prefer today's unwielding gangsta machismo to the androgynous hip-hop look of the late seventies and eighties when, as comedian and noted social commentator Charlie Murphy opined, it was fly for men to look like women. Back then, there were no black men to speak of, just a lot of neuters in Jheri curls, eyeliner, and lip gloss, pop-lockin' down the street wearing elf boots and Michael Jackson jackets. Small wonder the new hip-hop young'uns wanna man-up. But even I can admit—the machismo has gotten extreme. But I've often said that the vanishing of the male role model during the eighties—due to the aggressive misandry of post-feminist America pushing for an ousting of men from the home in general, as divorce rates skyrocketed—precipitated a generation of young men whose principal role models were all female or woman-like. I don't think that assertion makes me homophobic, and I don't know if we have more coincidence than correlation, but I think it's worth studying, if someone is so inclined. People are so quick to blame hip-hop for fucking up black America. I think feminism—which encouraged, to a large degree, single motherhood over the standard family structure—has some culpability. Why do single moms raise their sons to be beta males in an alpha world, and then wonder where all the "real men" are? Single moms raise great beta males. But we need alpha men to save our communities. They instill in them the best qualities of a woman and what you think are the best qualities of a man. Evidently, they are wrong. As a result, there are a lot of men cooking, cleaning, and doing needlepoint, but they don't have the cajones to stand and deliver. An alpha mother can only raise a really good Beta man—she cannot teach what she doesn't know. She can take her best guess, and as evidenced by the generations of lost boys, this guess is off the mark. Beta men in search of their manhood are forced into letting trial and error in a cruel and unforgiving world fill in the gaps. This could be why you have a generation of reactionary, emotional young men who would rather shoot than fight, who have no regard for authority or law. Maybe a generation without any men in the house grew up without any idea of how to be men, and began rewriting the rules in spray paint. Look at all the male images back then: Kashif (kind of like the Sean "P. Diddy" Combs of his day), Prince and his crew (The Time, Jesse Johnson, et al), Rick James, Culture Club, Richard "Dimples" Fields, Full Force, niggas running around in elf boots, chest hair, eyeliner, and shit on *Soul Train* . . . consider . . . for a moment . . . rap music's histrionic (yet unaggressive) masculinity (beyond the esoteric politics, et al.) is what marginalized it for the longest time. Men in makeup and perms were the predominant imagery back then. The culture of the eighties made it okay—even preferable—for men to act and look like women, and it affected what we have now, and how men represent themselves and their gender roles. Now, assigning gender value to some things is problematic, and I think androgyny is okay—any man with two feet of hair, who sometimes wears sarongs and is even sometimes mistaken for a woman would probably have to—but I wonder what happened to a population of young men without a reliable media filter, when all they see and are regularly exposed to are androgynous men?

Blues and jazz contained lyrics objectifying women, as did other forms of popular music. Not that it's right, but men have always paid tribute to women in song in ways that women didn't find particularly flattering. Blues was often graphic and raunchy. Jazz was more covert but no less explicit. Soul music was pretty sexy for its time, prompting white America to try and ban "race music" until it became rock and roll. Pre-feminism, the dominant message was that black men and women needed each other, and the music and media reflected that sentiment. Post-feminism, the message was "we don't need no man," "use what you got to get what you want," and the messages in the music and the media became confrontational and adversarial. It's kind of a "chicken-or-the-egg" thing, and I don't know if we have correlation or coincidence.

Women who perpetuate the perceived problem seem to

bear no accountability. I always wonder, while we are decrying the no-good black men, who's keeping the women in check. What are women doing to help each other be better role models . . . like Karrine "Superhead" Steffans, for instance, the best-selling author who made her mail telling tales out of school about all the dick she's sucked. She says "don't try this at home" but the trappings of her lifestyle suggest to impressionable young women that dick-sucking is laudable, a profitable ticket to fortune and fame. Her first book, *Confessions of a Video Vixen* decries the choices she made, then her second book, *The Vixen Diaries* celebrates her life of continuous hoe-hood, and the life her bad choices afforded her. It's a bait-and-switch hustle at best, and an ugly dichotomous argument for promiscuity at worst. Not only was Karrine Steffans covered by magazines like *Essence*, but women like Oprah Winfrey held her up as some kind of "this is your brain on drugs" type of role model. Steffans even started a girl's club at some point like some kind of Girl Scouts for young dick-suckers, which she later pulled the plug on. The most troubling thing about Steffans isn't her horrifying backstory of sexual abuse and exploitation—which is a tragedy and far too common—but the idea that she wants to suspend your logical mind and convince you (and your daughter) that her first, best option for providing for her son was sucking cock, when everyone knows there's work at the post office that might involve some licking, but not a whole lot of dick-sucking. She was too good to loan-up and go to college like the rest of us, and decided to use fellatio as a social-climbing skill. And while she touts her book as a cautionary tale, she's printing up a new one called *The Vixen Manual*, where she will teach you the tricks of the trade. Like Eddie Murphy's Velvet Jones used to say: "You too can be a high-priced hoe." *Essence* should be exposing this chicanery. But apparently, Steffans has many lessons to teach.

In the pages of the Keyshia Cole issue of *Vibe* magazine, she offered counsel to young girls, letting them know that they shouldn't be afraid to, you know, "give up the butthole" to keep their man. What kind of advice is *that*?! Never mind that basically, only kids read *Vibe* anymore. Why is *Vibe* cosigning that? I don't cosign anal sex for kids—WTF? For adult women? Hey now—that might be some sound advice. But I digress. When it comes out in the wash, I'm sure it'll all be some black man's fault.

Responsibility is a critical part of the women's empowerment and liberation movement that is missing, ladies. You want to fuck around, pee standing up, and be as trifling and stupid as men can be, well, there is often a price and some responsibility to be taken for that. It could help matters if women taught their daughters to take care of their black man, instead of bemoaning the dearth of black men in an abstract way. I guess it's just easier to call that brother a misogynist, accuse him of being an under-cover fag, or just in need of some rejiggering than to consider, for a moment, that the reason for the decline of the black commu-nity is probably at the beauty shop right now, on her way to buy a Coach purse with the child support check and scheming a new way to win the big butt contest. A community can't rise any higher than the morality, dignity, and aspirations of its women. That's not a hard and fast rule. But I think it applies here.

"What about your momma, Jimi?" you ask. *"She's a black woman too."* Right. My moms.

Well, like 90 percent of you, I wasn't planned. When my fa-ther left, she kept a job. Like, eight jobs. My mother is the hardest-working person, besides myself, that I have ever known. We were on public assistance for a minute, but she didn't get comfortable. And she didn't spend the money on bullshit. She had fun but wasn't laid up with a different man every week. Not even every decade. She was too busy working. She got off welfare and made a way for herself and her child that didn't involve stripping or exploiting men for free meals. Notably, she didn't complain. She didn't like life alone, but she held her head up. She didn't like my father—and she still doesn't—but she didn't try to blame him for the bag she was in. She's too proud and dignified for that. She bad-mouthed him a bit, but was cordial to him whenever she saw him. She accepted her lot and kept it moving. Today, she is a proud grandmother steadying for retirement, and while she is often mystified that I get paid to write, she absolutely is proud of her son, the writer, and admires his voice. So yeah, my moms did some dumb shit too. That's how I got here.

But, the generation she's from, they didn't bitch and whine, or try to get over on niggas. Well, I'm sure they did on some level, but it wasn't a cult then. Back in the day, they got their own shit together, and didn't blame anyone else for their missteps. Those were the days before *Essence* magazine.

If *Essence* doesn't get it together soon, I am going to launch some kind of boycott or call for censure. The editorial mission, to empower black women at the expense of black men, has not changed since *Essence* started printing. Enough already. You don't like strong black men. But why can't I find a strong black man? Must be because they are all homo, in jail, broke, or dating white women. Or all of the above. Right. We got it.

Enough already.

Hip-hop has always held a mirror to society, and society is sexist—it was that way long before any emcee ever picked up a mike. Sure, this pervasive message is problematic, but *Essence* attacks the music while seeming to dismiss the media conglomerate behind it. And if *Essence* burnt some shoe leather and got out into the streets to get opinions from people who aren't paid to think about it, I'm sure they'd find—yes—a lot of anger, a lot of concern, but also a lot of sisters too busy buying stretch pants for Big Butt Nite at the Drink N Jook to give the issue much steam at all.

There is always some war on black maleness afoot, and the simultaneous denigration and celebration of women in rap, for me, seems like a natural rebuttal to it. Black men love black women, but don't love the changes they want to put us through. From Oprah to Judge Mablean, brothers are always no good, down low, or thugged out—you'll have to look long and hard for any woman celebrating unapologetic black maleness. There's a real resistance to letting a black man be a man without reconstruction, and this fosters its own kind of frustration. Black women seem to want men to be more like fictionalized caricatures than whole people. Young black men feel increasingly impotent trying to convert to some woman's ideal of manhood, and begin to model the behavior of the mythical "pimps"—street-made men who mastered all women, one way or the next.

Sure, rap has got some 'splaining to do. But the idea that rap music has single-handedly marginalized black women from society is offensive. While I don't agree with the critics, I freely admit that there is a point to be made here. But *Essence*—best known in my barbershop for articles like "Did Your Man Leave You for a White Girl—Again?!" "That Dude's a Bum, Girlfriend," and "No Money, No Honey"—seems only too happy to put the evil black man and his music in check. This time, as with most others, they are more than a little misguided. Rap music, when it's good, lets black men express themselves unbridled. The Denzel Principle has disillusioned black women and trained them not to listen to their men, and *Essence* magazine has been at the vanguard of this mass hypnosis by insisting that every man can be Denzel Washington or the do-right man of the month, while berating those who are not.

The Case for and Against Marriage

For some people, marriage is an undiscovered country, an ancient mystery, or some kind of encoded parchment in need of deciphering. Something Leonard Nimoy used to go in search of on that goofy show "In Search of . . . ," where he'd go to the ends of the earth trying to debunk man's mysteries. I don't have to rely on Mr. Spock—see, I've demystified the mystery.

Been there. Done that.

People who get to know me well find out that I was married. Twice. I'm youngish, so you should see the look on people's faces when I tell them: it's a bemused mix of horror and pity. They don't know if they want to laugh or laugh harder. No, strangely, the fact that I am a veteran of two failed marriages doesn't engender as much sympathy as you'd think it would. At least, not sympathy for me.

When you're a thirty-eight-year-old man who's been married twice, people naturally assume you're defective: fucked up in some imperceptible way. The thing is, I don't know if that's true— I don't pretend to be anyone's Denzel Washington. I'm just a regular guy making an irregular living, regularly making mistakes along the way. I could very well be fucked up: it's completely possible that I am incorrigible and unmarriable. Possible, but not probable. If I was that fucked up, it would have been hard for me to land a wife in the first place, right? I landed *two*: convinced different women with nothing to gain that I was husband material. So obviously, there must be something lovable about me.

At least, that's what my mom tells me.

Sometimes, people gather at my feet like I'm some wise, old tree: tell us about his thing called "marriage," they say. It's as if they don't get the main thing—that my marriages were not successes by any definition. They were contentious relationships with bitter, unhappy endings. Still, they want to know what I learned, and they insist on all the macabre marital minutae I can muster. So I have written about it. A lot, to the point where colleagues told me it was bad form, and my first ex-wife once called an editor to complain that I was using my power of the pen to impugn her character. My second wife? She's indifferent. Given that neither has written their own account (although they may now), it probably seems unfair for me to write about it much more. But I don't give a shit. It's my story too, and I have just as much right to tell my side of things.

Looking back on my marriages, I have more questions than answers about why they failed. It probably didn't help matters that I went into married life with the wide-eyed wonder of a child, all the Disneyland happily-ever-after fantasies I could imagine, the most selfless intentions. I was determined that I wouldn't let my marriage crash and burn like my parents had. I told anyone who asked that divorce was not an option, to the point where it was a running joke of sorts—Divorce: Not an Option. But after my second trip to D-Town, it's clear that not only was it an option, but it was the B-plan du jour. My sense of commitment despite adversity, it turns out, was the running joke.

On the other side of all that, I'm a new man. Arguably, a better man.

A man who could recommend marriage, but knows he'll never get married again.

Even when I was very young I fell in and out of (puppy) love effortlessly. From Diana, the very first girlfriend I had in day care, to Penelope, the very last one I had in high school, I dated girls with the idea that we were building toward marriage. This is the kind of innocent stupidity only a child could have. If you think it's hard to convince a grown woman to put her career on the back burner and start a life with you, imagine trying to convince a fourth grader in pigtails to "settle down." I wanted what my parents had had: something in me wanted to fix that in one way or another. I thought I could have that, and formulated all my romantic ideals remembering my parents, or watching *The Love Boat* and *Love, American Style*. Watching Darla and Alfalfa on *The Little Rascals*, Joanie and Chachi on *Happy Days*, and watching Marcia Brady go out on dates on *The Brady Bunch*. I figured, this is the norm: whatever these guys have going on, this must be what the ladies like, if Marcia Brady is going for it. I think that is where my eternal quest for love got its impetus: prime-time television. Or maybe I was just half retarded.

Whatever the call, I always had a girlfriend, but it didn't always go the distance. And to this day, I can pretty much recall every girl I ever dated in my grade school years and the reason why we broke up.

Day Care: Diana Walters. Outside of graham crackers and orange juice, we didn't have much in common. How do you even keep toddler love alive? I dunno.

Kindergarten. I think I was too busy getting vaccinated to really notice girls, and they basically ignored me. Kindergarten is also known as my Long Dry Season.

First Grade: Theresa Woods. The only girl in class who hadn't peed herself, she never said more than two words to me: "Get away." An affair of the heart, I'd say.

Second Grade: Shawna Benson. I serenaded her with Rod Stewart's "Da Ya Think I'm Sexy?" I even told her I was Spider-Man—for *real*. Ultimately, we grew apart.

Third Grade: Kimberly Smith. The other girls teased her for liking me, and peer pressure precipitated a messy playground breakup (more later).

Fourth Grade. I had a pretty good crush on the fifteen-year-old down the street whose name actually escapes me. She got pregnant. I was *not* the father.

Fifth Grade: Karen King. I gifted her a flower and she socked me in the face with a dodgeball. That's playground-ese for "It's not you, it's me."

Sixth Grade: Elizabeth. Intro'd via three-way phone, and dated for about a school year. I met her in the flesh once and she was heinous. I got standards, man.

Seventh Grade: Karen King. Again, right? Our love was undeniable, but I was almost completely indoctrinated with the Jehovah's Witnesses. Jehovah frowns on tongue kissing.

Eighth Grade: Gloria Fisher. She was an ugly duckling turned swan, plus she was a Jehovah. Good match, on paper. But I couldn't get a blowjob? Seriously?!

Ninth Grade: Michelle Giles. Intro'd via three-way call, she was Karen's best friend. Didn't go to the Hall. Private-school girl. Her dad hated me. Her lips, however, love me long time.

Melissa Kennedy. First white girl. I was way outta my depth, here. Wanted a white girl because, essentially, all my friends had one. Went bad, somewhere. Go figure.

Tenth Grade: Amy Washington. Really nice, really cute red-bone from California, only came to town for the summer. This is before e-mail and cybersex, so, pen palling—eh. It got old.

Eleventh Grade: Michelle Giles. We fell back in style, some kinda way. Commitment wasn't her strong suit, so we fell out just as quick. My first serious heartwreck.

Paulina Grey. A really cute coed with an innocent façade. She maybe had one of the worst reputations in the whole school. I didn't care—it was true love.

Twelfth Grade: Paulina Grey. Things were great until she sucked off a good friend of mine, thus giving credence to the rumors. No sleep for a week. Heartwreck #2.

And this is how I grew into love as a young man, with a trail of hits and misses, which would not have been bad, had my expectations not been so lofty. I think the failed relationships left a hole that I tried to fill with other women. Lots of other women. The problem wasn't just that I didn't have any idea what I was looking for or what qualified as wife material, it's that I wasn't very bright. I was easily taken in by smooth talk and fast curves. I had just enough game to get damn near any woman I chose, but not enough to know hunters easily get captured by the game. I was gassed on the petrol of looks and youth: young, dumb, and full of cum. Not quite full, because I got my dick sucked in shifts: I had a 9 A.M., a nooner, and a suppertime hummer. By the time night fell, my balls screamed for mercy. But I was not so inclined. No ma'am. My motto was "Have dick, will travel." As long as there were condoms and I had the energy, I'd do my thing. Sometimes, my dick just said "hell naw" and fell limp. Most times, though, I was cocked and loaded. I was in and out of school, semi-gainfully employed. Just a loser, aiming my member around town like some crazed pussy-sniper in a dick-shaped clock tower.

Not much of a life.

But such that it was, my life was consumed by the catch and release of desirable women, and even some not so. I'm not bragging—it was a hella reckless way to live my life. This was during the heyday of AIDS and I didn't always condom-up. I'm lucky to be testing negative, thank God. But back then you couldn't get me to slow down. I had so many at a time, and I thought I would marry them all. That is, I thought they all were marriage material, that I was making a pool of women from which I could choose a wife. Me, the philandering dick-slinger was horny for commitment. It never occurred to me that any woman who would suck my dick while I stood at the bar probably wasn't the one to meet my folks. But some of them did meet my people.

My mom is hard to get ahold of, so mostly, the ladies in my life would meet my grandparents, Sweetheart and Buddy. I think my grandma Sweetheart didn't really take any of the young ladies seriously, because she saw so many of them. She didn't get that meeting my folks was a vetting process of sorts. My grandfather Buddy gave them all kinds of once-overs, but he didn't favor one girl over any other. To be honest, I can only think of two women he expressed any approval of. And they ended up being the women I married. My aunt Lara didn't care for any of them. She didn't trust their motives. She would ask me about the women, who normally had everything on the ball.

"Now, look at you," she would say. "With someone who got it going on like that, what could you possibly have to offer them?" That's a pretty fucked-up thing to say to someone: you're so fucked up, no one with any sense would want to hook up with the likes of you. Lara was direct: this was her way. I don't think she was being mean: I think she wanted me to be clearheaded about the idea that women don't just get with men because of love and affections. As romantic as the notion is, she wanted me to consider the idea that women may have ulterior motives, however subtle. I didn't get that, precisely because I thought I had so little to offer, and because I considered myself a student of the game who could not be took or shook. To be honest, I'm not sure if she objected to them for good reasons or mainly because a good portion of the women she met were white. The others were black girls in the middle stages of some sort of psychotic episode, often evident in the crazed looks on their faces. I didn't *need* my family's approval, mind you. But I wanted it. I wanted to do things the traditional way. Besides, most of my family are women, and while men are easily fooled, women can neutralize other women's game. I thought they'd be able to help me pick good mates.

Not so much.

I was looking for love in the wrong places for the wrong reasons. When I started looking for a bride, smarts and mental health were kind of secondary concerns. I wanted a fine-ass bitch to make my wife. I had a lot of women, but I just wanted one. The heart wants what it wants. My cock? Well, it has a mind of its own. Sometime in the early nineties, the two came to one accord, when

Frances walked into the Record Den where I was working just enough not to be fired. She arranged through a mutual friend to interview me about house music, deejay life, or whatever. I asked him how she looked, and he shrugged, and I knew not to expect much. But when she walked in the store, my ears rang. Frances was a warm brown, with long flowing blond dreadlocks, great eyes, a large smile, and a neck-snapping walk. Frances looked as if she could have auditioned for The Supremes or En Vogue and missed the final cut by *that* much. Beautiful woman.

Frances was a parochial school girl from Rocky River. She lived alone with her mother, and never knew her father. They only lived a lower-middle-class life, but Frances talked and be-haved like aristocracy. I think her mom compensated for the gap of fatherhood in her life by spoiling Frances and giving her an inflated sense of self-worth. She'd been a debutante, for Christ's sake, so she had this posture like she was better than most people. I ignored that shit. Frances had been a sophomore at Clark until she accrued so much tuition debt that she could no longer regis-ter for classes or request official transcripts. She came back to the Cleveland area to get her head together and try to save money to get back in school. She took tickets three nights a week at the lo-cal racetrack, and she was so close to the horses that she often brought home fleas. It was shit money, but a job's a job.

We had a lot in common off the bat: she was kind of artsy and bohemian, like I imagined myself to be. She was a writer— or at least, trying to be. Me too. We both liked Andy Warhol, Keith Haring, and fine film. She had an air of sophistication that I would've had, if I wasn't so trifling. And when I invited her to come hear me play at Numbers, the gay bar where I was deejay-ing, she didn't flinch. Didn't ask me for an explanation or some accounting of my heterosexual credentials—she got it. We started keeping company straight away, despite the fact that I was already in a pretty serious relationship with Heather, a white woman I was living with.

Heather was a college student at Case Western Reserve University, and we met at a college bar through a mutual acquaintance. Heather was very smart, very pretty, and very exotic, with a wonderful smile and incredible figure. Outside of our lust for one another, we had a mutual love of books and smart conversation. She was bisexual, and it made our sex life fun, as she allowed me to bring women home. Watching her make love to another woman was like watching some kind of strong, beautiful ballet. She didn't mind if I fucked other women—she was secure in what we had. All in, she was a keeper, in my book. We liked each other a lot and got on really well. This relationship had legs, I thought.

Whereas Heather had no problem with me having another girlfriend, being number two bothered Frances a lot. Not because I had another, but because she was playing second fiddle to a white woman. Like most black women I know, she had a distinct dislike for white people in general and white women specifically, and our affair was a blow to her ego and self-esteem. When we talked on the phone, she'd cry a lot about it. It drove her into a mild depression. I'd been honest about my situation, so I didn't have a whole lot of sympathy. This was the deal: I have a girlfriend and I'm not leaving her. So what if she's white? That was my line, up front. To be honest, I wasn't sure what Frances saw in me anyway.

My cavalier attitude broke Frances's heart, but it was hard for me to feel responsible, because I wasn't holding her at gunpoint.

I didn't even try to make her feel better about it. I asked her to accept it or leave me alone. She tried to break it off a number of times, but to no avail. So she found another way to reconcile the relationship. She explicitly refused to have sex with me. This was her, putting her foot down. It was fine: I wasn't with her for the sex. That's not the way she fulfilled me. She filled a spot in my soul that I had heretofore not known was missing, and she did it with her clothes on. She had a hellacious body, but I really fell for her from the neck up. And I think the feeling was mutual. After a turbulent college romance, she said she found it refreshing to meet someone who valued her mind over her body.

Which isn't to say we weren't physical at all.

She'd blindfold me, lay me down, pull my pants down to my knees, and blow my brains out on her living room floor. Or we'd lay in her bed kissing until her pussy was dripping wet. Or take endless showers together. One day she couldn't take it and I fell up inside of her. She was loud and grateful, and as her ecstasy rose, the neighbor kids were quickly pulled inside the house. It didn't matter how loud we'd turn up her stereo—we were the kind of lovers who disturb the peace. And so it came to pass that whenever the neighbor saw me get off the bus and walk down the street to Frances's house, she called the kids in and shut all the windows, like I was the evil antagonist in some long-forgotten spaghetti western. Here he comes! Hide your women and children!

S'funny.

None of the sex quelled Frances's hurt from being the Other Woman. It made it worse. So, by way of accommodation, I told her that I wouldn't have sex with Heather within twenty-four hours of having sex with her. This pact probably got me the best sex of my life, as Frances kept my dick limp with the idea of out-fucking Heather. Of course, this was a brilliant lie. Not only did I fuck them within twenty-four hours of each other, often it was within minutes, and my balls were sore and drained from the strain of it all. But a man's gotta do what a man's gotta do, I guess. I don't lie unless I have to. And looking back, that was definitely a necessary lie.

As time went on and months turned to years, I couldn't rightly deny my connection with Frances. She was a good lover and friend to me. But I was committed to my primary relationship. To short-circuit it, Frances mounted an argument that really hit me in the gut.

She politicized my relationship with Heather, and made it about me choosing white over black, when it was more complicated than that. But hers was a simple argument: a "real black man" would do the right thing and choose a sister for his life mate. This was post–L.A. Riots, Ice Cube was still a Muslim, and everyone was wearing African medallions. Black folks all around me were choosing sides. The more I tossed it around in my mind, and the more she hammered it home, the more it made sense. I had to make a choice.

One Friday night from the sound booth, I called Frances on my cell phone and asked her to marry me. A few months and a tumultuous breakup later, I was living with her.

I'm a personable guy, but I wasn't always the sweet guy you've come to know and love. Back then, I was a jerk and Frances's mother, kind of a reformed sixties-era radical-cum-feminist, was not as crazy about me as you might think. I'd once made the comment that any woman who wasn't married by a certain age was either lesbian or crazy—her mom having never been married.

She took great offense that I would try to offer a semiclinical diagnosis of single women, and asked me to keep my opinions— all of them—to myself. Frances concurred. And I, against type, agreed.

Love is abiding.

I had no car, a job and a half, and just enough credit to get a decent place for us to live. But all the time I spent being a sex machine had taken time away from my day job, so I got fired not long after Frances and I got together, and I was too proud to file for unemployment. I wanted to work for my money. That was stupid—I was entitled to unemployment insurance benefits and should have taken them. She worked retail, and I kept spinning records and investing (burning) money from my savings to throw parties in an attempt to double or triple my money. They were kick-ass parties, but none turned a profit. She resented the fact that I wouldn't use my savings to pay off her school debt. I told her I'd go in for half. That wasn't good enough, and she berated me for being selfish. I wasn't being selfish—I was being practical. I just wasn't going to be a sponsor or a chump. At least, not yet.

She and I started out as a bus-stop couple—brokeity-broke— and we were getting married in much the same way. She resented the fact that I wouldn't take some of the burden off of her and file for unemployment. Trying to manage our meager finances caused problems, and this is where our relationship started eroding.

Financially, we had come from two different black cultures: whereas I had been raised more or less in a state of near-poverty, she had the idea (whether real or imagined), that she was from a very bourgeoise background. She had a Cosby-like fantasy of what our life should be like. I knew we would get there after we both got out of undergrad, but she wanted to live the Cosby life now. Me? I didn't mind the idea of being broke for a while, because I knew I wouldn't be broke forever. As a matter of fact, I thought it would be important for us to live small while we got through college. I grew up with very little, and it's not how I want to live my life, but in the temporary, it don't phase me. While I'm kind of a survivalist, willing to sacrifice for the greater good and a common goal, she may not have been as willing to commit to some of those sacrifices.

We both agreed to help each other through undergrad, and we both acknowledged it'd be uncomfortable, a struggle, like it's supposed to be. I said that once we got married, I'd give her half on her $3,000 school debt and we'd work together to scrimp and save to pay the rest of the balance. To me, struggling meant having no food: for her, it meant basic cable. She spent money on frivolous things like pizza delivery when she didn't feel like cooking (maybe 90 percent of the time) and a $60 grocery delivery, twice a month. We weren't doing well enough to order in and have luxury services. But she would not be denied. She didn't like living on very little, and made it known. Loudly. Profanely. All this made me re-think my marriage proposal. But then, we'd have sex, and everything would be fine.

She wanted to have as traditional a wedding as possible and insisted that her pastor marry us. Since I wasn't a member, he couldn't marry us in her church, but he consented to oversee a ceremony elsewhere. A few months before the wedding, he sat us down to do a matrimonial interview to judge our readiness and suitability. Before we met with him, Frances offered up some loving advice.

"If you fuck this up for me, so help me God—don't be fighting in front of the preacher," she said. "I know what he *says*, but he doesn't really want us to talk about our problems. He just wants to know how fucked up we are. He wants to find a reason not to marry us. So, just pretend, and it will all be okay."

And I did. What did I know about preachers? This whole process was foreign to me. And I thought that marriage was its own space within the universe where love heals and grows strong, naturally. I believed this with all my heart: reformed player as hopeless love-slug.

So, we lied to the preacher. He didn't buy it.

"I don't want you to think I doubt you-alls love and commitment to one another," he said. "But I want you to be careful that you aren't falling in love with each other's *potential*." This was the nicest possible way to say we didn't have a chance in hell of staying together. We assured him we were going into things with our eyes open and I guess we sounded sincere enough, because he agreed to marry us.

Her mother refused to pay for the wedding, either in protest or just because she was mostly broke. So, Frances and I paid for it out of our pockets, which meant we got married at a public park in the middle of the day and served finger food to our guests. I invited family and drinking buddies. Her extended family filled out the tables. Everyone wore a bemused look of wonder and pity on their faces. All the guests were either terminally single or divorced: there was no optimism to be found there. Except at the wedding table, in my chair. I stepped out of a perfectly good relationship to be with my soul mate, and I was ready for all the adversity marriage had to offer. But the day was young, and it would be a few hours before the enormity of my choices became apparent. It didn't take long to realize that I'd made a mistake. Like, hours. Minutes, maybe.

As soon as we got home and started packing for the honeymoon, it seemed as if she rattled off a list of things she expected me to do: buy a house, buy her a car, give her credit cards, and so on. I'd never heard anything like it, so I couldn't know she was being unreasonable. She really had the expectation that we were going to live like the Huxtables right out of the gate, and that I would do whatever it took to sustain that vision of the good life, whatever the cost to my wallet or personal agenda. Me? I wasn't on that, at first. Stick to the plan, I'd say. She'd graduate first, then me, then we'd be ballin'. In the meantime, it was lean-time: scrimp, save, and stack chips. But she said if I loved her, I'd put my needs aside. I'd do anything for love, and she knew it. So she convinced me to play along.

After we got married, it didn't take long for all that pussy I was getting to dry up. I became a sexual camel, forced to subsist for months at a time on scant and obligatory sexual encounters. For reasons that are still unexplained, my wife started smacking me around. Not just playful love taps, but the way Joe Pesci slapped that cowboy in *Casino*: hard, with the intention of keeping me in line. At first it was funny, then peculiar, and then, as it crept outside of our apartment and into social or public situations, embarrassing. It wasn't like she'd haul back and threaten me with the back of her hand, but if I didn't want to do something, or was in any way noncompliant she would deliver a flurry of open- and closed-fisted blows until I relented. People who witnessed this mistook it as *Bickersons*-style antics for their amusement. I guess they couldn't know that this was a part of my married life: I felt like a battered husband.

I know, I know—it's gotta be hard for some people to get their heads around the idea that a woman can abuse a man, certainly a five-foot-ten, two hundred-odd pound brother who has seen many a street fight and lost nary a one. The idea must strike you as funny—it struck most people as funny, and that prevented me from really talking about it. Instead, I alienated my friends and family so they wouldn't see me humiliated like this. Between the punani deprivation and the browbeating, I was bent the fuck up, losing all consideration for anything that didn't benefit her, including my future. I was pussy-whipped, without the pussy. All the emotional abuse and sexual deprivation abuse was sufficient to break my spirit, but the physical abuse added all the humiliation of the first two with an element of unique, emasculating degradation. I didn't want out of my commitment—I wanted someone to help me deal with this. But who's going to listen to a black man in an abusive relationship?

Nobody.

"So, when you say she *hits* you," asked her pastor, "you mean like, *hit* hit?"

"I mean, she hits me in the head, man, in the back . . . I have to block my face."

"Well, you two are still young and have a lot of time to find other people," he said. I didn't think dissolving the relationship was a very pastoral suggestion. So I had a talk with her mom, and begged her for advice.

"Well, James," she said, "I suggest you handle that situation the best way you know how." I thanked her and hung up the phone, completely shocked and confused: what the fuck did that mean, exactly? That's probably the stupidest fuckin' advice you could ever give a newlywed young man in my situation. What exactly is "the best way"? I know she didn't care for me, but my mother-in-law should have cared enough for the welfare of her child to give more thoughtful advice than that. I was smart enough to know that if I hit this young lady back, the cops would take me away, regardless of the story attached. So I never, ever raised my hand to Frances, unless I was fending off an assault from her hands, fist, or household cleaning agents. But the damage was done—she wore me down into a nub of the man I had been. I wasn't perfect, but I had been a man. But after awhile, I didn't know who I was anymore. I did anything to try and make her happy, in hopes that she would just leave me alone. I didn't have what she really wanted—money. But I had just enough.

After she bullied tuition money out of my savings account, she paid off her school debt, went back to school, busted her ass, and graduated. During this time, I dropped out, trying to generate as much bread for the household as possible, by working as many jobs as I could. I was a janitor at my Masonic hall, which they rented out. And I had to pull used condoms from the clogged toilets after every party. I also worked the cash register at Caribbean Sea, a seafood place in the hood—kind of like the ghetto Red Lobster-to-go. I made change for drug dealers, civil servants, and crackheads too poor or too lazy to get food at a real fish restaurant. The big seller was the White Boy—a whiting fish sandwich with fries and coleslaw. I also worked at a record store and was still deejaying. Everywhere I went, I smelled like fish, drawing hard looks and turned-up noses. "We sure wish you'd bathe" said my boss at the record store. I didn't care. I worked hard and honorably, because it was a small sacrifice for love. You do what you can to make your mate happy, and soon enough it would be my turn to get back into school, and once I graduated,

Frances and I would be the black power couple of the future: well-educated with a union sealed with love and ambition. And all the used condoms I pulled out of the toilets at the lodge, and times I burned my hand on the heating lamp at the restaurant, and long nights I spun records until I dropped, and crappy CDs I sold: it was all worth it to me. After all, these are the sacrifices love is made of.

Graduation day came for her, and I was proud to watch her walk the stage. I hooped and hollered from the stands. "Thank you for helping Frances make this happen," her mother said. It felt good to hear that. And I knew Frances was grateful too, even if it seemed she intentionally wouldn't say.

After all the celebrating was done and we made it home, I reminded her that I needed to get registered for class, because now it was my turn to concentrate on school.

"I don't think so," she said. "Why don't you just do you? From here on, why don't you take care of yourself, and I'll take care of me." I thought the reason we got married was so we could belong to each other. I was confounded, confused. At a complete loss.

When it came out in the wash, she wasn't willing to help me because she didn't think I was college material—I'd languished in junior college so long, she probably figured I wasn't smart enough or worthy of a college education. Any time or money I spent in that pursuit, she reasoned, would be wasted. She thought, like my high school counselor before her, that I should learn a trade, go work in a factory. Something that didn't require a lot of thought. I couldn't have been serious about going to college, right?

"Well," I said sheepishly, "I was thinking advertising . . . but now, I dunno. I think I want to be a journalist . . . a writer of some sort."

"A writer?!" she said. "Listen, you'd *better* be trying to get a job at a factory or something, because you will, never *ever*, be a writer. There aren't many things you could do, but trust me, writing is not one of them."

Three months later, she took care of herself and bounced, taking just about everything but two plates, a spoon, a fork, some of my clothes, and an old solid state black-and-white TV.

When she left, I was broke with school debt of my own, no woman, no job, and no prospects. I lost three thousand dollars and a lot of dignity trying to make my marriage a success. All those years I should have spent in school, I was helping someone else fire their dreams. I felt like a chump. I got punked.

I vowed I would never marry again.

Things were looking up after my divorce, by my standards. I started a new job schlepping checks for an investment firm, and I felt important. I was renting a small hole of a room with an antique shower in the bathroom—chicks loved the shower. It was a tall Franklin shower from the late twenties sitting in a marble stall: a huge, curved showerhead with caged brass pipe work that made it look like the skeleton of some ancient Argonaut. My widowed landlady said her plumber husband installed it for her mom, back when my room was the in-law suite. She'd turned down offers of $60,000 and up for it, which probably means that the shower was worth more than the entire house. It was old and sexy, a bitch-trap, like dinner at Benihana or a '57 Thunderbird, except much, much faster.

"How does it work?" they'd ask.

"Only one way to know for sure," I'd say, pulling off my

pants. Soon they were undressing, and together we lathered up as I put down some plumbing of my own. This is how it worked. Every time. Candy's dandy, and liquor's quicker but an invitation to bathe in an antique shower is the best way to get women naked.

There were a lot of women in my life, post-divorce. They rallied around me with food and sex, both things I needed in great quantities. They'd arrive with heaping plates of chicken and fish, completely made-up, dressed in tiny black numbers with black stilettos, as if inappropriately dressed for a funeral: as if someone had died. Many were trying to fall into that wife spot, not because I was this great, wonderful catch—because carless and ashy with a bullshit job, I wasn't—but because good guys are hard to come by. I guess.

My ex had always said I was a soft touch: too nice. Never again.

When women got on my nerves, I kicked them out of my pad. Quickly. It seems they were under the impression that I was hurting for pussy to the point where they could act a fool. They were mistaken. Pussy, I had—I needed more, like peace, pussy, and good company. It was tough to find the trifecta, because I wasn't for the bullshit, disrespect, or loud talking, the trio of emotions I seemed to encounter the most often. You can go out and loud-talk the guy on the curb, I'd say. But if I wasn't going to treat a woman like a bitch, I sure wasn't going to be anybody's bitch. Not again. Fuck that.

Some women took that mantra as a challenge, like it was a game, and tried to see how long it'd take me to raise my voice. They learned the hard way. Others respected my unadulterated insistence on being treated like a man, and I returned the favor in kind. But my fuse was short in those days, so they all saw me point a finger at the door at one point or another. I didn't get angry, raise my voice, or even give them a chance to apologize. I just pointed a finger, and she had just a few minutes to put on her panties and shoes and get out. Men that get all upset with women can't always articulate their emotions, and end up with high blood pressure or trying to beat on a woman. Those men are punks. Real men don't hit women, and I'm too much man for that. Don't need any drama in my life. So I watch them walk away, wounded and bewildered, and it was empowering. I felt like I was taking my life back and I was doing a public service by teaching them a lesson: wiles, ways, and wagging hips don't always work. Sometimes you pop fly and you end up agitating the gravel.

Simple lesson. It's hard but it's fair.

Strangely, even with this kind of assholery, I didn't want for company—single life was good to me. And I think some women get off on rejection. For a while, I needed the attention to affirm my virility and viability: I needed to find the manhood I'd lost to my first wife. After a few months of fun and games, it was too much keeping all the women straight, and they were demanding of my time. But it wasn't like when I was a younger man, when women were a hobby—after my marriage, women were more benefactors and happy distraction. I wasn't looking for another wife—never again, I said.

And then I met Leslie.

I met Leslie working as an assistant to a broker that I schlepped checks to. She was tall, fair-skinned, and exotic with her large atomic-red Afro, tan silk top, skintight brown slacks, and pumps to match. She was exceptionally attractive. I couldn't see all of that from my vantage point. What caught me off guard was her smile. Full-lipped and completely genuine, stretching her lipstick across an unusually pretty face. That smile was the thing that got me to peek over the counter to see what this shorty was working with. And she was working with quite a bit. So I chatted her up. It turns out that we had a lot of mutual interests, like reading and writing. She said she was just working for the broker part-time, for medical coverage for her and her son. Just a twenty-five-year-old single mom trying to make it the best way she knew how.

Now, I had a rule about women with kids: *no kids*. As in, no thank you. I wasn't interested in playing house, or having some broad trying to mack me for money or fighting off somebody's baby-daddy. I had enough problems. But she lived with her babysitting parents and siblings, so the truth was that she'd always be coming to my house, and I never had to see the kid if I didn't want to. So, after a few phone conversations—and she met my shower—we started keeping company.

She'd get off work, hop on a bus, come to my crib, and we'd make love. She was the aggressive type who liked pushing me down onto the bed, but that shit didn't fly for long. I'd push her back, snatch down her pants, rip off her panties, and fuck her like a dog. And after a good spanking, she took a liking to Jimi'z law. Between rounds, we'd lay back in the covers listening to the soundtrack of *Love Jones* on repeat, over and over again. Talking.

She was good to me, good enough where I didn't need any other women in my life. She gifted me with food and nicer underwear. When she came by, she'd cook, clean, and fuck. And leave. Up to this point I'd never been treated so well by a black woman. It softened me up and wore down my defenses, but our relationship didn't have any legs until her son's third birthday.

She invited me to her son's birthday party, and I took a pass. I wasn't that interested in getting to know her well enough to know her kid, and since she and I didn't have a future, it seemed inappropriate. But she convinced me as only she could, and on the appointed day, I hopped a bus to her parents' house. Even though I'd begrudgingly met women's kids before, this was my first kiddie party. Truth to tell, if it violated my personal protocol, I didn't think it was a big deal.

Walking up the drive of her parents' modest suburban home, various kids sat on the stoop. Music blared from inside as I knocked on the door. Leslie ushered me in, but there was no smallish child to be seen. "Where's the tyke?" I asked. And then a young girl—Leslie's youngest sister—came tearing around the corner with a cute little boy in hot pursuit. This must be him.

"Hey Little Man," I said as I caught him midstride. "What's your name?"

And he spit on me. Right in the face.

I put him down, and he leapt back into the chase. I wiped the spittle from my face. And that's how I met Preston, Leslie's son.

"I'm sorry," she said. "He's in that spitting phase."

"Yes, of course," I said. "That spitting phase." I took a seat in front of the TV in the living room, marking time. As soon as the cake was cut, I'd cut out. Toddler spit was not my kind of party. Minutes dragged until the cake was cut, and I started looking at a bus schedule when he began to open his presents. One was a video game—Crash Bandicoot—an absurd gift for a three-year-old. Preston went to the TV and put the game in the PlayStation console. As it turned out, at three, he was old hat at video games. Me? I hadn't played since Pac-Man.

Then, he turned to me.

"Watch me play?" he said with these disarming big brown eyes. So he found a place on my lap without a formal invitation, and I watched in amazement as he whopped the shit out of it. I was entranced. The party went on around us, but he and I sat there in front of that TV.

"Watch me?" he asked. Yes.

Night came before I knew it, and Leslie's dad offered me a ride home. It was time to go, and Preston walked me to the door, holding my hand. I looked at down at him in the stairwell. What a great kid.

"See you later," he said. Without thinking, I picked him up and kissed him on the cheek. Today, I don't know why I did it, but at that moment, both our faces lit up with smiles. He looked me in the eye, and I saw myself for a moment. Then I saw something greater than me. The unspoiled emotion of a child. He was a heavy fucker, so I wanted to put him down, but I never wanted to let him go. And for one moment, there were only two of us in the world. I made it a rule not to date women with children, but when he asked me if he'd see me later, I knew he'd see me later.

Such a sweet kid deserved a life with a mom and dad, not living in his grandparents' attic. But Dad was in jail or otherwise incognegro, and the attic was the best Leslie could do. As we grew closer and closer—Leslie and I—I began to feel myself falling in love, and all I could think about was that great kid and that wonderful smile. She was good enough, but Preston? He deserved better. It all began to make more sense.

One day in the afterglow, Leslie and I decided to commit to each other and start a serious relationship that would include her son. We decided to start building something like a family. Against all my best instincts, not only was I falling in love with this woman, I let her son take my heart as well. It took some time, and some long, hot sessions of persuasion, but eventually I just laid back and accepted the fate of the lovesick. I can remember the moment I put my defenses down and smiled freely. My instincts told me to run, but I had to let go: her little boy and his incredible smile freed my heart. She was great, but as long as he smiled, I had no worries. One day, it just happened. I put all my guards down, was free from all my inhibitions.

And now, I was in.

We found a place where we could all live, and we became a family. She was the mommy, Preston was the baby, and he stopped calling me Jimi, instead opting for Daddy. The future looked bright for this found family.

That's around the time it fell to shit.

I'd thought Leslie to be industrious, what with being a single mother and all. I was sure she knew something about a hard work ethic. And for some time, it looked like I was right. She was working hard, and I was doing the best I could pasting together checks. She was a good woman—patient, as I struggled to find work—despite what her family told her. She wanted an addition to our family, but I told her there was no way for that, until I made more money. Well, one day, my life as a writer took off, and there were no more excuses. We had a child together and were looking forward to the future . . . until she decided that maybe she wanted to start a family with another guy. Without warning, she snatched up our kids and moved in with this zero, packed up all our furniture, and there I stood, again. Alone. Trying to scrape my face off the ground. I'd lost it all. Again.

What a fall it was. But it was the last fall like this I'd take, I promised myself. This time, for real.

I'm thinking that the next time I get together with someone, and we think it's love, if we just have to be together all the time, I'm opting for the Shack-Up.

I've shacked-up with a few different women. And it was magical: cow, free milk? Check. No papers obligating you? Check. "The Man" not regulating your love affair? Check. When I was living with women, everything was hunky-dory. Nary an argument about money, sex, or the weather, because it was understood that if you don't like how it's going down, you can always opt out. In my circle of friends, the average marriage lasted four years, maybe. Man, I have friends who have shacked up with people for ten, twelve, fifteen years or better. Some of them are still going strong. The most interesting thing about that is, most of those couples are *gay*. That makes me wonder why gays want to get married, lately.

As gay marriage becomes legal in California and New York recognizes these unions, it won't be long before other states have to deal with the issue. Other countries are much more tolerant of homosexuality than America is, and I think it's time our country articulated a policy. The problem is where does gays' right to marry cross over to some people's right to be morally offended by it? Do you just have to go to everyone's gay wedding? I've been to a few, and let me tell you, it's something.

As a rule, I didn't do weddings, mainly because I didn't think anyone could afford the inflated fee I would charge to put up with that schmaltz. But as a guest in the gay community, doing weddings for free was one way I showed my appreciation. The black gay community is poor, so nine times out of ten, these ceremonies were held in Numbers, the gay club I spun at, right after or in place of the weekly drag show. No expensive china plates, linen napkins, or champagne toasts. There was a small cake and chicken wings, *maybe*. The couple-to-be would walk onto a platform near the dance floor and exchange vows that they had written themselves. The butch lesbians would wear suits and the femmes would don dresses, and I gotta tell you, they made good-looking couples, in the main. Men usually wore tuxes. Sometimes people got married on the fly, and would be wearing whatever cross-color outfit they had on that night. I always respected these couples, but I didn't take the marriages seriously because by and large, the community didn't either. There was often an emcee, but never any judge, mayor, security guard, or religious emissary officiating— the ceremony was mainly for the couple and to serve notice to the community to *leave this piece of ass alone*. It was not so much a political statement as just another level of commitment. As I mentioned, some of these unions lasted a long time, but mostly the couples ended up in heated, public, and violent divorces. Makes me wonder what the point was.

Marriage, as we have always understood it, is a union between a man and a woman, largely for the purpose of procreation. I think it's important to be able to have a bond between you and your beloved that the law recognizes, but what the nature of that union should be is another question. Call it something else, because it isn't marriage—it's its own thing. When attitudes and mores change, so too should the terminology and the law.

I haven't been to a gay wedding in recent years, but back

in the day, I did get to one wedding that went all out—an extravaganza, relatively speaking—and it was an event to remember.

The ceremony was in the living room of a smaller home all decked out with flowers and pastel sashes everywhere, and violin music lilted through the air from a boom box. There was a makeshift altar of beautiful flowers, with seating for about twenty or thirty people. The cake was set just to the left of the altar. A gay pagan dude who officiated gay weddings as a side hustle mingled with the guests, who consisted mainly of friends, family, and curious workmates. The brides were elsewhere getting dressed.

A glance into the peanut gallery gathered to witness the blessed event delineated two general moods. The friends of the brides? Anxious and excited. The family? Dumbfounded and perplexed. This was one of the many lesbian interracial marriages I've attended, and the colored folk in attendance are always confused. But it never fails—there is at least one black relation who starts tastin' a lil early, and doesn't mind letting everyone know what they think. "What the fuck am I doing here?" mumbled one elderly patriarch, looking about at the surreal circus of a room, where it appeared as if the casts of *The Cosby Show* and *Queer as Folk* had exploded. "This is some *bullshit*."

Soon, the brides made their way down the stairs, decked out in white gowns. Not bridal gowns per se—more like better cocktail dresses. As a hush fell over the room, the pagan Reverend Doctor Gaylove spouted off some mumbo-jumbo, leaving the brides themselves to offer more thoughtful, heartfelt words in their vows. As he pronounced them spouses for life, they turned to kiss each other, and you could hear a mouse shit on cotton—the room froze, and then burst into applause as the two made their way back down the aisle to prepare for the reception.

Now, every kid you know loves a wedding reception, because it guarantees free cake, free food, and a chance to be king of the dance floor. But as we all began to disperse and get on our way, at least one child was confused. "Uh . . . I thought she was getting married," one little girl said. "So where's the boy?" Someone yanked her arm and whispered a reprimand as we all piled into cars on our way to the reception.

Normally, wedding receptions are held in a Masonic hall or the basement of a church. But most gay weddings I've been to end up at one of those hoity-toity, gay-owned restaurants with a French-sounding name, and this was no exception.

Note to gay couples planning weddings: at the reception, everyone is eager to get their eat-on. Couples with a lot of little nieces and nephews on either side should not serve food that looks back at you, still moves on the plate, or requires subtitles. Nobody is checking for that. At this wedding, noses were turned up, faces were broken, and children were pointing at their plates crying. While all the brides' friends chowed down, somebody's uncle made a run to Rally's—hey, ya gotta eat!—and once the bar was opened, a good time was had by all. And that couple has been together a long-ass time—as of this writing, they are still kicking it strong, as far as I know. But I don't think the ceremony had anything to do with that.

Lately, I'm opposed to marriage in any form: a commitment between two people that requires the state to cosign it seems doomed from the beginning. I think gays had it right when they were content to just shack up and live together. Also, I think homosexual politics shouldn't put itself at war with what are considered to be hetero-normative institutions like marriage. This could only stoke bad feelings and misunderstandings. I think everyone can find their place in America without stepping on the next person's toes or beliefs. Gays should have the right to live and love freely, but heterosexuals should also have the right to stand by their moral convictions, if those morals tell them that homosexuality is wrong. Live and let live, I say. You can't always change the world to suit your lifestyle. We are all here together and have to find a way to make it work.

I don't know if gay marriage is the answer. Many people can only see the Judeo-Christian picture of a man and a woman in a blessed union—how does God feel about Adam and Steve or Frances and Tonee getting married?

I don't know, but I know I don't want to be the one to ask him.

I have relations that have married two or three times, mostly, I believe, so they could fuck and be right in the eyes of God. I don't give a damn about the eyes of God so much: hey! He gave me a penis, so he knew no good could come of that. I got married twice, and it's obviously something I'm not particulary good at. So I'm over it. I always laugh at people that say they marry because they crave intimacy. These folks never stop and think that there are some things that you don't *want* to know. Well get your mind around this: your wife? She farts in her sleep, man— so loud, you'll duck. And she doesn't always smell like Chanel No. 5, but then neither do you, Musty McCrusty. Welcome to intimacy.

All that in, I still think there is a case to be made for and against the whole love and marriage dealy.

PRO: It's nice to have someone to come home to.

CON: When you get married, it's hard to have your own space.

PRO: No more one-night stands.

CON: Sex either comes in heavy waves or not at all.

PRO: It's nice belonging to someone.

CON: Codependence can be unhealthy and scary.

PRO: Being single sucks.

CON: You get a lot more pussy when you're single.

PRO: It's noble to dedicate yourself to one woman for the rest of your life.

CON: The rest of your life, God willing, is a long time to be with one person.

PRO: Married life has a quieting predictability.

CON: Married life has a quieting predictability.

PRO: When marriage works, it is the most wonderful thing in the world.

CON: There is no way to know if your marriage will go the distance.

PRO: If it doesn't work out, you can always get divorced.

CON: Gunshots are less painful than divorce.

PRO: You find someone to bear children with.

CON: Getting married to have children, or because of them, is basically asking for a divorce.

PRO: You'll never be lonely again.

CON: When you are married to the wrong person, marriage can be very lonely.

PRO: You split the bills.

CON: Your mate may not work for the white man. Which means they don't work.

PRO: Guaranteed home-cooked meals.

CON: This assumes somebody can cook, and the cooking is edible.

PRO: All your friends are doing it.

CON: Who cares?

PRO: You finally have some stability in your life.

CON: Nothing is as unstable as marriage.

PRO: You can finally relax.

CON: Even the bad marriages are a lot of work.

PRO: Free jewelry.

CON: Can't think of one just now . . .

PRO: No need to hire a dog sitter for business trips.

CON: She makes you babysit her cat when she's out of town too.

PRO: Marriage, failed or not, teaches you a lot of hard lessons.

CON: Marriage, failed or not, teaches you a lot of hard lessons.

*   *   *

The first lesson I learned about marriage I learned while me and my ex were dating: always trust your instincts. When I met my ex, Frances, she was free—she had a fuck-buddy, but nobody staking a claim—and that should have tipped me off immediately. Why is this fine, intelligent black woman virtually alone? Some folks are alone by choice, and that's cool for you, because you can tell right up front they're sick. No normal person, given a choice, wants to live life alone—that's a life of Ex-Lax, multiple cats, and *Matlock*. People are alone normally because they're fucked up, and nobody can deal with that shit for longer that it takes to bust a nutt, get dressed, and leave.

As it happens, when I met her, I was already occupied, and that isn't uncommon. Anyone with anything at all to offer already has someone trying t'stake a claim. Not that I was the bomb catch, by any stretch . . . but I had certain charms that discerning women covet.

Second lesson I learned: recognize girls with more game than you. I thought my exes were suburbanites who couldn't compete with my club-tested, ghetto-approved, street legalese. I don't know how I could have been more wrong. They were sophisticated players in their own right with long, internationally known reputations. I got taken down by love. Very early on, I was in love. I know because I'd been around it a bit. I mean, love had come and gone, and love and I went to the same parties and danced at all the same clubs: we'd even shared cocktails after hours. I knew love pretty well. I'd been smitten and bitten by a woman before and come out on top, so if I resolved to avoid it, it wasn't going to happen. Not to me. But it did and took me under in short order.

Lenny Kravitz said, "Let Love Rule." My ass. Keep your head on straight so you can see game from the curb.

The third lesson I learned is that love doesn't pay the rent or fire ambitions. Somebody has to have a job and/or an ambition to have more in life. While poverty has its own distinct romanticism and there is nothing sweeter than starting at the bottom and ending up on top, not everyone is feeling that approach. Not when the bills come due.

Right after I took my vows, everything changed. Those women went from being my partner to being my owners, my adversaries. Kissing the bride was like firing the starting gun of a race to divorce court, it seems. Women are smarter than men in every way—I say that a lot, and it's true. Especially emotionally, women have a greater grasp. I wasn't ready for the disappointment, the rejection, the feeling of being disposable and replaceable. I never thought I would hurt the way I did, or bruise so easily. I did. Women can mask their pain. I, on the other hand, have a hard time pretending I wouldn't like to be in love again. If only I could trust love again. Not that those women were the loves of a lifetime, but they were supposed to be. When you give that away and it boomerangs back and knocks you to the ground enough times, you learn that's a game you'd rather not play. The Denzel Principle has taught me one thing: I am no Denzel Washington, and I could never be. I can only be myself, and hope that's enough.

Sure—I'll love again—I've loved since. But it's like going on a virtual roller-coaster instead of mounting the ride and actually taking risk. Love's not the same ride without the risk. Divorce changed me. Love and marriage were so traumatic that although I haven't been married in years, my life hasn't leveled out or normalized. I just adjusted to a new normal—alone. All the guys I know are always talking about what bitches their ex-wives were—not me, Jack. I have good taste in ex-wives. Since they sometimes pop up in my work, people insist that I provide them with an identity, but I don't. I am happier not married to them but I am not happier alone. Love isn't a renewable resource: sometimes people take it from you and use it all up. But I remember love. And sometimes, I desperately want to know it again. But it's easier to be single, both feet on the ground. Standing in line but never taking the ride.

Her Peeps

Men don't really listen to women, though we should. I know—
we think we're attentive. But the truth is we tune women out soon
after they begin talking, leaving them few choices if they want
to be heard. But even when we do listen, and offer feedback, most
often that feedback falls on deaf ears. Women, even your woman,
thinks everyone in the world is worth listening to but you. Dr. Phil,
Jerry Springer, Jenny Jones? These people are brilliant. You, on the
other hand, are a fucking idiot as far as your girl is concerned. I
know, you think you got your woman in check: you pimp-by-dick,
and got the game on lock. Maybe, but not likely. Chances are better, no matter what kind of guy you are, her friends and family
run her life. Women crave attention and the approval of their inner
circle. Just because you are her man, don't think for a minute
she listens to you, respects your opinion, or that you can comment
negatively on or discredit her sphere of influence. You matter, but
not much. When she really wants some advice, or some clue as to
what to do next, she turns to her friends and family.

She relies on the counsel of her people. Whether she needs
advice or not, she always listens to her peeps.

NOTE TO THE LADIES: No one is as likely to break up your relationship as your mother, sister, or best friend. That's real talk. Your moms, who couldn't keep your dad in the pad; your sister—the lesbian—and your BFF, whose man is down low, fresh-out, and fucked up, every which way? They all have great man advice, copious and free of charge. Now, I know you thought you were happy, but you were wrong. FACT: unhappy people are drawn to content ones with the intention of disrupting their happiness. Miserable people want you to be miserable too, so they offer you the same advice that got them in the bag they are in, ostensibly because it will probably work better for you. Right. They keep you hip to the latest gossip, looking out for you: they saw your man talking to some white girl, or thought they saw him coming out of a bathhouse with a drag queen, or heard he was dealing drugs on the side, or coulda swore they heard some other bullshit to put your shit on tilt. Meantime, dude was at work. Or chilling at the bar with his boys. But don't worry—you can do better anyway. Why are you settling for *that* loser? From what I have observed, black women are their own worst enemies in that regard. They can always be counted on to give each other bad, tainted advice.

Onward.

Now, I've never had a good relationship with my girlfriends' friends or family. Not ever. Young in the game, I was always too much of something and not enough of something else: lips too big, too poor. Too quiet or too outspoken. Too much hair, or not enough "down there," the bookish kid who knew too many big words: an all-around social misfit who didn't really tickle anyone's fancy. Probably not the natural choice for kickball captain or class president. That kind of thing gives most kids a complex. Instead, it emboldened me with a false sense of superiority. See, there's a real power in being a square peg: you can't disappoint your peers because no one has any expectations. When you're an outcast, you keep your own counsel, so everything you do is a surprise. It's like, you're Machiavelli, except without the charisma. You can't manipulate people so much as situations, based on what people in your environment think of you. It's like, passive-aggressive mind control. I know—I've probably spent too much time analyzing playground politics, but I had a rough time of it. If you see me in the street . . . give me a hug.

Please?

But I bet you never thought being a playground crank was so complicated, huh? I bet Stalin wasn't a well-liked kid either.

When I did get a girlfriend, I tried to keep it a secret from my group of friends and their girlfriends, so word wouldn't get out and her peeps would stay out of our mix. Sometimes, you just want a love that the world will leave alone, even when it's just puppy love. The way things are in grade school with all the busybody bathroom sessions and cafeteria chatter, it's pretty hard to pull off a clandestine affair. That never worked, and it wasn't long before they'd be off in a corner of the playground chattering and giggling, rolling their eyes and pointing. Making up jump-rope songs about liaisons in trees. It's hard to keep your relationship off the radar with people singing about it. Singing is normally a celebration, but not on the playground. It's more like high-tech hazing. I learned early on that a bunch of women in one place, talking, means something ain't right. The spirits are aligning, and nothing good can come of that. Hen sessions lend themselves to messy, public breakups. Even in grade school. Like my first breakup.

I got fired by my third-grade girlfriend because her friends laughed at my hand-me-downs, my crusty chapped lips, and the way I was always wearing "high waters" or "floods"—pants whose legs didn't extend past the top of the ankles. It was one thing to wear hand-me-downs, her friends reasoned, but another to advertise it. So to make a statement, she fired me in front of the entire playground.

Me, hopeful and helpless. Wanting it all to be some kind of joke. This kind of humiliation doesn't happen often in a man's life: to be belittled and rejected by the opposite sex in the presence of his peers in a moment of cheap-seat street theater. No allies, as my crew watched from afar, huddled, too afraid to laugh, afraid to move, for fear they'd raise the ire of the girl-mob. When it does, there's an indelible mark that never goes away. I can't forget her—pigtails, funky-fresh green Garanimals hookup, no-name sneakers, with the entire female population of school revolving around her like she was the queen bee of some evil, prepubescent lip-smacking, neck-rolling she-hive of Amazonian killer bees just hungry for the sting. The girls split their numbers like simple division leaving Kimberly facing me over a huge chasm of sand and grass. I don't remember her words, but I know that it wasn't clear what I'd done to deserve this, or why her friends did not approve, or why I didn't measure up to her expectations (and more importantly, the expectations of others). But with her neck-roll and a snap, it was clear to me that I was dismissed. There was a cheer of "Huzza!" as she swished off into a horde of proud young coven of future heartbreakers: this was her coming out. She was so happy to have finally completed her initiation into womanhood: she trapped, caught, and killed her first boyfriend. And they call it puppy love, but I was wounded by the revelry and dark celebration of a downed man-child. This man was done; this romance was over.

Because her friends say it is so. Until I became a man, this scenario would play itself over and over again. When I became a man—when I became of age—the ritual was still the same.

There was the genteel flirtation, where I let her know, but not know, I could be interested. Maybe a look, a *stare*. Just a certain brand of kinetics that says without saying, "You should be mine." The kind of invitation a gentleman puts out to a lady, knowing that she makes all the decisions. Whether or not she gives you time has nothing to do with you. Women choose men—this I know— I'd let women choose me. Let them look back, walk that walk. Play those games.

Then the quiet conversation from prying eyes—I'm a firm believer in the "quiet place to talk." Sometimes, it's a coffee house, or my favorite restaurant, where all the staff know me, know the game, but no one else knows my name. We can be alone to talk about the things people talk about before they take the dive into an adult chat. We don't have to rely on other ears interpreting our chitchat. It's all about us as we get to know each other. You make the first move. I make the first move, but it's more like a race you're winning, right? After all, women choose men. This not to say that you're in control. This to say that I'm the boss, and I defer to you. This is the way you like it.

We try not to talk about each other, but we do, and my friends—men—are indifferent. But your friends—women—are invasive. Who is he? Where is he? What does he do? Where does he go? How does he get there? How long? How short? How tall? How fat? They put everything you know, everything you tell them through the sieve of their own experiences, and always their worst experiences. Soon they are whispering supposition in her ears, and I'm answering for crimes I haven't even committed. They know us, and watch us when we are together and they can't put their finger on it, but there is just something about me they don't like. Despite the fact that you seem happy and they say they want you to be happy, they don't want us to be together. You smile too much around me, and that ain't good. Misery loves company, and if you are happy, who in the world will they have to commiserate with? So they effortlessly tear us down.

And it isn't quite the playground, but it is the playground of our virtual world: our circle of friends and aquantinces. Some are shocked, some know it was too good to last, and some of your peeps just love to watch the drama. Love the chance to see a man melted to nothing. But I know this game so rather than step forward into the hive, I keep my distance and just let you slowly walk out of my life into the throngs of cheering lady friends waiting in the wings with gallons of ice cream, bottles of wine, books, and movies that will do for you what it has done for them: make them happy, lonely.

Your peeps are lonely people whose only means of connecting to others involves making sure the people around them—people that they call their friends—are as unhappy or more so than they are. This is the way of women. I don't know any *Sex and the City*, giddy, spare-ass-Annies in Manolo Blahniks living life and getting good lays. I know groups of successful women who have spent their lives building careers, looking at the other end of forty, bitter that they can't keep a "decent" man for more than one night. Often, a woman's family and friends conspire (intentionally and by accident) to diffuse a woman's happiness by scrutinizing and criticizing her choices in men.

These people think it's their job to keep watch on her virtue and guard it from unscrupulous types. They have the best interests of your girl at heart, but their definition of "best interest" probably doesn't involve you, or any other man for that matter. Women generally want a man for practical purposes, but don't feel as if they need a man. So when you and your girl look to be going too well for too long, her peeps show up to throw a wrench in the works. Women fill out their social circles with a coven of unhappy friends.

Women generally have a few different types of peeps in their circle of friends:

- **Aunt Esther.** LaWanda Page immortalized the wig-wearing, testifying, Bible-thumping Esther Anderson on Norman Lear's *Sanford and Son*, but her peeps are not quite as subtle and laid back as Page portrays on screen. Her peeps say that if you take her out for a drink, you are drinking Satan's ejaculant, and if y'all go to the movies, you are putting her under the influence of darkness. And sex?! Oh boy, it's not bad enough that you fornicate, but if you both put your mouths in unclean places—clutch the pearls! Both of yous are going straight to hell. And she reminds your girl of that every chance she gets.

- **Evelina.** Evelina may or may not have a man, but she doesn't have a good man. Or maybe she does, but that doesn't stop her from being angry all the time, and she brings that energy around your girl. She's always bitching and moaning, and encouraging your girl to join her in the madness. She doesn't like you, or anything about you. No good reason—just because you're breathing.

She's had a rough life, and she wants to make your girl's life rough too.

- **Dr. DonHavamon.** The doc has five degrees, three cars, two houses, and has joined the vibrator of the month club. She don't *need* no man, and don't know why you think you do. She's spent so much of her life trying to be Ms. Independent, that she gives off an air of superiority and high maintenance to any real man. She wants your girl to go back to school and get a suitcase full of degrees, so that she never needs a man to take care of her. Yet and still, the good doctor is always home every Friday night watching Tyler Perry DVDs and eating sorbet. She hasn't learned that success need not come at the expense of your social life. But she knows that she needs some company and wants your girl to be it.

- **Woman in the Shoe.** Everyone knows that children are a blessing—but not when you have more than you can afford. Her peeps in the shoe keeps telling her that all she needs to do is have a baby, and she'll be *set*. She can lay back on your support check, the state will pay for her schooling, and she will have herself a beautiful baby. Of course, Ole Girl tried that out one too many times, and now has a child by every man on her side of the block. And she says she wants more. She loves kids, but don't need no man telling her how to keep them clean and fed correctly. She can do bad by herself, she reasons. She wants your girl to join the club.

- **Divorcee.** Marriage was the worst thing that ever happened to her peeps, and now that she is divorced, she wants to make sure your girl doesn't suffer the way she had to. So every time your girl sits down to talk about your relationship (despite the fact that you tell her not to), Divorcee will take some nugget from her story and draw a comparison to some scenario in her own failed marriage, like your problem putting the seat up. See, when Divorcee was married, her husband left the seat up and one night when she had to shake the dew from the lily, she sat on the toilet and sprained her pussy bone: true story. Now that she is divorced, and it's just her and the eight cats, she doesn't have that problem. But if your girl isn't careful, Divorcee says, she will.

- **Miss Cleo.** Miss Cleo is one of her peeps who claims to be clairvoyant and somehow connected to the spirit world. Everyone knows that person who claims to be some kind of magic negro because they can guess all the right totals on *The Price Is Right*. It's like that one friend you have who claims to be half-Indian because they have "good hair," knowing full well all their people are from Detroit. Okay. So anyway, this chick claims to have a portal into another realm, despite the fact that her spirits didn't tell her she would be fired from her assistant manager's job at the Dollar Store. She thinks she can see the future, and things look bleak for you and your girl, she says. When the fuck is she gonna keep her a man and get herself a job? Funny—the tea leaves never seem to know.

- **Dear Abby.** Abby always has the best advice, but her own life is fucked up. Still, she mounts such a good argument and her words make something like sense to the point where people—like your girl—will always listen to her. She's a cancer, with this strange power to influence—like the Jim Jones of beauty salons and hen sessions. She's a menace.

- **Dee Dee Downer.** Dee Dee imagines her life as fucked up and wrought with misfortune, and she presumes the worst for everyone, including your girl. If the sun is out, she's afraid she'll get sunburned. If she won a million dollars, she'd bellyache about the taxes. And whenever she gets a man, she worries him to death to the point where he leaves just to be done with the nagging. She nagged a hole in his head about every little thing, and she does the same thing with your girl, trying to worry her about every little next-to-nothing. If you buy her some jewelry, she says it probably ain't real. When you prove it's real, she says you probably stole it. Show the receipt: she says you are fucking the jewelry store manager. And on and on. Dee Dee Downer takes bad energy wherever she goes. And she's always up under your girl.

- **Sister Soldier.** Sister Soldier is super-black. Never voted in an election, preferring instead to get down with a sixteen-point plan to save the black nation and uplift the family. The problem is she can't afford bus fare to the revolution for herself, her boyfriends, and her kids. She's so caught up being black, her life is in shambles. Yet, she tries to impose her plan on others, and questions everyone's blackness and the blackness of their union, whatever that is. Unless you and your girl are dreadlocked-out, wearing dashikis and sandals, chewing bushwick, your blackness is suspect. When she turns up homeless, she wants to crash with your girl. Trouble ahead.

- **Opal.** Like Spike Lee's Opal Gilstrap from *She's Gotta Have It*, this is the lesbian in her crew who's always throwing shade, because, truth to tell, she wants to munch on your lady's nookie-cookies. Now, because your girl is so smart and progressive, there's no convincing her that her peeps is trying to knock her. Months after you break up, they're at the jewelry store picking out commitment rings and figuring who's gonna get impregnated turkey-baster style. Oy.

- **Nola.** Nola Darling, the protagonist of *She's Gotta Have It*, lives a sex-positive life where she fucks who she likes, when she likes, and everything is peaches and cream. Her peeps is living that same spare-ass-Annie scenario, and she talks about it like it's such a fabulous life, and this makes your girl wonder if the thing you really need is an open relationship, so she can fuck your friends and half the NBA. The secret is that Nola is fucked up emotionally, and probably the next candidate to turn up positive.

- **Jealous Jenny.** Jealous Jenny makes a lot of good points about how you're slipping, and adamantly argues for your dismissal. The thing is, on the low? She listens to the way your girl degrades you and knows that your girl doesn't know how good she has it. So she talks you down, in hopes that your girl will dump you and then she can come by your pad, put the pussy on the monkey, and claim you as her own. Come to think about it, Jenny might not be so bad . . .

- **Dee Elle.** Dee is constantly accusing you of being gay. She says you display all the signs: you're black, you're male, and you like big asses. Obviously, you're a homo on the low. The thing is Dee Elle is kinda mannish, and she's always looking at girls in a wanton way. She swears she's not gay, even if she's been known to make out with her "best friend" when she gets drunk—every Friday. Dee is struggling with her sexuality and trying to deflect that onto you.

- **Earthquake.** Going out with her and her peeps is always a recipe for disaster, and when Earthquake comes along, it gets to be a rolling boxing match. Your girl doesn't want you to get into it with her friends, but Earthquake tags along with you all just for the sport of goading you into a fight. If you ignore her, you get in trouble, if you engage her, you get in trouble. If you ask your girl to kick her to the curb, you look like the bad guy. Given time, Earthquake will bring your relationship crumbling to the ground.

- **Lazy Linda.** Lazy Linda gets six checks a month, has no kids but has madd scams to squeeze money from your local human services. She hasn't held a job since that lemonade stand she had in first grade. Her life is consumed by collecting Coach purses, staying ahead of government investigators, dating on MySpace, and trying to convince your girl that she is living *The Life of Riley*. Lazy Linda wants nothing out of life, and wants your girl to get nothing out of life.

- **Juliet.** One of her peeps reads all the romance novels, sees all the romantic movies, and is looking for love just like that, and rags on your girl for settling for less than the ultimate romance. Juliet is waiting for Romeo or Prince

Charming. Anybody. Somehow, she always ends up with Prince Alarming, a man anyone could see is a mental case, but may have looked good on paper—the toilet paper he wrote jailhouse poetry on before he got let out. She's going to make him into her Harlequin Romance. He may make her into a hand puppet.

- **Oprah Junior.** Oprah Winfrey is a rich black woman perpetually engaged to a brother who looks crazy suspect. So how in the world she gets anyone to put any stock in her relationship advice is beyond me. Yet, Oprah Junior owns every recommended book, subscribes to all the e-mail blasts, shops at the Oprah store, and hangs on every word Oprah says or has ever said. The problem is that Oprah is batshit, but her peeps repeats her advice like the gospel, trying to convince your woman to join the cult. Some of that madness sinks in, and next thing, you're carrying your girl's purse and walking her dog, Stedman Graham–stylee.

- **Nunja.** Nunja is worse than a busybody. Not only is she in your business, but she insists on offering her advice, and for some reason, your girl always listens. You try to tell her your problems are nunja her business, but she turns it around like you are trying to be controlling. Nunja imagines herself as a referee but she's really an instigator.

There are variations and combinations between but these are the ones you can clearly recognize. Dealing with friends is one thing. Dealing with family is quite another.

I was a little taken aback when I heard that the president was thinking about moving his mother-in-law into the White House.

I can't think of a faster way to bring the country down than for a president to move his mother-in-law in. He wouldn't be the first, but damn. Now, I know she's helpful with the kids and such, and that's a good thing. But having a relation—any relation—crash at your pad is bad for business. It's simple physics, really: if you have a compound that is the family and you add an element that could throw off the balance, then you risk disintegrating the compound—doesn't matter whether it's your trifling brother, Uncle Mudbutt leaving skidmarks everywhere he sits, or the mother-in-law. Now, MILs get a bad rap for a reason: they nag, they are notoriously nosy and meddlesome, and they will give you advice on everything from the right way to raise your kids to how to spread mustard on a sandwich properly. This is a well-worn trope, but like every stereotype, it has its base in common sense and apocryphal knowledge. Moving your MIL into your house, unless she is sickly and in need of care, is bad for business. There's no exception to this rule. If Obama needs child care, he'd be better off paying for it than having a live-in mother-in-law. He's going to spend more time managing her than managing the country. She'll have her girlfriends up in there playing Mahjong and Tonk, sitting around gossiping about the comings and goings and classified information. It's bad enough having to deal with your MIL on the holidays and family occasions. Could you imagine that the country is in the middle of some global crisis, and the First Mother-In-Law is in the Oval Office giving advice? Holy crap.

Unfortunately, Barack can't use the "we don't have any room" excuse that works in most cases. I can't be the only person out there who thinks Obama moving his mother-in-law in could go really bad, really quickly. He doesn't come across as one of those milk-sopped "Honey Do" brothers who lets women rule his roost, and I appreciate that about him. Michelle has already let it be known that she intends to fall back and let her man do his thing. Let's hope her moms got the memo. One thing I know for sure is that there is a double standard at play. Because if Obama's mother was alive and he was talking about moving her in, he would be universally panned as a mama's boy. People want to racialize this topic and make it about turning the White House into the Huxtable compound, and I'm not on that. This isn't about T-shirt politics or the black woman. This is about relationship dynamics and the construct of a successful nuclear family. Sister, just ask yourself, do you really want his mother telling your kids the opposite of what you tell them to do? Or having to manage and push back against someone else's sphere of influence with your children and your man? Seriously. There aren't many women in the world who would let their husband move their mamas in the house. Family is tough and moms are toughest. That's why they have their own house. I wish Obama well with his trip into the unknown.

There are basically a few different types of mothers:

- **Moms Mabley**—Like the comic laughtress of the "Chitlin' Circuit," every time you see her, she's fucked up, but at least entertaining. She cusses up a storm and causes a scene in every restaurant asking for an extra glass of water for her dentures while she gums away on chicken bones. At one time, she was fine as hell and had it all on the ball. But she fell off the horse a few good times, and never got back on. Now she's collecting an SSI check, trying to send you to the store for beer and rolling papers. Moms Mabley is sweet as apple pie. The problem, of course, is that the apple doesn't fall too far away from the tree. Her peeps is harmless, cool, and a lot of fun to get high with. She's toothless too with a butt as large and flat as a Sony TV. Welcome to your future.

- **Bitter Mom**—This is the mom who got pregnant at thirteen and spent the best years of her life raising a child. She eventually married and divorced a shit-heel of a man, for the sake of the child. Now she's lonely and pissed off at the world, determined that her daughter avoid her fate. She thinks she wants her daughter to find a good man, but she thinks all men are bad. She's pretty fucked up, trying to fuck up her daughter, telling her to do and say dumb shit to put you in her pocket.

- **Independent Mom**—Independent Mom has been both mom and dad so long, she doesn't know how to just relax and enjoy parenthood a bit. Granted, being both Mama and Papa Bear is stressful. But if Mama wants her daughter to find a man, she needs to back up a little. She's overbearing and obstructive, feeling a need to approve (never) or disapprove (always) of everything. She's single and keeps company with eight cats and a ferret named Oscar. She has convinced herself that she doesn't need a man, and her daughter doesn't either. When you're dating a woman with a mother like this, love is a battlefield.

- **Mr. Mom**—Your girl is one of the lucky ones—both of her parents are still together. But between her peeps, Moms wears the pants. Moms is the Deebo of the house, cheats on her dad like a pimp, shot-calling everything from what her dad does with his paycheck to when and how he should pee. Your girl looks up to and admires her moms and hopes you and she can share a love like her parents. Lucky you. Hope you like wearing an apron.

There are also different types of dads:

- **Sergeant Dad**—Dad may or may not have any military experience, but he demands military bearing from his children and his household. Which would be right on point except for the fact that he wants to put you under his thumb too. He wants to run his house and your house too. That, you can't allow to happen.

- **Punk Dad**—He's not a man. Just a paycheck, maybe. Product of too much refiguring and an *Essence* makeover, Dad is just a shadow of a man, flinching any time anyone in the house raises their hand too quick, for fear of being slapped around. Even Sprinkles the housecat has Punk Dad in check. Spends a lot of time in the basement masturbating about the life he could be having if he was a man. Your girl really admires this cuckold and says you could learn a lot from him. *Not*.

- **My Pal Dad**—Pal Dad is a rare find indeed. See, Dad used to be you when he was young. He knows the game, knows all the rules, and he keeps it gulley: stays out of your business, doesn't take sides in arguments, and loans you money to help with the bill when you need it without vig and on real reasonable terms. Prides himself on his ability to stay out of your business. He's the kind of dad you can have a drink with.

- **Ghost Dad**—Ghost Dad is a picture on the mantelpiece or in a family photo album—he isn't around and has never been around. Her mother rarely speaks of him, but your girl wishes on his name: wishes she knew him, wishes she could call him—wishing she'd ever spoken with him. She's never had a man in her life, or any significant relationship with a man who wasn't horizontal. So either she's got the Dizzle and expects the world from you or expects nothing at all. Both scenarios make your life hard.

Seems like every woman I've ever dated, her mom was in our mix like a bad deejay. Everything we did, everything I said, anything I wore, she had an opinion on. There were times when I was madd broke, trying to gift my girl, but her peeps always had something smart to say, always scrutinizing and devaluing me and my tokens of affection. I bought one of my girls a stuffed animal with a gold earring in its ear, and her moms was like, "What are you, in grade school?" When I bought one girlfriend some candy, her peeps said, "Why the fuck he buy you some Lemonheads?" Didn't matter that it was her favorite candy— my thoughtfulness didn't count. When I bought another girl Godiva chocolate, her moms convinced her it was too exotic and put it in the freezer, where she would fetch it a year later during an emotional case of the "lonelies." I asked one dad if we could have a man-to-man talk and he said, "You better speak to my wife." I asked another father the same thing. He looked around, confused. "We could," he said, "but I think we're a man short."
Hmph.
You expect her parents to be critical, but you don't expect them to be combative, interfering, or destructive. It's not that I'm sensitive but it's hard to pitch woo when someone is standing on the sidelines rating your efforts. The truth is, you can probably

dodge and dismiss the friends. But you have to deal with her family—there's no way around it. Trust me—I'd know if there was.

When the holidays roll around, I've always taken a deep breath. Not because I'm about to be besieged by my relations—as a Jehovah's Witness, one of the religion's perks is that there is rarely an event that rallies all the kinfolk. So I never have to see my peeps if I don't want to. I've never worried about dealing with my folks during the holidays—instead, I worry about breaking bread with my girlfriend-of-the-moment's people. Because nothing can make trouble like idle dinner chatter . . . with her peeps.

If you've played the dating game like I have, it means, come holiday time, you are the accessory of choice and the man of the hour at all her family functions. I've dodged this responsibility when I could—referencing my staunch religious upbringing to explain my unease in the presence of unfamiliar pagan rituals. Which, of course, is bullshit. In the end, if the relationship lasted over a week, and that week fell in the fall, I would find myself at someone's dining room table begging off seconds of broccoli and chocolate-chip casserole. You know if you get around some colored people, somebody's mama will burn down a kitchen correctly. This is the big upside of eating with her peeps: maybe she can only cook a hot dog but her moms knows what's up. It's hard not to wonder why she didn't pass that particular skill on, but probably impolite to ask.

However, there was always that one play-aunt who would break out a recipe she clipped from a double issue of *Good Housekeeping* back in '72, and then the dinner got real long. A napkin can hold only so much food, and when that culinary concoction came repeating on me, it was nothing nice. So after years of experience, I would always take strategic trips to the head with a napkin in my pocket, dumping uneatables into the toilet. Most times though, I got my eat-on just fine at the family functions.

Back when I was young and in the game, and even when I got married, a home-cooked meal was hard to come by. Single, I basically subsisted on cooking potatoes in chicken grease. And when I got married, Pizza Hut was the house specialty. So around holiday time, you could usually find me a whirlwind of fingers, forks, and elbows at her family dinner table, while her people looked on—disturbed—and my woman of the moment masked her embarrassment. Fingers and elbows? That's right—I'm not much for airs—I don't get off using the right forks and spoons. My dinner manners aren't Cro-Magnon, but if there is fried chicken, I eat it with my hands, and if the getting is good, I *will* lick my fingers. Grab a roll and toss me one, Grandpa, f'real—we all family, right? Then let's keep it family and eat like we're hungry and not like we're teaching a class on the Food Network—pass the Trappey's Hot Sauce and shut the fuck up.

The actual consuming of food is the easy part of holidays with her peeps—as long as you can keep your gas silent and evenly dispersed, you're in the clear, as I see it. It's the before and after that'll get ya, when her peeps are getting to know you . . . getting to know *all* about you. Be advised: this is a trick bag. You are an idiot if you indulge it, and an idiot if you dodge out of it. I just tried to keep my mouth full of food, but sooner or later, I had to start talking.

Predictably, that's when things slid downhill.

When you're a stranger in other people's homes, they have a bad habit of wanting to interview you. Entering her people's house around the holidays feels too much like pulling back the curtain at the old *Tonight Show*, as you're expected to wave and smile like Sammy Fucking Davis Jr., greeting everyone with a wink and a point: who loves ya, baby? Immediately, you're called to the couch for chitchat, but there's nothing of substance to talk about.

The approach I've found works best for chick-relation conversation is to stick to the basics: name, rank, and serial number. I don't follow sports and any talk about religion or politics is likely to go south. Mainly, I've said little past "hello!" and "what time is dinner?" until my girl's people eventually began referring to me as "the robot," as in, "you're not bringing 'the robot' to dinner this year, are you?" and that was fine by me. Because the raw truth is that no one really wants to know what you think—about anything. In the courtship phase, all her relatives see when they look at you is somebody playing the doggie game with their little girl without the benefit of marriage. And even if you're married they don't like you much, and they would eat your liver for holiday dinner instead of Aunt DeRosa's double-dry turkey, if only someone knew who seasoned it.

In a weird, cockeyed way, I owe my career to her peeps.

At one family function, I was trying to be personable, animated—like a man with a pulse, not so much the machine— and I engaged in conversation. I made the mistake of talking to my then-girl's peeps about how I was working on some essays— thinking about changing my focus from a career in copywriting to more creative works. Her peeps—Moms, a couple of family friends, and others—looked confused. After all, I hadn't graduated from community college yet. How did I expect to be a writer? Well, they wanted an example. I mentioned this one essay about interracial relationships I was writing and how I was largely indifferent to whom others choose for a mate.

At that moment, one of her bootleg relations asked me how I felt about them. I said what I pretty much always say—that it *was* my choice, but it wasn't anymore, and that it was no skin off of my back—live and let live. "If you believe dat," he said, "then you even mo' uva punk than I thought you wuz."

Okay.

This old coot, only one scheme away from being a hobo—selling bootleg FREE O. J. T-shirts from a gunnysack—called me a punk, as everyone's face broke around me. Now, this is why you don't say much at her people's gatherings, because heaven forbid you have to rock someone's yacht for intentionally disrespecting you—giving you the wide-eyed "whatchu gonna do?" look and all.

What did I do? I clammed up.

But I resolved that from that point forward, I was going to be myself with whomever's people—no holds barred—and let the teeth fall where they might. A man can only be so many punks in life—trying to play the game with her peeps, I played myself out. Never again. It took me awhile to refine this approach.

Years later, another one of my girlfriend's peeps—mother, this time—cornered me and inquired as to how we were getting along.

"I don't give a fuck how *we're* getting along, because I'm not dating you," I responded. "The best way to keep me and your daughter happy will be to stay out of our mix, and let me be me."

Now, I actually regret putting the monkey on her forehead like that—I apologized to her years later for the intemperance. But she had to get it straight, right? It was tough but it worked very, very well. Strangely, I got along with all her peeps famously—better than most of my own. And while her family used to say,

"That boy sure don't talk much," now all they say is, "Will that boy ever shut up?" They found a way to navigate and decipher my idiosyncratic behavior without offering any unsolicited input, while lending a helping hand when needed, and you gots to love people like that.

Mothers almost universally dislike me, but if your girl ain't got no menfolk, it's a thousand times worse. Nothing beats a bunch of hens pecking at you from every direction, asking about your money, your schooling, and your baby-mothers. Women without men in their lives are bitter and suspicious of every man, and have a tendency to put the kibosh on their best girlfriend's happiness—even if that best girlfriend is a daughter. When you have a choice, choose a woman with a father in her life. A dad really helps the communication string along, and opens a space for a man-to-man talk if it becomes necessary on either end. Seriously. A girl with a dad in her life who isn't too fucked up is a rare find, and a good catch. Like it or not, you've got to deal with your woman's family and friends—it's a package deal. If you can short-circuit the Denzel Principle and all the unreasonable expectations that come with it, with any luck, her people will be your people one day too.

Baby-Mama Drama

Like most baby-mama drama, mine started on my mother's kitchen table.

Like every other kid you know, I already knew where babies came from by the time I was thirteen. Heck, at eight years old, my mother had already told me about the birds and the bees.

"You came from my rear end," she said. "My rectum."

"I came out your booty, Mommy?" I queried. "Like dookie?"

"*Just* like dookie," she said.

My dad didn't come around often or stay long enough for conversation, so naturally, I turned to the playground, where the finest young minds of my time debated sex, politics, and lunch box aesthetics. While my mom's explanation didn't pass muster, it gave me just enough information to take back to the block, debate intelligently, and weigh other theories critically. Some were still thinking it was the stork. Since our mailman was his daddy, Fred naturally assumed babies came in the mail. Nine-year-old Santana—a fine thinker and expert on all things lurid and profane—seemed to have the best line on the female anatomy and the miracle of birth. He had an older brother who showed him all the ropes. During one of his lunchtime lectures on booty-cracks, I interrupted his lesson to assert the theory that babies came out of girlies' buttholes. There was a murmur of discourse as Santana gave me a knowing smile and pulled a page of his brother's *Player* magazine from his Scooby-Doo lunch pail. A dainty young brown lady was bent into the camera, as if bracing for a cervical examination.

"Nah, man, you're fucked up. Not *that* hole," he said pointing to the young lady's anus. "*That* hole." And all the boys drew in hard to the page, staring wondrously at Miss December's angry pink vagina.

School bell rings. Class dismissed. Lesson learned.

As I've mentioned, I kinda grew up as one of Jehovah's Witnesses—those annoying folks who knock on doors saving souls at the most inopportune times imaginable? Yep. Those were my people. I say "kinda" because although my mother's side of the family was almost entirely J-Dubs, my mom didn't fall in the fray until late in her twenties—just in time to repent for the disco years. I went to the Kingdom Hall and even out into the field service once or twice, but I was never quite indoctrinated. I went because I had to, and all the other parents warned their kids to stay away from me, as if I were Satan himself. As kids are wont to do, I kept up the best appearances, and did what I needed to get by. Like the one-on-one Bible study assisted by aides from the Watchtower Bible and Tract Society.

I was thirteen, sitting across the kitchen table from Carl Williams, the young guy who ran my bible study. We studied a bible aid called *Your Youth: Getting the Best Out of It*. Of all the literature that young Witnesses dread studying—and there is *a lot* to dread—the little red book, called "The Youth Book" for short, is up near the top. "The Youth Book" was the second of two books directed toward kids and pre-teens, and it represented the first serious dose of the doctrine: the first full glass of the Kool-Aid the J-Dubs are selling, and you're either drinking or you're gagging. You buy it or you don't. "The Youth Book" is chock-full of hooey about why God wants parents to beat the shit out of their kids, effectively disown and ignore dis-fellowshipped family members, and snitch on friends and kin. It espouses the virtues of disavowing college in favor of settling for a low-paying job, living in your parent's basement, and cramming "the word" down people's throats in your spare time. I'm exaggerating of course, but the essence of the hard sell is to do what God says, or he'll rip you a new one. So you sit there, at the kitchen table, reading this book penned by the hand of God or one of his assistants, absorbing this instruction on growing up, obeying your parents, and eating your vegetables, all allegedly based in biblical admonition. Later, you'll realize this was your last chance to ask questions like "Does a blowjob count as sex?" and "Why is God watching me jerk off, anyways?" But you don't, because your God-given parents have permission to beat the snot out of you at their discretion, especially if you ask stupid questions. So you smile, nod, and feign acceptance. Like me.

As a young Witness, you get to the two chapters in "The Youth Book" called "Growing into Manhood" and "Becoming a Woman" and you are stuck on the other side of a kitchen table talking about sex with someone who is not your parent. Someone we presume to be a mentor but in reality is something closer to a taskmaster: Jehovah's Gopher, whose intent is to transform you from a free-thinking, open-minded kid into a close-minded Bible schlepper. He began to unravel God's truth about sex and sexuality from across the kitchen table, and there was nowhere to run. This was to be my fate, and as Carl and I sat at the precipice of this critical moment of my convergence, I got the farts. My bowels churned.

What I couldn't say is that I already knew the mystery of life by the time Carl and I sat down for our genteel discussion of conception. Aside from Santana, there'd been a few "show me" sessions with the neighbor girls and, of course, the teenaged female twins who babysat me and demanded I watch while they masturbated. They were all sorts of demanding, as it turned out, and trained me well. So for years, I knew the basics, the mechanics, if not the actual genetics and biology of it: I knew that the same place you put your penis is where babies came from. Nonetheless, Carl and I struggled through the text and discussed how, when a man and woman are in love, a man puts his "urine hose" in the woman's "birth canal" and releases his "love elixir" to create God's greatest gift to man and wife: a child. Sex was bad, jerking off was a hot ticket to hell, and I had no business talking to girls about anything other than Jehovah. At all.

The next day, at same said table, I come in from walking my dog to find my mother sitting with my blue book full of phone numbers. I'd put it in my special drawer, with my comics, some love notes, and my Michael Jackson collection, but Jehovah, as it turns out, doesn't really believe in respect or privacy for kids. Go figure. At thirteen, I was indignant. All these years later, as a parent myself, I can dig it. Kids need dignity, but not necessarily privacy.

"I know you and Carl talked about sexual intercourse in 'The Youth Book,' and they teach it now in health class. Do you have any questions?"

Questions? For my mom? About sex. Yeah, right.

I shook my head.

"Good. Because the only thing you really need to know," she continued, "is to keep your pants up and your zipper zipped." She held up my phone book. "What does a thirteen-year-old boy do with girls' phone numbers?"

"I dunno."

"I don't know either," she said as she tore my phone book into tiny little pieces and threw them on the floor. "Now clean that up." That phone book held the numbers of over one hundred young ladies met at The Hall, at school, in the street, and happenstantially, ladies eager for chitchat and conversation. I was proud of it. I bragged about it to my friends. It made me king of my section of my subset of the playground. Even at The Hall, other Witness boys gave me the nod. Phone numbers were sexless, harmless trophies of would-be player status. It's harder to get a number than a sucker-bite. At least, when you're thirteen it is. I coulda been a contender. All my playboy wishes and gigolo dreams? Gone.

This abject lesson was the last of my formal sex education.

I hear on news reports and talk shows that young black men impregnate as many women as possible as a rite of passage to showcase their virility. While it sounds sexy, the fact is I've been black a long time, and I can't say I ever met any dude in high school giving high fives around the cafeteria because he knocked up his girlfriend. More often, they were weepy and scared shitless. In my crew, we laughed at guys who'd gotten someone pregnant, because they were *fucked*. Anybody we knew with more than one kid was just fucking stupid, and we stopped talking to them altogether. They were too stupid to roll with "the crew" and never had any money to chip in for beer. No back-slapping or grand huzzahs. If anything, we'd dump liquor on their behalf, in mourning. No more kicking it, no more bullshit: their life was over. You were locked forever to some chick you nailed in a back hall somewhere, whose last name you could scarcely remember. That shit ain't cool. They were dead to us. I've sat across the bar from grown-ass men dropping tears at the prospect of spending the rest of their lives connected to a booty-call. Seems too easy to run down to the drugstore to get a condom to prevent that sort of thing. Not that I'm the expert on planned parenthood.

Early in my sexual life—like, high school—I used two methods of birth control. Three, if you count prayer. For a minute, I was doing it Lunchables stylee, using sandwich bags as condoms. This, so my mom wouldn't find any condoms in my room and know I was having sex. I ate the sandwich in my bag lunch and put the baggie in my wallet . . . you know . . . just in case.

Pretty brilliant, huh? You can't really get a ton of pussy like this—just the sight of you pulling a baggie out of your wallet will either make girls laugh or pull their pants up in disgust. Of course, if you do it doggie-style, she's none the wiser, until you are trying to fish it out of her cooch afterward, and even then, she need not see it once it's recovered. Now, this is the kind of maneuver asshole guys run on horny coeds, wisdom passed on in locker rooms from senior to freshman. Not so proud of it, but it was cheap, they were handy, I was horny, and dumb as a bag of rocks. And, at the end of the day, a sandwich bag was probably better than nothing, although the bread crumbs probably gave the girls the mother of all yeast infections. I was a kid, and in a back hallway, or deserted restroom, you have to improvise, right? I was too embarrassed and scared to go buy rubbers from the drugstore, but at least I was thinking on my toes. When I got the gumption to buy rubbers, like every high school boy, I used Trojans until I found something better. As an eighties club rat I switched to Mentor—no, no, not the Freshmaker—the condom with anti-viral Nonoxynol-9 that came in a small cup with the funky applicator and adhesive. It sounds like some crazy shit, I know. And it certainly wasn't made for a wallet. But that condom was the shit back in the day. You'd whip out a Mentor, peel back the seal, and women would watch you put it on like you were transforming into Voltron: a horny Voltron. Like, Holy Jesus: what kind of Space-Age shit was this? That shit never slipped off, and it sealed like Tupperware: never an air bubble. Mentor condoms were the Mad Hatter for baby-batter. I don't know why they stopped making them: putting one on was actually as much fun as having sex.

When I didn't condomnate, I used that old-school, Quick Draw McGraw technique—aka the "stop n squirt" or "doin' it porno stylee." The key to that maneuver is in the timing. This was fun because, try as you might, you were never sure how much distance you'd get, how much nutt you'd fire, or where exactly it would land. At first, I was just concerned with getting the beat right: did I pull out quick enough? Where is she on her cycle? What this girl's name again? Later on, I was Lee Harvey Oswald with the nutt, and could land sperm on the tip of a girl's nose from the back. In the dark. Not like it was sport or anything. This was an emergency form of birth control that required precision and concentration.

And then there was the prayer.

It says a lot that I've never been burnt. It says I'm picky and I'm really, really lucky.

The two most beautiful words to come out of a woman's mouth are "I'm cumming." The two worst? "I'm late." And I've been on the other side of that phone call. Boy have I. I can vividly recall all of the times I've been pregnant, and the lessons I learned:

#1 The Fan
Lesson: Never take her word for it. On anything.

When I was in high school, I worked at the local college radio station producing a show and cohosting on weekends. Sometimes the host was out, leaving me to actually helm the show. This is kind of a high school dream for anyone: to have thousands of people listening to your every word, dancing along as you spin the tunes. I flirted with every female who called the show, but Jennifer actually flirted back. We talked a bit when she called in for a request, and that eventually led up to a meeting at her house. She lived off in the cut, with her sister and mother, who worked late at night. When her moms went to work, that's when I hopped a bus and clocked in on her couch, making time as best I could with Baby Sis cock-blocking. Somehow, we managed to get our fuck on, and the first time we had sex, she put the rubber on me—backward—and it came off inside her somewhere. I didn't think much of it, hoping condom juice and the power of prayer would protect me. All the rest of the time, I got the rubber on without incident. Of course, she got pregnant, and I was scared out of my mind. I knew I wasn't the only one she had sex with, but I just presumed that with my luck, the baby was probably mine. As if this wasn't bad enough, she called me and invited me over to meet her mom, who was eager to meet and file charges on the college-aged gentleman who'd knocked up her thirteen-year-old daughter. I had to shake a shit-brick from my pant leg: I was sick with guilt, fright, and confusion. I thought

I'd get in trouble—don't ask me what kind—if I asked my mother for advice, and my dad's advice about women was always coarse, if almost always right on the mark. But I didn't need coarse: I needed a plan. I was at a loss: I didn't know much about the law, but Jennifer told me her mom was serious, and it really looked like I could go to jail. I didn't know what to do, but there's something about the words "statutory rape" that induces a compulsive flight response. Sadly, that's what I did. I was scared, so I went underground. I regret that decision. By the time I realized I'd made a mistake she'd gotten married and left the state.

Cleveland's a small town, and years later, we ran into each other at a mall. She was long-since divorced, with boyfriend and my son in tow. It was amazing to see him, after all those years. We exchanged numbers and in the course of our next conversation, I stepped up to do the right thing. The right thing, as it turned out, was for me to give her money upon demand without the benefits of scheduled visitation, child support based on my actual income, or regular parental rights. I had the right to give her money, but not the rights afforded me by law. It didn't seem reasonable that she and her boyfriend should be able to shake me down for contributions and refuse me access to my son. I wanted to go through the state child-support system to secure my rights, and she said she would refuse to subject Richard to a blood test. She didn't like that idea.

Ultimately she told me my son was not mine. I didn't believe her then. I don't believe her now. I just think she didn't want to give me my rights. I pushed for a blood test but inexplicably her boyfriend jumped in the mix, and there were words exchanged and it became clear to me that with all the drama and harsh words going back and forth, there was a good chance someone could be hurt (not me). He jumped out of his car onto me while I was on my way home from work one day, and I thought that this was about the end of it, because he was trying to Deebo up on me, in my neck of the woods, not knowing that I had some real hitters in my crew that would cut him into dog chow. So I backed off. I thought the best thing for me to do would be to take her at her word—I couldn't see much good in forcing the point. It must sound silly, that a girl would use a child as a meal ticket while refusing the father any rights. Ludicrous, right? We'll get back to this.

#2 The Near Miss
Lesson: Some things aren't meant to be.

As a club rat and nightlife pseudo-celebutante, I met a shapely German chick from the West Coast named Fran. She was tall and statuesque, with kind of a big ass. Easily colorstruck, she got passed around the male niggerati and soon enough it was my turn. We started kicking it, and she became my girlfriend, kinda. I thought it might turn serious. But I say "kinda" because when Fran told me she was pregnant, she tacked on the fact that, oh, FYI? I'm not exactly sure whose baby it is. Kudos for keeping it real, but damn. I was scared, angry, and confused but willing to step up if I had to. She had an ectopic pregnancy due to fibroids, and ended up needing surgery to terminate it. Which was the best thing for everyone involved, which was like, half the dudes in my crew. Not that I was Faithful Fred, I'm just saying. I fucked around, but I had sense enough not to fuck her friends. She had an indiscriminate thing for black guys, and that was a real turnoff. As you might suspect, our relationship ended on a bad note.

#3 The "Fuck Buddy"
Lesson: Platonic female friends are underrated.

Right after my first divorce, me and my ex-girlfriend Beth started diddling around again. We dated off and on for years and fell in and out of style. In those days, we were just friends who cared about each other a great deal—enough to never date again, enough to fall in the sack with no strings or acrimony. That's right: she was my "fuck buddy." She did her thing, and I did mine.

One night she called to tell me she was in a family way. Again, with the "not sure whose it is" rap. This wasn't as cut and dried as before, though. I loved her dearly, even if a relationship was not in the cards. A baby is not a good reason to get hitched, and I realized that I didn't love her in a "til death do us part" kinda way. More like a "can you hand me my socks, I gotta go" kinda way. Not just that, but my shit was fucked up. I was broke, without a degree, writing for eight cents a word, practically selling blood just to pay for my divorce. She was doing better, but not by a lot. We may have been able to make something work, but I didn't want a baby with her like this. Moreover, I didn't want the talk-show "blood test" drama that would not only try our friendship, but playing "Who's Your Daddy?" might end with it not being the man she'd hoped it would be. Me, in this case. Together, we decided to take a trip down to ye olde abortion clinic, a place she'd been at least two times before with other men. She picked me up early on the appointed day, and we rode silently.

Naturally, the place was surrounded by pro-life zealots chanting and holding up three-foot pictures of aborted fetuses. I tried not to look, tried hard not to think about what was happening. The clinic was a brown, nondescript, three-story building on a hill, where the parking overflowed onto the street. We registered and got ready for the long wait, and I wanted to be anywhere in the world except in an abortion clinic waiting for a nurse to call my friend so a doctor could go inside her body and kill our baby. It was this or bring a child into a world I was struggling to feed myself in, much less a woman and child. I had a cool demeanor, but inside, I was torn. I didn't like the choices much. We were not enough of a couple to effectively coparent a child: this was the pragmatic solution—no sense in catching feelings. But I did. I can't speak for all men, or even most, but for me, deciding on an abortion was not an easy thing. Not in this case.

We sat in that dry waiting area with all the other couples, watching an older TV with a mixed bag of irresponsible young people, single women and their mothers/friends, and older couples who seemed to be wearing the exact same expression of dread and anticipation. There wasn't much talking in the waiting room. I guess there wasn't much to talk about.

The nurse called her number and a few hours later, she emerged. I smiled. She smiled and we left. I kissed her on the cheek as she dropped me off and we went our own ways. I called her later, but she wasn't much for talking. I don't have any regrets, and I'm glad to live in a country where we can make choices for the greater good of an unborn child. We're still friends today. I think we stay friends because we don't talk about that day.

#4 The Ejaculation Negotiation
Lesson: Condoms are cheaper than lawyers.

Men under forty-five get most of their first ideas about coitus from porno films. That's where a lot of the dialogue our women hear—"You like that big black cock, baby?"—comes from. Before the advent of home video, I doubt women were ever entertaining questions like "Where do you want me to cum?" because the choices were so obvious, and before the Pill, limited. Either in there, or over *there*. The Pill opened up some options, but pornography got the dialogue started.

"Where you want me to cum, baby?"

When you think about it, it's a stupid question. One that I've asked too often, or maybe not often enough. Depending on how you see it.

I fucked Susie occasionally. She lived in the projects near the steel mill, and I'd call on her from time to time. She was my friend and hood piece between relationships, between classes, between the between time. Birth control wasn't a problem, because not only was I the Jedi master of the "stop n squirt," she was on the Depo shot. Depo-Provera is a birth control injection that a lot of women on public assistance seemed to opt for in the late nineties. I'm told it wasn't compulsory, but Sue told me her work made her get it. Supposedly, it lasts for twelve weeks, but it takes fourteen days from injection for it to kick in. This is a detail very few remember and woe to she who miscounts.

Like Sue.

Once it became apparent she was pregnant, I didn't believe it was mine. Sorry. Not to be too much of an asshole, but Sue had what could politely be described as very casual, very liberal attitudes about sex that suggested to me that there were probably a few other candidates. This wasn't at all like knock-up #1: Sue was legal, I was smarter, and a lot more eager to work with her and figure out the right thing to do. So I stepped up, kinda. I say "kinda" because I wasn't sure the baby was mine, but I didn't want to be a jerk. Not this time. Besides, whatever the case, there was only one option really, and we both knew it. Sue and I were not in love, or vertically compatible and while friendly enough, didn't really like each other enough to coparent a child. Besides the fact that, yes, I was still broke. Even if we got along, the kid has to eat, and moving to the PJs trying to scratch and survive just wasn't an option for me. At first, we were of one accord: abortion. It was the only option that made sense. Then she changed her mind, citing her lukewarm Catholic convictions. Okay. So, adoption. Yes, adoption was really the best option, to give this child a better shot at life. Lord knows, I had so little to offer.

This is the point where the plot got thicker, as adoption required a different degree of commitment from me. I had to agree, without the benefit of any genetic testing, that I was the baby's father and be willing to sign my parental consent to an adoption. I was hesitant, but too stupid to see the downside of being buffaloed into paternity by default. So we agreed, I signed the papers reluctantly, and that was that. If I wasn't going to parent the child, then whether or not I was the biological dad seemed academic. I didn't take it as seriously as I should have. But that would soon change.

Sue changed her mind shortly after the birth and decided to keep the child. By that time, I was in another relationship, and as excited as you'd expect about the prospect of having to explain this development to my girlfriend. When I insisted on a blood test, Sue told me, inexplicably, to leave her and her daughter alone. She resented the insinuation and didn't want my money. There would be no test and if I didn't stop calling her pushing for one, she'd call the police. I figured that someone else was the father. So I stepped off. Of course, the question lingered in the back of my mind for years, but I went on with my life, and she went on with hers. I saw her occasionally on the street with other dudes, with that pretty little girl of hers whose face was starting to look more and more familiar as time went by.

Three years later, I get home from work and my second wife is opening up a letter addressed to me from the Child Support Enforcement Agency requesting a blood test—this, not long after we'd wedded and just after our youngest son's birthday. I hadn't mentioned this lingering question to her for lack of concrete facts and an ignorance of how to resolve the issue of paternity. This letter had the worst timing imaginable. Even if the child had been conceived during a bad patch of bad road in the courtship, it's hard explaining a lie of omission to a new bride. I stood in our bedroom, tears flowing from my eyes: she was as understanding as she could be. It's not a scenario I'd wish on anyone.

She wanted to accompany me to the blood testing facility, to show that she would stand by me and not be run off. I wanted to go alone. I didn't want to share this indignity with anyone I cared about.

The CSEA testing facility has a waiting area that hasn't been upgraded in fifteen years or better. The women who wait wear sad, determined faces. Children play with toys. There's a TV, a guard, but no couples. The room self-segregates by gender right down the middle. Silent. If you're here, there's probably not a lot to chat about. The doctor swabbed my jaw and three weeks later the test came back.

It's a girl.

Once paternity was established, I promptly began paying child support. I tried calling Sue to establish a visitation schedule. Her phone was disconnected. I tried stopping by, and she was never home. Whenever I did manage to get ahold of her, my daughter was always too busy to see me or come to the phone. For years. No, of course, it didn't make sense, but I felt helpless. After my second divorce, I was unemployed for a year and got behind on my payments, and she stopped taking my calls altogether. She moved. I moved into a shitty job situation (it was the ole recruitment bait and switch), but I sent money when I could and called and called and called trying to set up visitation. Later she would tell a judge she was "busy." Sue, with no job, no classroom, and nothing to do but eat was busy. Screening her calls. For two more years.

You'd think I was smart enough to know my rights, but you'd be wrong. Street smart, yeah. Book smart? Kinda. The problem is the streets—surprise!—don't hold classes or seminars on fatherhood, and when it comes up, they don't get it right, and up until recently, there weren't any books on baby-daddy rights. The truth? I knew I had some rights—because I made the kid, so it stood to reason, but I had no idea exactly what my rights were or how to enforce them, and I couldn't afford a lawyer to help me sort it out. I barely had enough money to cover my support. I tried to DIY it, but the way the system is set up? You need a lawyer. You can't get in the fight for your rights without a lawyer. If you could afford to hire a lawyer, you would probably be up to date with your support payments, right? In my opinion, the system makes it as hard as possible to be a complete father and not just a paycheck. This is the puzzle, the endless maze of it: women can use children as pawns and fathers don't always have the resources to secure their rights, or they become disconnected from children borne of women they never cared much for in the first place. This realization didn't stop me from giving it a shot, sans legal counsel.

I called the clerk of courts and no one I talked to seemed to be able to help me out. They were all equally confused: "You want to secure your parental rights? As a father? Uh. Hold on." Often, they wouldn't come back to the phone. And this went on for some time, until finally I spoke with a kindly clerk who walked me through the process and sent the paperwork out to me. So, it didn't cost me much to file, but I spent thirty-five dollars getting ahold of my daughter's birth certificate, and with the filing fee it topped out at about a hundred bucks, all said and done. But it was a great feeling to get the ball rolling.

Now, when a court is handling a divorce or custody case, they set up a mandatory parenting class. Some will let you attend in another city or state, some demand that you are there in person, as was my case. I took a day off work, rented a car, and drove 369 miles to attend.

This class was set at the clerk of courts office in a side area that looked like it may have doubled as a lounge area or break room. The room was full of the most despondent, flat faces you could ever see, just ready for it to be over. Mostly couples, all white. Except for me, a fact not lost on a security guard who inexplicably moved closer to where I was seated. I was late and the sandy-haired lady at the front of the class was lecturing on not saying ugly things about the other parent, if you could help it. A young hipster clerk-chick came over to check me in.

"Is the mother here?" she whispered. I nodded.

"Where is she?"

"She's over there," I said, pointing. "The big blond one." And Sue was big. Just kinda zaftig when we met, she'd ballooned to close to three hundred pounds.

The clerk-chick gave me a stack of handouts, and I tuned out.

Forty-five minutes later, we broke off and the litigants met with a magistrate ostensibly to work out a compromise, thus eliminating the need for a court proceeding. This was the part I came up here for, really. I was pretty sure we could work out the details without standing in front of a judge. I just wanted to be able to talk to my daughter on the phone and schedule visitation every so often. No biggie. I was hopeful we could reach an accord.

Some people bring a lawyer to this proceeding. She brought her mother. This was the first sign of trouble, and one of the most important laws of baby-mama drama: you are never gonna win a fight—any fight—that involves just you, your baby-mama, and her people. Never.

So, me, Sue, and her mama retire to the chambers, and the magistrate—the "hipster clerk-chick"—took her seat. A black guy in a room with three white women—and that guard again!? Prima facie, these weren't great odds. Plus, I bad-mouthed my baby-mama to the magistrate.

This wasn't going to go well.

As we got started, Sue whipped out a statement whereby she accused me of calling her names, not paying child support, and being generally no-account. The magistrate didn't care about that. Why, she wondered, didn't she allow me contact with my daughter? "Contact and visitation aren't contingent upon regular support payments or congenial relations," she said. To her credit, she got to the heart of the matter. What she couldn't understand is that I wasn't willing to leave court with anything short of a court order because Sue could not be trusted at her word to schedule regular visitation.

During the course of mediation, it came out that while she knows of me, my daughter had been kept from visiting me for her entire life and needs to be able to do so if she is ever to get to know me better. The magistrate scoffed, informing me that I would only be able to see my daughter for a few hours at a time because "[your daughter] doesn't know you from Mr. Black." And it was then that I packed myself up and headed for the door. Later, a straw poll of friends, colleagues (including a linguist), and legal professionals produced discomfort, shock, and disbelief, but no one had ever heard of "Mr. Black" as synonymous for stranger or unfamiliar person. Reasonable people might suggest that the magistrate's quip revealed a hint of prejudice, bias, and insensitivity.

I wrote the judge and received a nice apology. She reassigned the case to a black male magistrate who was at least able to feign an air of objectivity. The incident gave me a clarity I'd been missing to that point: the child support system was not designed for fathers.

When you have a child with a woman you aren't married to, you two can make a support arrangement that doesn't involve the courts, or you can go through your local social services agency and set it up. In most states, child support is equal to about 15 percent of the man's gross earnings. This is way more preferable in the likely event that there is some discord between you—as long as you have been paying your support through the courts, she can't really fuck with you. Some women prefer you to pay out of your pocket, but any cash payment is considered a "gift" if the state agency does not record it. But if you haven't or you fall behind, you'll have a real problem.

For those unfamiliar with the law, men who are $2,500 or more in arrears in their child support payments can have their driver's license revoked, their property sold at auction, or in some cases, be put in jail. Sure—there are a lot of irresponsible fathers out there who don't want to be responsible for their children. More often than not, fathers become unemployed. And if you happen to get a job making less money, child support agencies are not inclined to lower your obligation. Some men pay what they can, but if you are obligated to pay $490 a month in support, and can only pay $200, the other $290 gets tacked on. So the following month, you owe $780 smackers, but can still only pay $200. So you can see how easy it is to get behind.

Also, if you are unemployed, the child support obligation cannot be suspended until such time when you find work. The agency imparts an amount you should be earning, based on your past and calculates an amount you should be paying. This debt compounds the longer you are unemployed. The man can't petition the court for debt relief, but a woman can ask that a debt be forgiven. Most often, they don't. This is how men end up paying long after children are of legal age or end up in jail for criminal nonpayment of support—a felony—regardless of the circumstances. Mommy can put Daddy in jail, and Daddy has no recourse.

Child support agencies enforce a woman's right to money but not a man's right to see his kids. Women are not obligated to allow the father to see his children, and are rewarded with public assistance for having as many babies as possible, to the extent that it's become a hustle of sorts and a strain on resources. I'm not saying that men don't need to be held accountable, but the child support solution should be fair to all parties involved. Shouldn't we also hold women accountable for irresponsible behavior? The child support system needs to be changed so it doesn't reward women for having as many babies as possible and bringing the hammer down on men who make a decent effort to take care of their children. I can think of a few creative solutions to make the system more equitable.

- For every child the woman has, reduce her child support benefits by half, so women have a financial motivation to use birth control. This way, if a woman already has a child and is supposed to be receiving $400 a month in child support and she gets pregnant, her benefits are reduced to $200 a month. Then if she has another one, and she is getting $200 for the first one and $300 for the second one, both of those amounts are reduced by half, so she only gets $100 and $150 for those two children. Every child she has would reduce her benefits by half, discouraging baby-making from becoming a hustle and women from having more children than they can afford.

- Require school, vocational training, or gainful employment within six months to a year after the birth of a child. I think mothers should be required to have jobs and not be encouraged to lay back on child support payments—this is how Baby Mamahood becomes a vocation. Some women are back to work within a week after giving birth. As long as she can sit up, she can be a receptionist, a night watchman, or parking lot attendant. If she doesn't work, her benefits should be drastically reduced or she should give up custody of the child to the father or the state. If you can't work to pay for the care of a child, you shouldn't have them.

- After a woman has multiple children by multiple dads and still remains unmarried, there should be a fitness hearing that lets the father make a case to be the custodial parent. Love is grand and all, but you can't give a baby to every guy that takes you to Benihana. Children aren't door prizes, souvenirs, or a going-away presents. So, three kids by three different daddies equals automatic custody hearing, at the state's expense.

- Women must establish a joint custody arrangement and be held responsible for it or lose benefits. No more "pay to play." The onus would be on the mother to make sure her child sees the father. If the father is resistant or shirks his visitation, strip away his parental rights but still draw child support from him until such time as the woman is married.

- Forget child support that allows the child to live the way the father is living. That's ridiculous. If the child needs to be living like the dad is living, the child needs to live with the dad.

- Women should not be able to move any Chester Molester motherfucker into the home she lives in with your child without the benefit of marriage. How many times do we read about boyfriends chopping up and raping their girl-friend's kids? Also, why is he in there soaking up cable, food, and other resources that should be allocated to the child?

- As long as the father is making a good-faith effort to pay support—and by "good faith" I mean paying half or better of the monthly obligation—any arrears amassed should be expunged every three years. Women use arrears as a weapon and revenge mechanism to put men in jail. Men can't pay anything in jail, and they certainly can't find work with a felony on their record.

These are just a few ways I think we could change the child support system to make it fair to everyone involved. Is this plan without holes? Of course not. But I think it's a starting point to creating an arrangement that is more fair to all parties involved. After all, the government can't find Osama bin Laden but they will call Duane "Dog" Chapman, B. A. Baracus, or Hannibal and the whole A-Team to track down "deadbeat dads." But who does Daddy call when he can't see his little girl? Sometimes, the agency provides resources you can call, but these "resources" are toothless to enforce father's rights. When child support enforcement comes to wrangle you up, they don't talk much about rights, just your responsibilities, and the consequences of shirking said same. Only recently have books come out outlining the rights of fathers. There is a "father's rights" movement, but it's the virtual equivalent of a bunch of guys sitting at a bar, bitching. Most men are as ignorant about their rights as I was. So it's easy for women, like Sue, to convince idiots, like me, that visitation rights are attached to the status of child support payments, e.g., that contact and visitation are at the discretion of the mother, if payments aren't current. By hood logic, it seems reasonable. Everything is pay-to-play with women. So they do the "pay to play, or I keep away" hustle with babies, and nobody loses bigger than the kid. So, guess what? You gotta lawyer up. No way around it. Expensive? Hell yeah. Competent lawyers want two hundred dollars an hour, plus a retainer of two grand or better. In my scenario, between my paycheck and the kindness of friends and family, I was able to get in the fight ready to win. The thing is, I know a lot of brothers complaining about their baby-mama drama while riding around in cars with six-thousand-dollar rims on them. Those cats don't have their priorities straight. You could get real fine legal talent for that kinda money, with some change left over. If you're serious about enforcing your parental rights, it's money well spent. But condoms are cheaper than lawyers, and this gets me back to me and my mother's kitchen table, where all the drama started. How so?

In all the talk about birth canals, urine hoses, eternal damnation, and God's Holy Egg Yolk, there was no allowance for humanity and the outside chance that I could make a mistake. Just a lot of talk about saving "it" and not doing "it," but the harder you try to "save it" the harder "it" is to resist. And the girls my age were often in the same boat—they had something boys wanted, but didn't always know what to do with it. Very often, they gave it away to nearly anyone that asked. I don't know but I suspect that girls aren't being given enough information about how to manage their sexuality either. If the pictures and come-ons on BlackPlanet, YouTube, or MySpace are any indicators, we are in trouble. I think the glut of single motherhood is absolutely preventable: we have to acknowledge that our little girls are sexual beings, and equip them to handle that responsibility. I know that's rough. And I know because I have a nine-year-old daughter, a natural beauty. She's got a great smile, so I know it won't be long before little boys start ringing my phone and knocking on the door wanting her to come out and "play." I really want boys to be better people, but I was a boy once, and I know how powerful hormones can be. We like to blame boys, and I'm not going to rely on single mothers to talk to their sons about sexual responsibility, mainly because Moms is not home or awake enough between jobs to have that talk, and sadly, her sexual choices have not always been above reproach. I could hope and pray that my daughter's mom has "the talk" with her, but again, with the whole "behavior not above reproach" thing. So I'm going to have to do what more dads are going to have to start doing. The best way to keep our daughters from getting pregnant is for us to talk to our girls about sex. I'd like to ask her to abstain, but this would be a hard thing to ask in an age when a blowjob can make Daddy's little girl rich and famous. So I don't expect her to be an angel, but I expect her to behave responsibly or be aware of the consequences of her actions (i.e. baby and/or disease). I'm not going to pretend that this is the best approach—I don't have the solution, but one thing I do know: it's not about putting the onus on young men so horny they can't see straight. That simply will not work. We want to tell our girls to just say no, or maybe try to steer her toward "da lawd," but the most promiscuous girls I have ever known were church girls and PKs. Better to be realistic than be an early grandparent.

Times being the way they are, we must have a whole new kind of birds and bees conversation with our girls as they become young women. So when it's time for me to have that talk with my daughter—which, let's face it, will be any minute now—I'll use this list of talking points.

IT'S YOUR BODY: No one has the right to touch you without your consent. This applies to games of grab-ass and the like. Feel free to defend your body by any means necessary.

FLIP YOUR OWN FUNKY OFF: You don't need a boy to do it for you necessarily. In the privacy of your own room or wherever (like the bathtub or shower), touch yourself. Know what you like. It's your body. That said . . .

KNOW YOUR BODY: Sex isn't just for him. Know your body well enough to get yours too. If you don't know what "yours" feels like, why are you having sex anyway? You have brothers, so you know what a penis looks like, but just know that . . .

IT WON'T FALL OFF OR GO BAD: No matter what boys say, a penis will not fall off or explode if not properly relieved. Blue balls is not fatal or contagious.

SEX, IN AND OF ITSELF, WILL NOT KEEP HIM: I know he tells you it will. He's lying, of course.

DON'T GIVE IN TO PRESSURE: Fuck that.

IT'S NOT ABOUT LOVE: If he loves you, he'll respect you enough to wait until you are ready. There is nothing self-ish about saying "no." If he can't wait, tell him to step off.

IF YOU DECIDE TO GO THERE: Make sure to either have spermicidal foam for yourself or carry condoms for him. No matter what he says, sex with a condom on feels 150 percent better than sex with his hand or no sex at all.

RESPECT YOURSELF: Don't get talked into dumb shit. Don't find yourself trying to get (him) off in humiliating circumstances, like in the church closet, McDonald's bathroom, or school bus. Catch as catch can, but be smart. Also . . .

YOUR FAVORS ARE NOT FOR SALE: You don't trade or barter with sex. Dinner and a movie does not equal a piece of ass, a blowjob, or a handie, for that matter. Which gets to . . .

DON'T DRESS LIKE YOU ARE SELLING PUSSY: I know you want to show off your curves. But you don't have to give them away. Wear clothes that fit, but not too tight. Look cute. Cover up. And if you don't, I will make you change clothes. Seriously.

IF HE WANTS HIS DICK SUCKED: Uh . . . be selective. Don't suck everyone's dick, because word gets around.

Good idea to have a condom in effect—flavored, maybe, so that it doesn't suck too bad. No pun intended.

IF HE WANTS ANAL: I'm going to vote "no" on that one. Because young boys don't know enough about anal sex to make it enjoyable for the woman. Later on, though, maybe. Because you can't get pregnant taking it up the pooter. And experienced men know how to make it *nice*. So wait a while before you open up your butthole for business. At least until grad school.

KEEP YOUR HEAD STRAIGHT: Sex doesn't equal love, although ideally? I wish it did. But that's your call. Don't get sprung on any one dude, because there are millions of 'em.

IF HE DOESN'T EAT PUSSY: Pass him by. Like I said, what's sex if you don't get yours? Chances are good he doesn't know how to work his wiener good enough to get you off. It's hard to go wrong eating pussy.

ONE AT A TIME: What the fuck? Sex is not a group activity. No spectators, no cheerleaders, no play-by-play commentators.

IF YOU LIKE GIRLS: All these same rules (beyond the whole condom thing) apply. Be responsible. The only thing more uncool than a slut is a lesbian slut. I won't judge your sexual preference, but I'm not paying for any lesbian weddings. I will, however, happily give you away. You are my daughter and I love you. Be happy.

IF YOU DECIDE TO BE ADVENTUROUS: and start having group sex or sex indiscriminately, hey . . . it's your body. You should be safe, first and foremost. You should also be prepared for the backlash that comes with promiscuity. As sex-positive and progressive as it may be to be a freak, no man wants a wife with a porn-star history. I know you think you can move away from your history, or perhaps change your name to conceal your identity but, no. Men talk. And someone always recognizes your face, and a reputation is hard to outrun or change. So be as freaky as you want to be, but be careful, and be responsible. Along those same lines . . .

DON'T BE BRAGGING ABOUT YOUR SEX LIFE: What you do behind closed doors is exactly that. And while we are on that subject . . .

NO FILM, NO PICTURES: If he wants a memento, make him a T-shirt (not really), but video is forever. There is no reason on earth to film yourself having sex.

IF YOU GET BURNED: Tell somebody. It doesn't have to be me. You need to be taken to a clinic immediately so you can get treatment. It happens to better people than you (not me, but you get the idea) but just know to protect yourself at all times. Or at least until grad school.

IF YOU GET PREGNANT: If you're under eighteen, we have to have a talk. Not a talk about why or how, but a talk about what happens now. Does the boy step up and be responsible (not likely) or do you make your own choice? I will try to help you live with whatever you choose. The fact is, I don't want to be a grandparent before I have to be. But I'll be there, as best I can.

IF YOU DECIDE TO GET AN ABORTION: I'll understand: having children is not a game. Your mother and I almost decided not to have you, but I am glad you are here. This is to say that you can always make a way if you have to, but it's rough. I'll support your decision, but will expect you to be more responsible going forward: abortion is not a viable form of birth control.

My problem is figuring out how to tell my daughter that it is okay for her to responsibly explore her sexuality in any way she sees fit without sounding like it's okay to be a slut. How do we have realistic conversations about sex with our little girls without feeling icky? Better to have them than not, though. It's part of our jobs, as fathers: keep our daughters off the pole and put them on the Pill. That sounds extreme, but so does fifteen-year-old single motherhood. Yes, I'm going to teach my little girl to respect herself enough to protect herself and to govern her own sexuality. I'm going to make sure my daughter knows the deal and has enough game to neutralize game. Oh, yeah. I want her to control her urges and have the ability to fight off—physically, if necessary—the urges of others. But I'm also going to make sure she knows what birth control is and has access to it.

Truth to tell, like most young men I knew growing up from the playground and beyond, once I figured out how it worked, I was likely to point my penis at any young lady who wouldn't run. Girls grow up much quicker than any of us would like, so from sixth grade on, you can get a blowjob, a handie, or on some rare occasions, you got lucky. Sometimes you condomed up—if you knew how—and sometimes you didn't. If it breaks, is defective, or there is an error in judgment, what do you do? How do you cope? That information didn't make it across my kitchen table. I fucked everything that moved because I was young, human, and flawed, not understanding the potential consequences of my actions. The discourse never seemed to touch on the very real possibility that you could impregnate a woman who was, in fact, something less than a gift from God. Amidst the flowery words espousing the impenetrable bond of God's yoke—and the ham-handed admonitions to abstain—there was no talk of worst-case scenario.

I got caught up in the Denzel Principle, which makes women think that any man who isn't the Dizzle isn't qualified to be a good father. That's when the games begin.

Sex gets political very fast: there is the birth control accord, the ejaculation negotiations, and the anal embargo. The recriminations start from the moment she is late, and they never stop. Smokey Robinson sang that his mama told him to "Shop Around" and that's advice all women should teach their man-child. My mom did me a great disservice by not preparing me to deal with young ladies in a cautious, responsible way. A word about doling the dick out discriminately would have saved me some of the baby-mama drama I went through.

Confessions of a
Former Sellout

Slightly taller, darker, balder, and thicker than average, Big D is my barber and friend. He told me a familiar story as he shaped up my hairline: he was dating a real nice sister—the same one he'd brought to my second wedding—until she started giving out free ass-passes in the street. Flagrantly. He didn't have an explanation—who does?—but I know him as a reasonable guy who bounces back quickly. He was single, owned his own shop, and was an all-around nice guy who would hop right back on the horse.

"Fuck these bitches," he said, buzzing away. "I'm done."

He turned the chair around so that we were eye to eye. "You're not goin' all *Will & Grace* on us, are you bro?" I asked. He looked around the barbershop for a moment and then: "I'm not dating *black* women anymore, son," he said. "That's all done. White girls, all day, all the way." Headz in the shop nodded affirmation. I couldn't believe it. I'd never known any black man who'd conciously given up on black women. No one besides me, I guess. Fifteen years ago, I too had given up on sisters and decided to exclusively date white girls. I couldn't see where I had a choice.

I thought white girls would be different, don't ask me why. I only knew them from television, and that's how I drew my conclusions. I really liked Janet Jackson as Millicent "Penny" Gordon on *Good Times* but damn if I could find a black girl who was always that happy, loyal, and optimistic. Jodie Foster, in *The Little Girl Who Lives Down the Lane* seemed so even-tempered and congenial. Sure, she killed her mother, but what a great smile. White girls literally ran from me until junior high school—my clothes were old, my attitude was street, and I just wasn't the kind of black guy you take home. But I found one who did exactly that.

Her name was Jenny. Pretty and portly, she lived in the better part of Shaker Heights. She was monied and top-shelf: I'm not sure how I piqued her interest, but I have my suspicions. I think my street sensibilities made me seem more authentic, and this seemed to be the thing young white girls were looking for, above all, maybe in an attempt to punctuate their suburban teenage angst with some excitement. So I went from being an outcast to the D-list guy you date to piss off your parents. I wasn't a first-stringer, but it wasn't for lack of trying: I was from the hood, sexually active, rapped, and up-rocked. I think it was the poetry and essay-writing in between that softened my image. At least I lived on the other side of the tracks—literally—I'm not sure how much Jenny cared. I wasn't the dangerous hoodlum she was looking for, but she feigned interest as best she could.

I was really excited about the upgrade. She was everything I'd ever thought about white people: she was rich, sophisticated, and even had royal lineage. This relationship was over pretty quick, and never consummated. I got my first vanilla kiss, and it was long and predictably uncomfortable as my overanxious plus-sized lips devoured most of her face. Even after we'd broken up,

I felt as if I had crossed a threshold. Aside from the fact that I'd gotten no pussy, it was a pretty smooth ride. I got a peek into a world I'd never known, and I was hungry for more.

At eighteen, I took stock of my dating episodes. Wasn't doing so great. A girl I had been dating off and on since the fifth grade was pregnant by another guy. Another schoolboy crush cheated on me brazenly, throwing me into a deep depression and nearly a week of lost sleep. There were others in between who didn't take anything but my maturing self-esteem: they were inexplicably angry and disagreeable for no good reason. They challenged me, in a put-up-your-dukes kinda way. That's right: I got kicked, hit, punched, and scratched by my girlfriends. Not because I was doing anything wrong. Mostly they hit me because I wouldn't hit them back. A girl broke up with me just because I wouldn't hit her back. The ones who didn't hit liked to humiliate me in public and cuss at me like a stray dog at every opportunity. And I let them. So they just punked me out: took my kindness for weakness. All the insults, physical blows, and degradation I'd suffered took some toll on my self-respect. Why wasn't I good enough to love without all that extra mess, I wondered—often aloud—and frankly it scared my friends.

These young ladies had only one thing in common: they were black.

This observation led to an unconscious color association: I associated every black woman in the dating pool with aloofness, rejection, and humiliation. Black women were robbing me of human dignity. I felt like I deserved to be treated like a man, even if I was still discovering what that meant. I suspected that white women were different, but didn't have a lot to go on. Once I discovered the nightlife, things changed.

One nightclub let me in when I was seventeenish and often for free, and after a few years of this, I'd become a celebutante—a club kid—one of only a few black regulars. I was living by myself and not working, but a trust fund from a childhood accident kept me in bar tabs and fancy clothes. The Aquilon was progressive and catered to those with eclectic taste in music and people. It was the post punk-disco era, and everybody was looking for a thrill. Populated by the coolest people in Cleveland—bankers, lawyers, waitresses, and creepy, sexy nightcrawlers—everyone was a star under the strobe lights. You dressed to undress on the dance floor, to be baptized in the drums and sweat. It was a motley den of musical convergence and debauchery: seventies-era disco decadence in the throes of death. It was just a club to some, but for me it was a reason to be alive. I was somebody in the twilight. I was out at the clubs five nights a week—I partied 'til five and slept 'til four every day. It was a cool life.

This club rarely saw black people, because they'd come in, hear the house music bumping, take a look around at the mostly white faces, and retreat. There were never more than two black women around, but there was a plethora of white women of every shape and social distinction. This was my opportunity to meet them in a controlled environment, and it wasn't hard.

I became something of a predator: smelling out the scent of attraction, baring teeth as I made my way to the prey. I fed ravenously on the kindnesses and sexual favors afforded me, but it felt like fair exchange. I would serve their paternal needs, if that's what they wanted. I would be a father figure, disciplining them when necessary. They could have a suave black stud on their arm: I didn't mind being an objet d'art. When I tired of them, I discarded them, because there were many eager to take their place. I mixed and matched them into my daily schedule according to what needs they met. Some mothered me, so they were always the overnight stay or the weekend escape. Some were too ugly to be seen with in public, so they were the late-night creep. Some complemented my good taste, and I took them out often. Not proud of any of that behavior, but it is what it is. You're only young once, right?

My first real sexual encounter with a white woman was at an after-hours hookup. I was a bus stop pimp who didn't drive, and after the clubs closed, I often needed a ride home. A girl I'd seen around, purely pallid, of Irish decent, obliged. We didn't know each other well, so we spent the short ride trying to decode each other. She came up for a bite to eat, as I had offered a late-night snack in return for the favor. I cooked her a turkey burger while we kibitzed about the club life. It got later and she asked if she could stay the night.

As Funkadelic's "Maggot Brain" came screaming from the speakers, we began.

It was slow and predictable at first. Some kissing, and the strange but oddly enticing taste of her flesh. And suddenly, all at once, I was elsewhere. In my head I smelled hay and farm animals, and heard wolves conferring in the woods just beyond the edge of the trees. Everyone was asleep, and she had come for me in the night to violate me . . . to be violated. I was the beast, and I devoured her. The next morning I was different. As I watched her sleep, white and naked, strewn across my haggard single bed, I wondered what I had done, who I had become. I hated myself. This vision would come back often. The feeling of taking the master's daughter as my concubine was a new sensation.

Yeah, I know. Weird.

Black women ignored me but white women were easygoing and available. I think this is how some black men develop a preference. They take their experiences, negative and positive, and pull out the common thread. I didn't hate black women or have a color complex, white women just treated me better. They were a little more kind and not as hell-bent on arguing about every little thing, holding my feet to the fire just for the fun of it. So dating white women was not only the path of least resistance, it was comfortable and, after awhile, normal. I was a man-child trying to find my manhood and I had no desire to be hurt, fought, or humiliated along the way.

There were concessions I made at first while dating white women. Like most brothers who date interracially, I had to imagine a new beauty paradigm. I'd been surrounded by black women my whole life, so I had to get accustomed to the idea that white women are just different physically and adjust my gaze a bit.

Allow me to elaborate.

Most people have certain physical preferences. Black men are no different. Generally, we like women with full hips, round behinds, and firm, spherical breasts. If you don't believe me, look at some of the women black popular culture idolizes: Pam Grier, Chaka Khan, Lena Horne, and the list goes on. Even white folks know these sisters are fine. Thus, brothers who date interracially find themselves changing their standards. The scales vary, but it goes something like this: if a white girl has any ass at all, flat, fat, wide, whatever, she gets about four points. Black women and white women have totally different types of asses. A black girl's behind is the symbol of ethereal sensuality: it's an event. It's the gyroscope that set the whole world in motion from the beginning of time itself, the presence that leaves whole blocks of gaping men asunder. Don't ask me how a woman's behind could move me to lush prose. All I know is that black women in thongs make everything in this world so much more bearable.

Don't misquote me—there are some white women with incredible behinds. I know, I've dated nearly all of them. However, they just don't move the same way; their asses don't demand the same respect. A white woman can have the same exact measurements, wear the same clothes, and put on the attitude, but her subpar posterior pales in comparison to the natural grace of a Brooklyn queen. White girl booty, just like black girl booty, comes in a few varieties:

White Chocolate aka Black Kryptonite. This is that rare booty among white women that is full, bulbous, and well-formed—the kind of butt you see on most sisters. The booty, together with the easygoing personality, is hard for a black man to resist. This white girl can't get the time of day from a white man, but she walks into a club and every brother there tries to angle a way to get her number.

The Jedi Mind Trick. You see this white girl from the back and the booty is banging. But you get a side view, and the butt reveals itself to be flat and bounce-less. Most often, this kind of white woman gets over in Da Club, where the lights are low and dimensions are hard to make out. You only find out you've been had once the panties come off. Damn.

Farmer's Daughter. Only found in the Midwest and the South, these are white women from agrarian backgrounds whose family history of farm labor reveals itself in the jeans.

Hers. Farmer's Daughters have the kind of booty suburban women spend hours and hours on a Stair Master
trying to get. These butts are round and tight.

Trailer Park Pancake. Indigenous to the trailer park, the
Trailer Park Pancake booty is the kind of ass that's not
too flat, not too fat, and all kinds of double-wide. Frequently, the woman is missing teeth, which in some practical ways, is a plus.

The Half-Crack. Also known as Muffin Butt, this white girl
has too much fat and not enough booty in back. It's hard
to know where her waist ends and her ass begins.

Ass-Sack. This kind of booty is round enough, but gravity
is having its way. The butt is getting longer instead of
rounder. A lot of "liberated" white women have this kind
of booty—they spend too much time sitting at a desk
and not enough time on the StairMaster.

If a white woman has either big breasts or small perky breasts,
she receives another one or two points. Boobs on women are generally run-of-the-mill, and for whatever reason, don't have the
same ethnocentric distinctions that butts do. Why? I dunno, and
I don't care—I'm an ass man, and that's not changing. Let the
boob guys figure it out. I bet there's some scientist researching
that mystery right now. If she looks decent, if she has two eyes, a
nose, and a mouth, they get a point. The truth of the matter is
she doesn't have to be a ten if sex and some short-term, exchange-
based relationship is the goal. This scale doesn't say that white
women aren't beautiful: on the contrary. A "scale" of sorts makes
white women able to be judged against each other as opposed to
being compared to black women, which just isn't fair. To some

this summation may seem derogatory and racist, and in some ways, I suppose it is. Life has taught me that this scale applies to all women, not just white women. Why reduce women to a scoring system? What can I say? I know what I like . . . and I'm just kinda fucked up and mannish like that. All this is not to say I didn't have any meaningful, three-dimensional relationships with white women—I had plenty. They didn't quite go the distance, but color was never an issue. My relationships with black women always seem to crumble for the most arbitrary of reasons. It's weird that black men and women ever get together at all, given that they are both bringing similar baggage to relationships. White women bring baggage, but not the kind attached to any racial pathology.

In any event, it's important to be discriminating. Sadly, nowadays brothers are hooking up with anything, and that's God's truth. If you're two hundred pounds overweight with six kids, on welfare, and *white*, there is a brother for you. Now, the average brother wouldn't be caught dead with a *sister* like that. Yet, you still see these brothers walking arm in arm with the dregs of white femininity. I've certainly caught myself out there in that bag, and I can't say I know why. I could've done better. Just didn't. But it seemed to me that only the corporate brothers get the "top shelf" white girls with good educations and all their teeth. Joe Average brother cats like me get the "dirt road" white girl or the art chick, or the maternal older/younger white girl trying to save him from himself, or the white girl trying to be "down." With her pants sagging and her sister-girl haircut, she's blacker than black, always on the hunt for a "ruffneck" brother straight out of the latest rap video. There are a few variants in between, but not many. The scary thing is that there I was, bouncing from one

"Debbie" to the next—and my friends were speechless and my family was noticeably uncomfortable. What to say?

I didn't care. Until Buddy, who's never at a loss for words, said to me:

"Yeah, *all* you pseudo-black revolutionaries are nearly alike: talk dat black shit but at the firs' chance you get, you on toppa some white girl. Yeah . . . Malcolm, Martin . . . dey all had a white ass on da' side. FBI knew dat shit too. But you know who Mrs. X and Mrs. King was, right? . . . Don't you forget it neither, boy."

I remember sitting there, stunned, as he turned away abruptly to finish searching *TV Guide* for a golf game. I had nothing to say. Nothing that would make him understand that I wasn't a sellout, that in a very real way, I was afraid of black women and all they would require of me: they seemed to have unattainable expectations. Nah, I couldn't really tell him how nice it was to be worshiped and respected without having to work so hard for it.

I sat there in his home, while my grams fixed us a snack. I looked at them both on that day, and while they don't always get along, I realized they have something. And I remembered the better times between my folks. I knew that there is no love like the love we have when we are together: a black man and a black woman. It's cosmic and unearthly, holy and inspiring, like a new birth or Isaac Hayes on a hot buttered evening. Black love is its own entity. I was young, and not sure I could ever have anything like this with a white woman. Ever.

While I'm sitting here waxing romantic, it probably bears mentioning that black women can be difficult, and they come with a special brand of drama. For one thing, it's hard for them to disagree without becoming disagreeable. About the weather, let alone anything of substance. The man is wrong, all of the time, according to black women. Doesn't matter what the topic or point of contention, some black women will holler, scream, and knuckle up to be right, whether or not they actually are. They are prone to unpredictable fits of anger and emotion that, in my experience, have often required police intervention. And if they can't beat you up, they will curse you out. No one wants to be abused, verbally or otherwise. But sisters seem to have mastered the art of verbal assault and draw this weapon at the slightest provocation. White women typically don't go through all those changes.

Black women call themselves "queens," as if to allude to some kind of royal stature, but outside my family, I haven't met a lot of queens. I've run across black women in one of two extremes: absolutely self-sufficient *feministas* or opportunistic high-tech prostitutes. Either they don't need you, your dick, or your money or they are using their beauty to further their position in life. Few of them have been taught to be queenly and fewer of them have been taught to recognize the king in you. So when a good black man crosses their path, they can't tell. The hard fact is that a brother could spend his life looking for a sister and never find her. And if he's waiting for a sister to see the king in you, he could be waiting a long time.

In fairness, though, there are not enough kings representing. There are a lot of knuckleheaded brothers out there.

Many would-be kings are selling dope, walking the streets with no job or classroom to go to, or have found the perfect sister . . . in another brother. *Not* that there's anything wrong with that: if you are fucking other men in the doo-doo clipper, it just is what it is. Also, sisters sometimes look at the quantity of material possessions as a gauge of manhood. However, sisters should remember the man they're looking for could be working at

McDonald's Hamburgers or McDonald Investments: standards are important. But finding a mate should be about compatibility and commonality, not measuring prospective mates against impossible criteria.

This piece is about me, lest you've forgotten, and I should be quick about getting back to the subject as opposed to attempting to speak for all the brothers. That's a bad look.

A white fuck-buddy suggested I start at the root of the problem. She found the way I lambasted black women in her presence offensive and disturbing. She didn't mind getting fucked, but didn't like feeling like a last resort.

"Call your mother. Get that shit straight," she said. "I wanna know it's *me* you want and not my skin color."

Now, my moms and I have not always gotten along. Women were never meant to raise children alone, and I think the pressure of rearing a young man by herself took a toll on both of us. Women always go overboard asserting their dominance over their sons. So she did what she had to do to corral her rambunctious young man's spirit. I just left, and went to go live with my paternal grands. We were really too much alike to get along, but after years of questionable speaking terms, my mother and I reached a point from which we could begin to heal our relationship. I decided to dump my white girlfriend in favor of finding a black woman. I thanked her and we went our own ways, she to the next brother, me to find a sister.

The sisters that I did manage to date ran the full gamut of every psychosis known to mankind. One woman changed her name three different times (and later again) and took a job at the local zoo. I don't want to say she was psychotic, but she liked to play with steak knives around my genitals. I ain't no punk, but we can all probably agree that this is a little more than "kinky."

I spent many sleepless nights at her crib, while her psycho cat attacked my 'locks while I tossed and turned. Sure—I could've woken up dickless—but I was trying to give this sister a chance. I asked her to marry me, and she promptly hosted a foursome— with two other people—to celebrate. Well, that wasn't the engagement party I had in mind. Why did I ask a crazy bitch like that to marry me? I thought I could save her. This was my fault: you can save drowners, chokers, and smokers, but you can't save crazy. But crazy is hard to see from the curb.

To wit:

Another sister was a thirty-nine-year-old virgin, and ready to take *that* step. She heard from her (white) artsy girlfriends that I was a freak (what can I say?), so she figured I'd make a good teacher. My interest in her was nothing more than physical, but I wasn't doing anything else important, so what the hell?

She got attached. Scratch that. She got *whipped*, right off the button, and I hadn't really taught her much. I backed off to mess around with a few of my old white girlfriends and sure enough, she went loco. She started crank-calling my home and leaving strange, dripping packages at my doorstep. She came by my mom's house while I was washing clothes and started ranting, the whole time ripping up pictures she had taken of me. When she left, Mom came downstairs and was like, "What'd you *do* to that girl!?" I told her, gently, what I'd taught her.

"Leave that girl *alone*. I mean *alone*, you hear me? No ass-fucking, no head, no nuthin'!" she said, shaking her head as she picked up the ripped photos. "You think you can get copies of these for me?" I shrugged. Later on, this sister found religion and became a nun after having a vision of being sodomized by Satan. True story.

These were only two in a series of wack women I would run

across. I wasn't looking for crazy, but somehow crazy always found me. One day my Aunt Lara, to my dismay, suggested that I was getting what I was putting out, that my appearance and demeanor attracted a certain kind of woman. I was an "alternative brother" (whatever that means), one that didn't easily fit into a "type." While white girls find this type of brother earthy and deep, some sisters find them obtuse and questionable. It wasn't about me going out to find a sister; a sister would have to find me.

If I wanted a sister, she said, I would have to make a few changes. Not a wholesale makeover, but a few real basic alterations. Like getting and keeping a job. Ironing my clothes. Bathing every day. You know, just the basics. Not that I was Pig-Pen . . . I just wasn't fly and crispy, like all the rest of the brothers out there on the prowl. I wasn't a bad guy, she said . . . *just kinda triflin'*. A diamond in the rough. So I did like she told me and I found the quality of women that were attracted to me began to change . . . but not by much. I was getting my thing tight, but the sisters I met didn't have their thing together, and that made me uncomfortable. They didn't have anything more on the ball than I did, and I had nothing on the ball. I just dressed the part. But I had some idea where I wanted to go in life and how I was going to get there, but most of the women I met had no ambition beyond buying a Coach purse or owning a Range Rover. Now, I like nice things, but the sisters I met? Material gain motivated their every action. They had their hand out at every turn, and demanded that I spoil them like their (usually absent) daddys never did. Me? Fuck that. I was broke as a muthafucka, and I wasn't digging on that shit. Now, there's nothing wrong with shallow if you like shallow. But I don't. And as a direct result of the fact that they were easily moistened by any guy in a flashy suit, they seemed to have problems keeping their panties up, if you get my drift. Sisters who wouldn't let me smell the pussy suddenly relaxed their moral inhibitions when a guy took them out for shrimp. Now, I don't think this is a problem unique to black women. The white women I was with slept around on the QT—and so did I—but the sisters were flagrant. The white women seemed motivated less by lures and bait than just getting fucked, which is the brand of infidelity, frankly, I can halfway respect. Because a slut makes a choice, whereas a whore can be bought by anyone. Neither is what I was looking for. Very often all me and my girlfriends had in common was skin color and a passion for shrimp. I felt like I was playing myself, like I was giving sisters a skin pass to be stupid and repressed. My boys concurred.

See, they weren't supportive of my search for a sister. At all. It should be about the connection, not the complexion, they said. While that slogan might look good on a T-shirt, its veracity and weight as a maxim was suspect. Still, many of them admired my courage, and discreetly—on their way out the door with their white girls—wished me luck.

But of course you wanna know . . . did I find the perfect sister?

Well, I went South already knowing I'd meet the right sister—I mean, that's where they grow all the big butts, right? I'd get me one with a PhD, some pearly whites, and forty-eight-inch hips and live out the rest of my days smackin' it up to flip it and rub it down—Oh yeah. That's the stuff. The thing is? I just resigned myself to stop looking. A good sister would likely find me. And find me they did.

You know, it's amazing how fast word gets around when a new, employed black man gets off a train in a small town like

Lexington, Kentucky. My dance card filled up rather quickly with ladies with big hips and the children they carried, who evidently kept preachers on speed-dial, 'cause they were hot to get married right out of the gate. Me? Not so much. Twice down the aisle for me is the limit. Oughta be a law. Had some great time on the *horizontal*. But we had nothing on the vertical. Or at least, not enough to write about it. So I got settled into life as a cat bachelor: just me, my cat Isis, and the occasional stray pussy that breached my doorway. I didn't want for company often, but I was lonely. Without my kids or a woman to call my own, my bitch-trap flat with twenty-foot ceilings and sixty-five-inch TV was closing in on me, one day at a time.

And that's just about the time I met Byrd.

I was in Louisville getting out of an elevator at a writer's conference and there she was in the lobby, fending off the advances of a randy pirate on Halloween night. She looked at me, I looked at her, and she waved me over.

Yeah. She waved *me* over and I immediately took to her swagger.

She smiled, and that was one of the first three things that drew me in. What kind of woman flags down a *man*, you ask? The confident, sexy kind. The kind I prefer. Now, me? My sexy was slacking. Me wearing a Johnny Cash T-shirt and a little day-funk, this probably wasn't the optimal moment to engage an attractive woman in heady conversation with any intentions. So I didn't really, but it became clear that the damsel needed rescuing, as she was literally beating him off of her. And it didn't take much conversation for me to defuse the punchy pirate, whose best line, evidently, was "Arrrrrrr." I didn't know her from any other woman in the room. But we got to know each other very well in a short period of time. And it became evident that we should proceed forward . . . together.

That was two years ago. Today, she's in the other room, writing. She'll ask me what I want to eat shortly and I'll say, "Whatever." It's a good life. Is it permanent? Am I psychic? If I was, I would have known that the perfect sister for me would be a white girl. Not by choice or exclusion, but simple serendipity. We are compatible, and we share common experiences. And no, I'll not curry together a list, and I don't owe you any explanation. She's not color-struck, and I didn't choose white over black: I simply made a choice to be happy and not care what you think about it.

I don't want you to think that now that I have a white girl, that I think that this is "the way," or I think I have all the answers. I don't. Because we're from different cultures, we carry different baggage, but we share some of the same hopes and dreams, some of the same problems, the same drama and shit everyone has. Just because I'm shacked-up with a white woman don't think it's Shangri-La—it's not. But we have much more in common than not, and our commonality and compatibility is the glue that keeps us together.

Sisters like to refer to brothers who date white women as "sellouts" because they are obviously much too weak to bear the brunt of hundreds of years of built-up resentment and dig through layers of pain into the inherent goodness and strength of a black woman.

T'yeah. It sounds pretty, but I'm not buying it.

Embedded in the Denzel Principle is the idea of racial solidarity: Denzel would never be with a white woman. Well, if I had Denzel's wife, I probably wouldn't wander far either. But I don't. I'm a single black man of substance, and I don't have to take guff in the name of being true to "Da Race." The legacy of slavery doesn't have as much to do with why black women can't keep a man as they'd like to believe. And even if it does, I can't live in that bag. I'd rather be happy than politically correct. I can't do love-by-committee: I am a man, this is my woman. 'Nuff said. I have nothing to prove to the race. My talents, gifts, and contributions to the community are not diminished by who I cohabitate with. I am a black man—blackness intact—strong enough to make my own decisions without apology. I deserve to be loved and respected. Anything else would be selling myself short.

Return of the Good Guy

It's probably important to say, if it isn't already obvious, that many of the concepts in this book don't just apply to black men and black women. Black women and white women like Nice Guys, for instance. I mean, I'm certainly equal opportunity.

I've not always been a Good Guy, but I've always been a Nice Guy.

Yeah, I know—stop laughing. It's true. I haven't always been willing to let people see into my soul and make myself vulnerable in that way, but I have been more than willing to lure women in and make them think anything they want to believe. It's not that I've been phony: rather, I've been guarded, and a lot of other men are as well.

Today, I let my Good Guy shine through. I'm not always the most polite, most genteel, most well-mannered guy in the crew, but the truth is I don't operate with malice: my intentions are always good. And that's really the hallmark of a Good Guy: it doesn't matter if he is well-heeled and well-behaved most the time, because all kinds of no-goodniks can fake the funk. Pimps, perverts, and serial killers are always described as "nice guys" by people who know them, until it's reported that they were exploiting eleven-year-old girls, or trying to lure little boys into oral sex, or the police found a severed head in the refrigerator. Then you always see the shot of some neighbor shaking their head: "I should have known something wasn't right," they say. Good job, Nostradamus. Maybe you'll know better next time that you can't judge a book by its cover, and the true measure of a good guy is the veracity of his intentions. Sometimes, it's clear as day, but more often than not, you really have to get to know a dude to know what makes him tick.

Some of the women I've been with have made it hard to be a Good Guy, and it's been hard for me to figure out how to navigate that. The solution was instead of being a Good Guy, I became a kind of prefab Nice Guy instead. What's the difference?

Well, plenty.

The difference between a Good Guy and a Nice Guy is that goodness just *is*. It's organic and comes from within. You can't learn it, buy it, or fake it. You know Good People when you meet them. The Nice Guy is accessorized and put on: his nicety is often a disguise, an overlay for a truly vile personality or a really sensitive soul. Sometimes, the Nice Guy is really a Good Guy, trying too hard. And the Good Guy is a Nice Guy trying to protect himself from being hurt. I admit, they can be hard to spot. Nice Guys are blindly loyal even in the face of adversity, like Red Sox fans or cocker spaniels. See, a Nice Guy is the standard gentleman: he pays for lunches, pulls out chairs. Buys flowers and candy. Writes corny, horny love notes. Walks girls to and from class. That guy was me: I was respectful, in all the conventional ways. Nice Guys are masking insecurity and hoping to distract you so you can't find it. A Love Puppy is head-over-heels in love with the love Keith Sweat, Gerald Levert, Luther Vandross, and Al B. Sure! used to sing about. He is a Nice Guy gone crazy. Those are the kinds of men women dream about, so says the radio. Love Puppies find themselves eschewing common sense to go above and beyond to find, please, and keep a woman. Women prefer Love Puppies over Nice Guys, although to most, the nomenclature is interchangeable. The aim, it seems, is always to turn a Nice Guy into a Love Puppy, because women think they long for a man who requires nothing but tries his damnedest to give them the world, who is prepared to work as many jobs, buy as many flowers, wash as many dishes, cook as many meals, or paint as many toenails as he has to in order to make his woman happy. A woman doesn't *really* want a man like that. Because that guy? Well . . . he's not a man. And most times, she is going to turn that Love Puppy into a Dawg. Nice Guys are marks who give until they have nothing left to give anymore. Good Guys keep their critical mind front and center and never give too much, to the point where there is an imbalance.

Early in the game, I was That Dude, buying my girlfriends candy and treats, picking flowers, and reciting bad, grade-school poetry. Most of the young ladies were not impressed, no matter how hard I tried. I was that one kid with the "bubble lips," always wearing floods, shirts with the Superfly collar, sporting the lopsided, lint-filled Afro. The only thing I had going for me was my smile. I didn't have that Jimmie Walker, Rodney Allen Rippy type of appeal. I was the boy girls dated for my "personality."

Now, I didn't necessarily know what that meant, but it never occurred to me it might be a bad thing. At that age, it seemed like girls had any number of superficial reasons to be with someone—they were good at sports, they had a tricked-out BMX, or maybe they always had the best brand-named snacks in their lunch box (Hostess Twinkies or Dolly Madison Zingers, as opposed to, say, best-value twin cakes or three-for-a-dollar cream pies, for instance). Maybe they had a Scooby-Doo, Fat Albert, or Speed Buggy lunch box, or another hot lunch-bucket-of-the-moment. I had none of that. I had old clothes and dandruff. I rode a bike with a banana seat and streamers on the sissy handlebars that fell apart every time I rode it. I took a Pelé lunchbox to school, and no one knew what cartoon he was on. I rarely had a snack cake in my lunch and got free milk from the cafeteria. So I didn't have to worry about girls wanting to be with me because I was popular. Nope. The young ladies dug on me for my personality. I was lucky that way, I guess.

In the years that followed, I'd hear about my great personality a lot, and I was so grateful that I took good care of my girlfriends. I mean, I wasn't a playground pimp or a Rockefeller or anything, but I did as well as any teenager could be expected to. And the ladies did dig it, but after a while, they'd get bored, and fire me to pick up some asshole who mistreated them. He was always the dopehead, the bully, or the jock, the kind of guy who'd ask a girl for a handjob in the back hall and not even bring her a nuttrag or Wet-Naps. I rarely got handjobs in junior high—at least, not from anyone else's hand. But I always had napkins, because I was just that considerate type of guy. Women seemed to like me—a lot!—but didn't want to give me the goodies. They liked me well enough to accept gifts and favors, but not well enough to give me some nookie. And they didn't know how to tell me, so instead they'd just cheat on me, drop me a note, and console the ensuing devastation the best way they could—as long as it didn't involve sympathy pussy. Or a handie. Or head. Just me, Mr. Fucking Personality, my "Dear John" letter, and my hurt feelings.

One day, it occurred to me that I was being used. Not for anything material so much as for comfort and affirmation. Looking back at the kind of women I was dating, it became clear I was a magnet for the fallen and downtrodden, the dock in a storm: or, not so delicately, I'd become a rest-haven for hoes. The girls didn't like me as much as they liked the way I liked them without judging them. I was their ego-boost and cheerleader, an ashy, one-man entourage during a lull in their fabulous lives. There I was, eager to please. I didn't know about the line between Nice Guy and Love Puppy. But I learned.

Let me break it down.

I think all women want a Nice Guy, but they don't want a pushover. They don't want a punk, but most women don't know the difference. The Nice Guy wears his feelings on his sleeve and is often guilted, cried, or deprived into submission. By deprived I mean he is deprived of sex. Women use sex as a compliance tool, and it works best with Nice Guys. Because Nice Guys don't necessarily know how to make a woman want them in an organic, seductive way. They only know intimacy as a service provider, and not as the consumer. Sometimes, they are skilled lovers, but mostly they eat a lot of pussy and end up jerking off. The rub is, they aren't particularly worried about getting off anyways— they only live to get you off, and to be robbed of that privilege is an unimaginable state of being, so they are willing to bend, break, or beg themselves back into your good graces just for a whiff—a sniff!—of the panties. They only desire, without knowing how to be desired, and live for the approval of their woman. Nice Guys have little or no backbone and are easily cajoled into all kinds of jacked up circumstances; from paying for school loans to donating a kidney, their kindness knows no bounds. They are selfless, but not in a good way.

Below the nicety is a profound need to be liked at any cost, including the loss of dignity and self-esteem. He loves her because she lets him do for her, and she kinda likes him because he does things for her. So he makes her number one and she makes herself number one too. The Nice Guy has no ambition of his own, and spends all of his time making his woman a better person. And while he is paying her car note, his bills go to pot. And when he's paying to get her hair done, spiders are nesting in his head. He spoils her and neglects himself. This is an unhealthy relationship that will only end one of two ways: she'll leave him for a new sucker with more money and resources to waste on her, or she'll be swept off her feet by some gorilla who wouldn't buy her an ice cream cone and treats her like a dog. Either way— and you knew this was coming—the Nice Guy finishes last. But let's suppose that doesn't happen. Let's suppose they continue on in something like a functioning relationship.

The Nice Guy is known for his "personality," and this is a kind of backhanded compliment, as it doesn't say much for the rest of his virtues. What it means, in fact, is that you are a mark: an easy touch. A nice person willing to do anything to please your partner as long as they stay by your side. From grade school to grad school, anyone with you for your "personality" is in it for what they can get. The Nice Guy gets weaker and weaker, until he's something a lot closer to a woman than a man: he can't brush his teeth, comb his hair, or get dressed without permission. Instead of being her complement, he's more like her shadow. Her manservant. She's the boss. She loves it at first, but soon she longs for a man. I mean, someone who can actually make a decision. The man she has broken is nothing like the man he may have been once. Now he is deferential, accommodating, and, unless he's taking out the garbage or changing a lightbulb, completely useless. Now that she has exactly what she thought she wanted, she's sad. Because she doesn't really, truly know what a man is. But she knows that the nutless wonder she calls her lover has lost his fire, and he barely qualifies for the job.

Naturally, she finds the polar opposite, leaves the old guy high and dry, and there he stands, no pride, no dignity, trying to buy his balls out of hock, feeling like he got caught up in a tornado and finally let loose. He wanders from place to place having no idea where he's been, and no idea how he got where he is. What he knows is he is angry. Angry that he was ever nice enough to let a woman take advantage of him. Angry that he let his guard down and let love in. Angry that he didn't see the heartbreak coming. You see, he knew the rules, but he gave love a chance. Night after night, he sits alone at the bar turning the events around in his head, saying "never again." Then everything he knows about women, both good and bad, finally comes back to him. And it all makes sense.

He washes himself off, gets his fits together, and straightens himself out. He gets his thing together until one day, he's a good catch, and all the ladies know it. In the depths of despair, he found the wherewithal he didn't know he had: his natural instincts start to kick in. And before you know it, he's a man reborn. But he's not the kind of man you'd want to be with, because you know what happened? Someone met a Nice Guy, turned him into a Love Puppy, dumped him off, and that Love Puppy grew into a Dawg, the kind of man with lots of game but little regard for women.

Women call men Dawgs when they do the same things women do: bounce from situation to situation at a whim, play manipulative mind games using their good looks, desirability, and sexual prowess to control and juggle multiple suitors at a time, often without their knowledge. This is the game women play. Dawgs are men who learn how to play it too. And they play aggressively and without remorse, like women. Turnabout is fair play, but try telling that to a woman scorned. A true Dawg misuses women and defuses any potential retribution for his action. They are not pawns in the game—they are Players. And men can only be up on the game after having been caught up in the business end of the game. After they have been successfully jilted by a few women. Bitches turn Nice Guys into Dawgs. We could argue the whole chicken-or-the-egg thing here, but there hardly seems a point to it—better to just learn to live around it and how to avoid getting caught up.

Even if men aren't Dawgs, women don't really seem to know how to choose good men. Sometimes, you can look at a guy and tell what he's about.

Rollo
LOOKS LIKE: Rollo from *Sanford and Son*
SOUNDS: too damn cool for his own good
YOU'LL KNOW IT'S HIM: when you are named as a co-conspirator
Like Nathaniel Taylor's character on *Sanford and Son*, Rollo is that good brother you know who is just a little too hood. He's not the kind of dude who would bring a forty to a Kwanzaa celebration. But there's a sense he's not above a little three-card monty or a quick game of craps. He's very often "fresh out" or "on paper"

(probation), yet somehow able to afford really nice clothes on his salary as a busboy. Has a knack for raising money quickly, and gives three contact numbers in as many weeks. Is often "visiting relations" for six-month stretches. He's very nice—charismatic, even—and respectful toward all the womenfolk in your family. The menfolk give him short shrift, making him that much more desirable in your eyes.

Ghost Dad

LOOKS LIKE: he's on the run

You meet this guy, and one of the first things he does is take out his wallet and show you pictures of his kids—man, they're so cute when they're babies. But these pictures are nine years old, and he hasn't seen or heard from his children in all that time. Now, there are a few good reasons why this could be. The mother could be playing "keep away" with the children and he may not have the kind of bread he needs to fight her in court. Or he doesn't care about his kids enough to pay support and/or fight for his parental rights. Now you may not be ready to date a man with kids, but you want to date the kind of man that will step up and take responsibility as well as all the joy and pain that comes with a single-father type of situation. You don't want a Ghost Dad or paper father who may pay his support but isn't trying to see his kids.

Rev. Hooten Holla

WEARS: too many gold crosses to take him seriously

DRIVES: a new Rolls-Royce. Every year.

It's weird that somehow, ministers always have a lady in their Cadillac, or sitting front and center in the pews. And what woman wouldn't want a man of the cloth—I mean, he's the man next to "The Man," right? The thing is, he's less holier than thee, thou, and the next muthafucka. Church leaders are notorious womanizers and sex freaks with underaged dick-suckers in training and prolific porno collections hidden behind trapdoors. These cats start out giving counsel, next thing they're getting head. These cats are steady pimping from the pulpit.

The Bar-Napkin Poet

LOOKS LIKE: he lives in a cardboard box

SOUNDS LIKE: he's whining, whether he's reading poetry or not

YOU'LL KNOW IT'S HIM: pretending to read Mao's "red boo"

You see this brother at all the poetry readings, cultural convocations, and Afrocentric happenings. He's draped in kente cloth and walks with a cane that he calls a "verb stick." When asked his name, he'll say, "I am called Talib," except that he hasn't legally changed his name, so his mama, when she calls him up from the basement for dinner, addresses him by his given name: Rufus. He can be seen at the open-mike functions sitting in a corner jotting down profundities on a napkin, with just enough poetic flare to get you to pay for the room. Nine months later, you'll be at open-mike, knocked-swole and angry, with your new girlfriend Riki in tow. You will raise your bastard child as "gender neutral."

Bartleby

LOOKS LIKE: a mailroom clerk

SMELLS LIKE: dirty khakis

YOU'LL KNOW IT'S HIM: he's driving your car

Like the main character from Herman Melville's short story of the same name, Bartleby is railing against The Man by refusing to work for The Man. Scratch that. He works, but kinda works The System, if you know what I mean. He works, just hard enough to keep a gig but not hard enough so anyone would notice. He's nice enough, if only he wanted something out of life. He goes to work (late) and becomes what people pejoratively call the "goldbrick-on-shift." He sometimes does enough work to get by, sometimes not. Sometimes, he lacks drive and just settles into a mailroom gig, where he can nap between mail runs. He often just keeps a job long enough to collect unemployment. He works fast-food sometimes—which is a laudable, honest vocation—and will sometimes get promoted to key manager (aka Straw Boss). He'll keep that key for ten years or better until finally someone asks him why he doesn't try to get promoted. "I prefer not to," he says.

Mickey D

LOOKS: tired and worn-out. From all the Fuck N Dash.

DRIVES: a bus pass

YOU'LL KNOW IT'S HIM: when your pregnancy test comes back positive

Guys like Mickey D have no job, no education, and only one ambition: to move from city to city meeting women and making babies, as if franchising throughout the inner cities of America. He's the Johnny Appleseed of the ghetto, dropping baby-batter like he's got the last sperm on earth. Child support isn't a problem for him, because he doesn't stay in one city for too long and he doesn't give you his real name. He's the king of the Fuck N Dash. And your house is his latest franchise.

Thuglife

Thuglife is smart enough to be anything in life he wants to be—instead, he aspires to live like rapper Tupac Shakur and die in a hail of gunfire. He's of the streets and stays in the street, shooting dice, hustling, and getting into trouble. If there isn't a fight in the club, he'll start some shit out of boredom. You're afraid to go to his house because somebody might shoot it up. He's almost always on his way to or just fresh off of a stint in the joint. Bailing him out of jail, paying for lawyer fees, and filling his commissary have become your new hobbies.

Dough Boy

All this brother knows is the dope game, and he knows it well. He's a former clocker pushing big weight and now he's a shot caller. He's got a nice house, a nice car, lots of money, and a lifespan of about half an hour. He's going to get knocked, and it's just a matter of who knocks him first: the police or the competition.

Burger King

LOOKS: cheap

DRIVES: a Hyundai

SCREENNAME: CUMMONBABEE

Burger King is often the guy you meet through an online dating service or in a chat room, and decide to take a chance on a meeting. He asks you on a date, and you're looking for a nice night out. He, on the other hand, is thinking about the cheapest possible way he can take you out and still get those drawers off. Looking for love online (as if), he presumes you are desperate and horny anyway, so dinner is just a pretext to what he's really interested in: going half on a room. The first sign you're with a Burger King is he doesn't spend more than twenty-five dollars—with tip—on a dinner date. The next cue is he takes a strange route home that just happens to pass a motel. Where it just so happens he knows the clerk by name, and they happen to have his favorite thirty-dollar-per-hour room waiting.

Nightcrawler

ALWAYS SAYS: "Somebody SCREEEEEEEEEM!"

You met him at a club, and he seemed like a nice enough guy. But the night you met was the only time you've been out together in a public place with good lighting. Inexplicably, he can only see you after a certain time of night and even then in clandestine, out-of-the-way spots where no one goes. And you've never been to his pad: it's either your place or the mo-mo. You ask him about it and he has a good line about the passion of the night, the romance of dark places, his place getting painted, and avoiding the crowds for a bit of intimacy. Legitimate excuses, all. But there is something he isn't telling you.

Fresh Out

LOOKS LIKE: he's been doing push-ups since 1986

DRIVES: your car

KEEPS: a topless picture of Tevin Campbell in his wallet

More and more brothers are going into the joint, and that means more and more of them are getting out. Fresh Out is that dude who's only been out a month or less, and is still trying to remember what female genitalia looks like. He's often erudite, well-spoken, and completely unemployable. He may be institutionally gay, but you are scared to ask. Besides, he bangs the pussy like he's settling a grudge. He ends up moving in, where you try to get him into some "fresh-out" job and trade programs. You end up pregnant, and he three-strikes-out on a petty theft charge.

Schleprock

LOOKS LIKE: he needs ironing

DRIVES: your car, with no license

YOU'LL KNOW IT'S HIM: when he calls you at work asking, "What you doin'?"

Wants everything from life but doesn't want to work for it. He's motivated enough to figure out elaborate ways to scam free money from the government via welfare fraud, disability claims, or selling cans, but he can't seem to figure out how to register for classes or fill out a legitimate job application. He's a sweet guy who picks (steals?) flowers for you and makes Valentines by hand and he might be an asset if it weren't for his aversion to waking up before 3 P.M. Very often, he has a variety of moneymaking schemes going at once, and occasionally one will pan out. Mostly, he is broke or nearly broke and doesn't care. You want to change him. You can't.

King of the Bar

Just like Partyman (see below), he's content to be a big fish in a little pond. Except that a lot of fish get shot in his pond. The neighborhood corner bar is a great place to build community, but makes for a sorry date. But this is where you find him, time and time again. This is where he meets you, and this is where you stay until closing. He's more than a regular: he's got his own voice mail on the bar's phone. Nothing wrong with hanging at the bar, per se, and he says he likes to watch the game with his buddies. But neighborhood bars are incubators for drama and bullshit.

Mr. Sweetbread

YOU'LL KNOW IT'S HIM: because you have to ask

I'm all for a man setting his own parameters for manhood and masculinity, but something's not right about this brother. Men raised by women tend to have a more pronounced feminine side, but this dude walks on air. It's nothing particular—nothing as silly as him matching his clothes or paying special attention to his grooming regimen. Rather, it is the peculiar combination of the effeminate way he speaks and a lack of traits we naturally attribute to men that makes this dude suspect. Too much Billy Dee Willams and not enough Jim Brown by a sight. He may not be bisexual. But he may be too close to a girlfriend to be man enough for you.

Lil Pimp

LOOKS LIKE: he buys his clothes at swap meets

SOUNDS LIKE: some kind of rapping idiot—everything rhymes

YOU'LL KNOW IT'S HIM: his suits need batteries

This guy is kinda dangerous. Not because he's a street brother, but because he thinks he's street, and could put the two of you in bad situations. He's got a lot of mouth and talks a lot of shit, but he's only about a buck twenty wet, and it's just a matter of time before he gets his ass kicked. The thing is, he's trying to impress you. Since so many women go for the thug types (see Thuglife, above), he feels like he has to represent. The problem is, he's Theo Huxtable in Rocafella clothes, with a fake gangster limp, throwing up gang signs he learned from watching *Boyz n the Hood*. If he could turn it off . . . well . . . he'd still be a punk.

Pimp Tight

This cat is always nickel-slick, dressing straight out of the book, with a nice car, and a decent crib. All-around good-looking guy, on paper. But you never hear him say he's late for work or hear him talking about his job. Strange, because no one's even sure he has one. His schedule is erratic and while he certainly disappears for long periods of time—like, weeks—he doesn't seem to have any shifts to clock in to or pay stubs to collect. Could be any variety of hustler. Or he could have inherited some money from a dead uncle. Nah—chances are better he's hustling.

Honest Abe

You just met Abe at a club, and it turns out he's not big on condoms—they cramp his style and dampen the sensation. You don't want to fight about it and besides, that dick feels so damn good, so you just make him promise not to come inside you. And he gives you his word of honor. Five months later, it looks on the ultrasound like he's also given you a baby boy, but his parents aren't giving you his forwarding address. He's moved out, and they have no idea where he's gone. Honest.

Sugar Daddy

LOOKS LIKE: your dad

SOUNDS LIKE: Barry White

YOU'LL KNOW IT'S HIM: when he collapses dead on top of you

Daddy-O is frequently the old guy in the club wearing a Chess King suit, playing Stacy Adams on his feet and Royal Crown on his dome. He's married, and has worked at the same factory for twenty years. Wifey's breasts are getting long and veiny and he's got the money to pay for the attentions of young ladies. So he sneaks out after second shift, goes line dancing at the club, and builds himself a stable of single mothers who eventually break him for rent, clothes, cars, and food, and he breaks them off thirteen minutes of lovin', if he can get it up. His wife finds a hotel receipt, they fight, make up, and it starts all over again.

The Black Jack Tripper

LOOKS: tired. And happy.

Jack is underemployed and his life is riding on fumes. He's three semesters short of a B.A., but he's a nice enough guy. You guys kick it for a few weeks, and like each other a lot. Next thing you know, he's moving his clothes into your pad. Next comes his PlayStation, his dog, and before you know it, he lets the lease run out on his studio apartment and he's living with you. It might be okay, except after books, bus fare, and video games, he's got no money left to spend on food and rent.

White Mike

SOUNDS LIKE: Tupac Shakur, circa *Juice*

LOOKS LIKE: he was pen-raped at a tattoo parlor

WATCH OUT BECAUSE: he's gullier than some real O.G.s

Mike is the white boy with the close-cropped haircut trying to pass for a light-skinned black guy. He's got the walk, the talk, and the attitude, all from watching hours of MTV's *Sucker Free*. He's blacker than you and your people, an attribute they find curious, laughable, and, that time he wore a dashiki to your Kwanzaa celebration, offensive. He's a new breed of white person raised with black culture as the dominant backdrop, and he thinks color doesn't matter. And it doesn't, when you're true to yourself. The problem is, you can't tell if he's really that ignorant or just faking the funk to seem blacker. He drinks a little too much man juice, taking on a little too much swagger, and has to be pulled out of fights and arguments occasionally. It's almost like he's synthesized the worst characteristics and stereotypes of black men into his permanent façade, and it's all a little disquieting.

Gordo
AKA: Big Poppa

You don't know what it is, but you like a fat man. Something about all that blubber and sweat makes you weak. You feel safe—and small—when he's with you. And he's a jolly fat guy, like most are. But you can't go to the mall, to the movies, or to the refrigerator without carrying a defibrillator. He's about one Big Mac short of a heart attack. You don't want a guy who's a gym rat, necessarily. But you don't want a guy who doesn't take care of himself either. Black men are prone to diseases related to stress and inactivity.

Itchy and Scratchy

This cat may be in transition from the streets to a home, from his mama's basement to an apartment of his own, or fresh out of the joint into a halfway situation. You like this guy a lot, so you haven't slept with him yet. Good girl. Don't get me wrong—he's an okay guy, except that he's always on his way to or just out of the clinic. He's got more medication and ointment than an old Jewish grandmother and every time you turn around he's scratching, itchy, or twitching—sometimes all three. You think he's grabbing his nutts because he's macho, but he may just be trying to quell the burn. Something ain't right.

Begging Billy

LOOKS LIKE: Keith Sweat, just broke

SOUNDS LIKE: "Please baby, please baby please."

YOU'LL KNOW IT'S HIM: because he smells like Chaps cologne

This cat is a throwback to a bygone era. He wears Karl Kani, South Pole gear, and a texturizer in his hair. He bought his 1996 Park Avenue from his stepfather and he's always blasting some New Jack Swing. He knows how to line dance and buy you a drink, and he knows how to beg a woman for sex and attention. Profusely. His game is lame and often in verse, until he eventually turns to offering the woman anything she wants if she'll just let him "taste it." You may or may not give up the draws, but will gladly milk this sap for gifts and favors. Billy buys four birthday gifts, pays two car notes, takes three women to Benihana, and has convinced himself he's a Player. Sometimes, he begs up on some pussy. Most often, he masturbates compulsively.

Smokey

SMELLS LIKE: weed

HE'S ALWAYS: ashy, with purple fingertips

YOU'LL KNOW IT'S HIM: because he keeps clean piss in his fridge. Don't ask.

Like Chris Tucker's immortal character from *Friday*, Smokey is worse than lazy. He's lazy and he smokes weed. Every day, while living at his mama's house. It's funny at first, but when he comes around your folks smelling like Cheech and Chong, it causes some embarrassment. You and he smoke socially. Soon, he reels you into this lifestyle. First, you get too stoned to make it to class. Then, you get fired from your job. Then you move in together to

Section 8 housing, and he has to start selling weed just to support both of your weed habits. Then you're pregnant, he gets knocked, and you're putting baby-formula money in his commissary.

Pierre Delacroix

Pierre thinks he is better than everyone, including you. He has a nice ride, an Ivy League education, and the personality of an English muffin: white and flat. With lots of nooks and crannies to hold the remnants of his blackness, that inherent connection most of us have with people of color from all walks of life. He's got an English accent even though he's only ever been to London, Ontario. The kind of guy who examines your grandmother's eighteen-year-old Persian Bokhara to see if it's a fake and boldly declares it so in front of your whole family. Pierre is a trifle dandy and intentionally doesn't exude any masculine qualities people might find offensive, leading people to call him "Dela-question-mark." Secretly, he wishes he knew who he was.

Hustleman

LOOKS LIKE: a ghetto-fabulous bootleg fashion disaster

SOUNDS LIKE: a TV pitchman, even in bed

YOU'LL KNOW IT'S HIM: because every time he parks his car, people gather around the trunk

Hustleman beat the system by selling durable goods out of his trunk. He goes to New York every few weeks, loads up on fake purses, jewelry, and designer fashions with the intention of bringing them back to your town to sell at a 180 percent markup. Sometimes, he is also a fence who sells items pilfered from Macy's department store or Macy's crib, your best friend and good neighbor. He's most often a security guard or mailroom clerk by day, with an aging certificate from some defunct technical school. He's flashy, well-paid, and not at all self-conscious about selling stolen and fake goods out of his trunk. Your family loves him because he gives them a discount, and you love him because you now own Coach purses in every color God created and a few he didn't. If he went to college and got a business degree, he'd be a good catch. But given that his vocation doesn't come with medical or dental, his marriageability is debatable.

Trick Daddy

This hardworking guy likes to cut loose after work and head to the strip club. That's cool, except he cashes his check at the bar and tricks a good portion of it off on lap dances and champagne-room shenanigans. He doesn't just go to unwind—he's kind of a professional trick. This is how he gets attention from women, and this is the only way he knows how to relate to women—as a customer. This might seem like a good thing, because this guy is accustomed to giving women money and gifts for their affection, and will do so for the woman in his life. But he only knows how to relate to women as objects, as service providers: the emotional game frustrates and confuses him.

Deebo

SOUNDS LIKE: Lurch, from *The Addams Family*

DRIVES: a huge truck, with a shotgun in the trunk

YOU'LL KNOW IT'S HIM: when you are filling out the restraining order

He's a big guy who makes you feel safe, and people move out of the way wherever you go. And you like that. But he's not the most articulate brother in the world, and you know he's got violent tendencies. So that means that every argument becomes a shouting match that is just a hair away from becoming physical. He's the jealous type who needs to know every time you go to the toilet, not to mention when you leave the house. He uses his stature to intimidate you into complying with his stalker ways. He hasn't hit you yet, and you swear he's a teddy bear, but you can't trust his temper. He's a bully. Get away from Deebo.

Waldo Faldo

It's okay for a brother to be bookish—we don't want to discourage intellectualism. But in order to survive in this country, a black man needs to know stuff you can't learn from a book. It's cool that he can do Chinese math, map out the universe freehand, and order appetizers in five different languages. What good is all that book learning if he's not fluent in all the tongues and dialects of the block? He reads too many books about black people, so he's afraid of your cousin Bootsy, Aunt May May, and other folks that don't appear to be from his country club. A black man needs a little street knowledge so he can get on with people from all races and sides of the tracks. This is a nerd who needs some soul.

Pig-Pen

BATHES: annually

SMELLS LIKE: he never wipes. Anywhere. Ever.

PROBABLY: has fleas

Dude keeps a dirty house, a dirty car, and a dirty body. Even when his body is clean, he's wearing dirty clothes. Sometimes, this is from lack of self-esteem. More often, he wasn't raised right and doesn't give a fuck. He leaves skid marks everywhere he sits even with his pants on. Could very easily be infected with something. Or everything. Nice guy, otherwise. Wish he had enough bread to hire a maid. Or HAZMAT.

The Arteest

He's very talented, and you know because he tells you. He spends all his time painting, sculpting, or painting sculptures. Or he's a rapper with a lot of great punch lines. You're attracted to his dark, emotional side. Or he's a writer, pouring his heart out in prose. He's about to blow up—they all are. The problem is they can't figure out how to monetize the passion—they sit back waiting to be discovered, instead of going out there and making an opportunity. The Arteest doesn't exhibit much, get himself published, do showcases, or make mix tapes. All his friends tell him he'll be large one day, and he might if he would just go get it.

Sweetdick Willie

LOOKS LIKE: any old Moe

SOUNDS LIKE: he's got game

YOU'LL KNOW IT'S HIM: because you're fucking him in the bathroom. Any bathroom.

Sweetdick Willie is every father's worst nightmare, probably because your dad used to *be* Sweetdick Willie. You never want your daughter to run into Willie because he has learned the secret of how to "pimp by dick." That is, he's got just enough good game to get your panties off and *pow!* spring you on some good lovin'. It's a hard trick to pull off, but once he gets it off, look out! Because he doesn't have to do much else to render you helpless. He's a cock man, slinging dick like a weapon of ass destruction. And you surrender freely, giving anything and everything he wants.

He's very often a Schleprock or Burger King in disguise, and he operates on the stealth. By the time you realize you are sprung on some good dick that you need to ween yourself off of, you're paying his rent and hand-washing his underwear. Your friends try to tell you, but nobody can tell you anything. Like any sickness, it's just a thing you have to let run its course. You'll come out the better end with stories for weeks and wiser for it.

Mustapha Osama Jihad Mohammed Watson

Farina Watson used to be a knucklehead, always in some mess, until he got turned on to this brand new place called "the bookstore" and proceeded to read every book about blackness he could find. He's changed his name and now Mustapha wears a kufi and a full-length African robe, carries a bag of bushwick and pears everywhere he goes, a militant scowl plastered on his face. He went from a pathetic to superblack in the course a year or two: he's trying to tell you what to eat, when to eat, and the Nu Afrikan way to wipe your behind. He doesn't vote in the White Man's elections or drive the White Man's cars. He stands around hollering about whitey this and whitey that and wonders why whitey won't give him a job. He's always trying to tell you what black people like you should do. The only thing worse than a little knowledge is too much, and a steady diet of books on the pathology of blackness will only make him angry and drive you crazy.

The Wino

AKA: Mudfoot, Dipsy

SMELLS LIKE: cheap wine and cologne

Dude cannot handle his liquor. He's fine sober—an affable guy who many find clever, charming, and entertaining. But when someone cracks a bottle of wine, look out! It's like, Dr. Jekyll and Mr. Wine. He's starts flipping out on people, picking fights. Spittle flies as he talks about your mama's lovely new wig and how he can barely see her freshly waxed moustache. You want to give him a chance to sober up, but your drunk uncle Loochie pours him another and his behavior gets worse. When he's not cursing, he's singing with Loochie and by the time he throws up in the barbecue grill, he's overstayed his welcome.

Partyman

This guy is a lot of fun—maybe too much fun. He leads every line dance, buys every drink, and is generally the life of the party. That's what attracted you to him, right? The problem is, the party is his life. He spends all his money on club clothes and grooming. You never go anywhere intimate and romantic—every date involves loud music and a strobe light. He's kind of Tony Manero, in the worst way possible. He's living for party night, which in some cities is every night, and the time between is just building up to the next set. This is his addiction, and he may kick it or not. You don't know if he's a Good Guy or not, because you've never had a complete conversation. Ultimately, he'll be that Old Dude in The Club, and you'll still be single.

Theo Huxtable

LOOKS LIKE: a fake bank teller

SOUNDS LIKE: he's trying to impress you

YOU'LL KNOW IT'S HIM: because your friends will tell you Malcolm-Jamal Warner immortalized the portrait of the suburbanized young black man. Theo looks good from the curb—he's handsome, smart, and well-attired. But privilege kind of made him soft in the middle. He knows how to pick a good wine or where to summer on the Vineyard, but won't drive down certain inner-city streets, and "those kinds" of black people shake him up. He looks down his nose at people—including you—and eats fried chicken with a knife and fork. He's a Bid Whist champ but has never heard of Tonk, Spades, or Bullshit. You can't bring him around your friends because he thinks he's better than they are and it's likely that he'll get kicked out, fucked up, or both.

Dagwood

Dagwood Bumstead is a character from the Murat Bernard "Chic" Young cartoon *Blondie*, and classic movie series of the same name. He's dutiful, doting, and pliant. More to the point, he's a milquetoast. He does whatever she asks, whenever she asks. Women think they want a man who will do what he's told, but is a man still a man with no backbone? Nah. He's a classic Nice Guy: a slug who can't think for himself, and before you know it he's asking for permission to use the bathroom. Women say they don't want a bossy man, but you want a man who's mannish . . . right?

Orphan Andy

You and Andy have been kicking it for close to a year now. Things are all good. You guys are in a good place. But when the subject of the future comes up, he seems evasive and unresponsive. You don't want to buffalo him into something he isn't ready for, so you fall back. Funny thing, though: you live in his hometown and he's never taken you to meet his people. He's met your people—begrudgingly—but he never mentions his folks having holiday dinners and such, and you never ask. He sees his family and attends holiday functions, just without you. You finally ask to meet his people and he says, "Aww, girl, there will be plenty of time for that." Two years in, and you can't be sure he even has parents, because you haven't seen or spoken to them.

Part of the problem is, women don't really know what they're looking for, and they want to blame men for that. It's become a topic for TV news and in-depth articles. I remember this piece in *The Washington Post*, part of their award-winning series on black men in 2005 called "Singled Out," about the struggle of black women to find "suitable" black men. First of all, the idea of a woman writing a piece purporting to discuss black manhood is problematic: women have no opinion of note on manhood, black, green, or purple. Not because they are women. But because if men are struggling to come to terms with manhood, women have even less of an idea.

The piece has one central focus, Robyn. Like most of the women in these kinds of pieces, Robyn's not *really* looking for a husband. Not in a nightclub, because that would be ridiculous. Nobody smart looks for a life mate in a nightclub. If the chances of finding a suitable husband just out in the street are low, how much lower are they in a situation where the main objective is to meet someone to take home for the night? The place you go looking for a husband is the same place pimps go to turn out housewives and strip-bar managers go to recruit. Square biz. It's true—people find their life partners in nightclubs. People hit the lottery too. But the odds are not in your favor. Yet, there she is.

So, against the odds, Robyn meets a nice cat—really digs him— and ends up breaking things off because of their class differences—

he's "too ghetto," you see. People come to you with prejudices about your background that they will dispose of, overcome, or embrace. Class is mostly in your imagination anyway. Class is about the ability to get down with people from all walks of life. Turns out that Robyn's peeps didn't dig her ex-boyfriend.

The conclusion of this piece suggests—like most of these joints do—that one day, black men will recognize how precious the black woman is and give her due props. Slavery and Jim Crow are somehow to blame, she intimates. Anything but some honest introspection makes sense.

The thing that always fascinates me when black women start to bemoan the lack of eligible black men is that they presume to be eligible candidates. I guess they sit around talking to themselves to the point where they don't know any better. They have this conversation in a vacuum that excludes men, and really think that they are somehow inherently better.

T'yeah.

The fact is that there are a ton of eligible black men out there, if "eligible" means gainfully employed, heterosexual, and non-psychotic. I think the ratio of sane black women to eligible black men should be examined. *The Washington Post* should do that piece. I think black women have esteem issues separate and apart from their relationships that start with Daddy (or the absence of) and follow them for life. Most of the dudes I roll with—big, bad, degree-holding, gainfully employed muthafuckas—don't want to play Robyn's psychologist. Nowadays, if you can just find a woman who won't go crazy and stab you in your sleep, you feel like you're "up" in the game. The myth of this progressive professional black woman with the fate of the race on her back is fallacious. I know madd black women out there with great educations, shitty jobs, and no ambition to do better. They are too busy trying to get up on whatever you've got going on, so naturally your instinct is to take them to the mo-mo and leave before they wake up. Because 90 percent of these women walking around who can't find a man are not wife material to begin with. She'll have a phat Wharton MBA, be managing a Wendy's, with six kids by seven dudes—six Fresh Outs and a "poet." No plan but to see what you got going on.

Many black women are not as eligible as they think, and you can generally pick them out too.

Aunt Esther

LOOKS: all buttoned up

ALMOST ALWAYS: is a bigger sinner than you

YOU'LL KNOW IT'S HER: because she's trying to get you to her church

Religion is a fine thing in moderation, but Aunt Esther doesn't know that. She never misses a chance to remind you that you need to get right with God. Forget the fact that you met her at a Bare as You Dare Contest, she insists on trying to make you into a man of God. Not that faith is bad: a real man is a man of faith. But that has to be his choice. Aunt Esther wants to convert you. She can't.

Career Woman

She has five undergraduate degrees, a PhD, and three cars, but can't butter toast. She is so focused on being a successful black woman that learning the finer points of the womanly art of wifery has slipped from her agenda. She can perform outpatient surgery, but can't keep the house clean and presentable. She can draw up a budget for the entire year but can't suck a dick to save baby

Jesus. Naturally, she expects you to play wifey and clean up the house, cook all the meals and such. And, as she often works late, you and Petey Penis are on your own.

Motormouth

Motormouth is the gossip queen, and she's always got her nose in someone else's business. Her mouth breaks up households, gets people fired and beat up, not to mention makes you look bad. No one likes a man with a woman he can't control, especially if his woman is a blabbermouth. She tells what she knows and even what she doesn't. She spends so much time with her ears to the streets that your needs go unattended.

Liberated Woman

She's independent and doesn't need you for shit. She's overly aggressive and will fight you about anything, anytime. She considers herself a feminist, but she secretly aspires to strap on a dildo and fuck you in the pooter. She says she's liberated, but she's really enslaved to an outdated ideology that requires women to subjugate their men instead of being his complement.

Crime Chick

SMELLS LIKE: bathroom soap

ALMOST ALWAYS: is involved in some scam to make ends meet

YOU'LL KNOW IT'S HER: because she knows all the local bail bondsmen. Biblically.

You want a woman with some street, but not more than you. You don't want a woman you don't trust alone in your house, or who you suspect may be setting you up to get robbed. Crime Chick is that kinda chick, and she's hard to make from the curb. Criminals come in all shapes and sizes. You may have met her at the library, but she could be using the library computer to use stolen credit card numbers. Some people like to pretend that black men have some genotypical predeliction to crime, but I'm here to tell you that I have met a few Crime Chicks in my day, and they were all up in the game. They had their hustle *down*. She's always cute and well-appointed, but she is doing some scandalous shit behind the scenes to float that lifestyle. I mean, ask yourself, how is she driving a new Lexus working the cash register at the Dollar Store?

Eve

Eve is the neighborhood incubator, and has several babies by several different men. Now, this may seem like the new reality lately, but it's not a situation you'd want to put yourself into voluntarily, because each one of her babies has a father with a personality that needs managing. Baby-mama drama is different from baby-daddy drama. As a man, you may not be explicitly asked to fill the shoes of a missing father, but if you get with a woman, you have an implicit debt of honor to make her kids into your kids. It's a hell of a responsibility, because you essentially have to put them ahead of yourself, and most guys aren't built to man-up like that. As honorable as it may be from the curb, taking care of another man's children is a trick bag to be in. You invest all your time, love, and affection in this relationship, and then may be pushed away, leaving you broke and lovesick for those kids. On top of that, conflict with the fathers is likely. Whereas baby-mamas always seem to get friendly with the woman in your life, old boyfriends and sperm donors want to come around and assert their ownership. And the other thing is—which is sad to say—there is no future with a woman who has multiple kids by multiple fathers. You don't want to add your seed to that menagerie.

Katie Kaboom

Katie likes to fight, and it doesn't matter what about. When she walks into stores, clerks scatter. When you go out for dinner, there's always a problem with her water, her fork, or her napkin. And she gets *so* pissed. She gets loud and out of hand, calling people's mama, cussing people out, raising Kane, Abel, and Uncle Ben, when it's really not quite that serious. To put it politely, she's got anger issues and rarely misses a chance to lunch out. She'll call you out anyplace, anytime, at the top of her lungs, and tell your mama you ain't shit. You can't bring her around friends and you don't want to introduce her to your moms because you know your peeps will cut a bitch for disrespect. If you and she disagree, she may threaten to throttle you in your sleep or castrate you with her teeth. She's cute enough. But she ain't the one.

Hood Chick

Now, there's no doubt she's hot. That's not the problem. The problem is that she doesn't have any fucking manners—she's hood type. She only knows the rules and social mores that govern the ghetto: which means from head to toe, she's a hot ghetto mess. The type of girl who keeps hot sauce in her purse and wears hot pants to a funeral. She lacks grace in social circumstances and often acts out in public. You are with her for horizontal company, because vertically you have nothing common. She's in and of the ghetto. Museums? Orchestra? Lobster bisque? You are speaking a different language. She's all good, all hood, and that's all she'll ever be. Might make a good chick on the side, but just know she is not the one to take to the company barbecue.

Chicken Pox
LOOKS LIKE: a million bucks
FAVORITE MOVIE: *She's Gotta Have It*
YOU'LL KNOW IT'S HER: because *everybody* knows it's her, dude

You meet this nice girl and bring her around your crew, only to find out that many of your boys already know her all too well. She's spread through the neighborhood like chicken pox—everyone has had her at *least* once. She's something like the neighborhood freak. Now, it's easy to get into this situation and think you've hit the jackpot. A woman who will put out on the regular without some kind of implicit remuneration is rare. But a girl like that is gonna have you in the clinic, and you'll be the joke of the neighborhood.

Bertha Butt
Bertha's a sweet girl with a big ass. That would be okay, except that the butt plays a big part in her life. There is that old adage about having it and flaunting it, but sometimes Bertha is a little over the top. The whole piece about dressing appropriately for the venue seems to be over her head. Every piece of clothing she owns is either low-riding, miniskirted, or form-fitted, to the point where it would be hard for the average man not to look, stare, and maybe say something inappropriate, effectively leaving it up to you, her boyfriend, to be on patrol: every time you go out, you know someone is going to say something crazy. She isn't hoochie-fied, so much as just immodest. Sure, you got with her

because of all that big, bouncing booty. But now that it's yours, she can probably tone it down a little, huh?

Coco Chanel

DRIVES: a 1974 Porsche 911 on mismatched wheels
WORKS: at the nail shop, as a receptionist. Got half a GED.
FAKES THE FUNK: with an English accent, when she's never even been to Detroit.

Coco always watches MTV *Cribs* and all those other shows highlighting wealth and wonders why she's not living like that. More to the point, she wonders why you are not man enough to give her that life. Next thing you know, she's at the mall with the credit cards she lifted out of your wallet while you were asleep, blowing up Lane Bryant and maxing out your credit. She tries to convince you to go along with this foolishness by telling you that she grew up middle class, and she only knows the finer things in life. Of course, it comes out in the wash that she grew up wearing hand-me-downs and grocery store sneakers, just like you. She's got steak dreams while making salami money, and she wants you to sponsor her fantasy.

Vanilla Ice

Fuck what Farrakhan says—there is nothing wrong with hooking up with a white girl. Love is where you find it, and people find it in all sorts of places—no reason to cheat yourself because of what people may think. It can go wrong when the white girl you're dating is blacker than you. That is, she's got the Technicolor updo, the bad attitude, and the urban patois working. It might be different if she was raised around black people, but she comes from a gated community—her ghetto fabulosity is fake and fabricated, picked up from many hours studying BET. She doesn't really know herself, so how can she know what she feels for you? Ice, Ice, baby.

Mother-Sista

LOOKS LIKE: she could use a good fuck. Right now.

TALKS LIKE: Mister Rogers trying to explain water to a three-year-old

DRAW THE LINE WHEN: she wants to cut up your food

This sister thinks she has her shit so together that she's going to do you a favor and save you from yourself, because you'd be perfect if only you had a "good woman" in your life. She proceeds to try and change your whole life, from your choice of underwear to your choice of friends. She tries to order dinner for you, but somehow you know that just isn't right. See, all you need is the love of a "good woman" guiding your steps, and she thinks that she's just the woman for the job. She's wrong. But that won't stop her from trying.

St. Pauli Girl

I don't know that there is anything worse than a woman who drinks too much. There is nothing unsexier than a drunk woman. Except when that woman is *your* woman. Don't get me wrong—it's nice to share a glass of wine over dinner, and go out cocktailing with your chick every now and again. It becomes an issue when she can't hold her liquor. You may know when to say "when," but she has no idea, and this makes your life hard. Because you can't really take her anywhere there might be liquor for fear that before the night is through, she may be up on the table dancing, cussing people out, or being just generally disagreeable. And you don't want her going anywhere by herself where there could be alcohol, because you don't want her to drive home, or worse, be in the position of needing a ride home from some dude trying to slip her a Mickey. Cocktailing is one thing, but if the girl's a lush, it's like a third job. If you tell her that she has a drinking problem, she may respond that *you* are the problem.

The Muse
SMELLS LIKE: patchouli and Kools
EATS: hummus. And pussy.
WORKS: Ha! Draws a check from some kind of work-study/ SSI scam.

The Muse is usually a reformed hoe of some sort trying to convince you that she's healed her life through the power of poetry. She spent half a semester in Creative Writing 090 and she quotes Hemingway, for Christ's sake. She normally has a typical name like Bobbi Ann or Faloojah but has taken to calling herself "Little Tree" or some made-up African name she found in *Ebony* magazine. She writes poetry and reads it at every opportunity. And this would be okay if she actually knew how to write. Her poems end up being mildly lyrical rants. She's so deep, she wants to guide you and your voice through the ancient waters of words to learn the art and craft of the written word. In the meantime, she's stopped wearing deodorant and decided that fellatio is "not the way of the goddess." Perfect.

Goldbrick
Goldie is nice to look at. She's ambitous, with big plans about big things. She wants to start her own restaurant, go to grad school overseas, and become a marine biologist. The reason

you got with her is because of her drive to conquer the world and make something happen. And she could if she would just get out of bed and make things happen. Instead, she lays around waiting to be struck by good fortune and is jealous of anything you may have going on. She's lazy and angry that you are too busy to commiserate with her. So she may even sabotage your shit just to see you fail and rub your face in it. She could be somebody, if she could ever get over her fear of success. She just got her Associate's Degree at Bryant & Stratton and wonders if she's too good for you.

Sybil

She was homeless at eight weeks and had to take a job shoveling elephant dung shortly after. By the time she was three, she'd been raped repeatedly by two of the local stray Dobermans, one of which she would marry in a Vegas ceremony. After her divorce at age eight, she became an alcoholic. Four years later, she was prostituting. On her fourteenth birthday, she was reunited with the mother she never knew, who turned out to be a post-op transsexual from Rwanda. By the time she turned eighteen she'd had fifteen abortions and walked the Twelve Steps thirteen times. On her twentieth birthday, she begins to get her life together and registers for classes, taking a day job as a receptionist, where you meet her. You can't tell by looking at her, but—yep—this sister has had a hard life, Jack, and it's making both of you batshit. She is tugging along truckloads of baggage. The problem isn't the baggage: it's the fact that she's resistant to getting some professional help trying to unpack a life of unfathomable hardship. And as part of the deal, you are expected to help her drag this life from place to place. No, thank you.

Daddy's Girl

Honey wants a man who can provide for her like a father, and treat her the way a father should. But Honey didn't have a father, doesn't know her father, and never knew her father. So she has delusional, fantastical ideas about what a father is that no man could reasonably be expected to live up to. Or she has a father who is either Bill Cosby or a complete loser, and wants you to model your relationship after how her parents get along, except that her dad's a punk who lets her mother run the house while he sucks on a Miller Lite in the basement trying to remember where he left his balls. This is her picture of a man. T'yeah.

Uptown Girl

The Uptown Girl gets with someone she perceives to be "hood" because she needs some excitement in her life. She doesn't really like you, and lets you know by talking at you straight down her nose. She's slumming, and everyone knows it.

Chickenhead

The Chickenhead is worse than the Hood Chick because the Hood Chick knows her behavior is a problem. The Chickenhead celebrates her lack of social grace, laundry soap, and her sexual promiscuity. She's entrenched in the culture of poverty like her mother before her, and is proud of it. Often she has a number of children of questionable paternity. To her credit she lives off in the cut in a place wifey or mutual friends don't go. And the Chickenhead sucks dick like a champion.

Ricochet

You meet a wonderful girl, and everything seems to be in place—but you find out you're just the latest cat in the mix. See, she's recently out of the most fulfilling relationship she's ever had in her life. Somehow, somebody fucked up, and now she's single again. But she misses him, and is thrust into the single scene not exactly sure what she's looking for. So she bounces from man to man in quick succession, in hopes that one of them will give her the feeling she lost. She haunts the clubs, and after a few laps around, she's exhausted the options and ends up trying to reel in men anywhere she can find them. The truth is, she needs to get back with her ex, because she'll never find that kind of love again.

Rehab

You meet this girl who's kinda got loose morals—she's a hoe, essentially. Not only does she like sex, but she likes sex with everybody. And everybody knows it. Well, when you're taking your turn and basking in the afterglow, you find yourself in a space where you imagine this tart could change. With the right kind of guidance, healing, and forgiveness, she could be reborn as someone's wife. Your wife. So you start by taking her clothes shopping, buying her books, maybe even taking her to church, trying to rehabilitate this lady of leisure into a respectable woman. You spend all your time and money trying to reanimate this woman's consciousness and make her into someone you think could be a better person, and contribute something to society besides used condoms. But she eBayed all that shit and kept on fuckin'. Everybody. Because you can't change a person if they don't want to change. And she likes being Sally Suckworth too much to be Holly Homemaker.

Daria Gray

LOOKS LIKE: who knows?

Daria is banging—every time you see her, her look is on point: hair, makeup, clothes, and the like. Straight out of a magazine.

But then you two get into a committed relationship, and you see her without all the accoutrements. And without all the makeup, she looks like Freddy Krueger's lost twin sister. Just sexier. She wears so much makeup that you can't really be sure what she actually looks like. She's spent so much time and money on paint and polish that she hasn't developed or cultivated a natural beauty. Without makeup, she's horrifying. It would be nice to be with a woman who doesn't have to run to her makeup drawer the minute she gets up. But she's been known to sleep in her makeup, just so you don't know she's butt-ugly beneath the surface until it's too late.

Dee Elle

LOOKS LIKE: black Peppermint Patty

Dee is a cool chick, and she's even kind of kinky. She talks about you all having a threesome with another chick, and you're kinda down, but that's not really your thing. That's not your lifestyle, and you aren't trying to make it your lifestyle. But she presses the issue, until finally she tells you that she and a girlfriend "experimentally" fell into the sack together. And she liked it. Dee doesn't really know if she wants to be with men or women, and she's not particularly honest about that personal conflict. So you have to find out on the street, or put two and two together. For some reason, we only think black men are closet bisexuals. But girls who do girls break up homes and spread diseases too. Best for everybody to come clean, I say.

The Denzel Principle posits the theory that women are the ones who have it bad because they can't find a Denzel, but they don't have it nearly as bad as men do. Men can't find a Halle Berry either. But see, at least black men *know* they are fucking up, although we are eternally grateful for the constant reminder. From everyone. But black women have no idea they don't measure up. Many of them are deluding themselves, holding men to a higher standard than they themselves can measure up to.

You'll see the return of the Good Guys when good women make a comeback.

Living with the Dizzle

WAYS TO KNOW ON SIGHT SHE'S GOT THE DIZZLE

1. She asked you to buy her a drink—WTF? Buy me a drink.
2. She's wearing a T-shirt with the image of a man—any man—on it. Idol worship is *bad*.
3. Her jeans are too tight—it's like she's advertising.
4. She's wearing too much makeup—what is she covering up?
5. She's traveling in a crew—what's up with that?
6. Her moms is in the crew—ugly.
7. Too much fakery: fake nails, fake hair, fake eyelashes, fake teeth.
8. Traveling with a lot of children, no man in sight—this is a sad, sad sight.
9. Looks to be on the hunt—*run*.
10. Smells like an Avon product—she's either selling it or buying it. Both are bad.

WAYS TO KNOW YOUR GIRL HAS THE DIZZLE

1. She's renting a lot of Denzel movies.
2. She keeps trying to make you over.

3. Swoons whenever Denzel is on the tube.
4. Lots of laughing and hee-hawing. You enter the room: it stops.
5. Spends a lot of time at the club with her girls.
6. She quotes Denzel movies randomly. In bed.
7. Denzel screen saver.
8. Cuts out the faces of famous black men and inserts them over your picture.
9. She spends a lot of time trying to get backstage or into the VIP room.
10. Pictures of other men in your bedroom.

WAYS TO SHORT CIRCUIT THE DIZZLE

1. Throw away all of her self-help books—*today*.
2. Take a getaway with just you two—spend some money, dude. Detroit doesn't count.
3. Keep her moms out of your business—with all of your being.
4. Keep the rest of her peeps out of your business—make it a part-time job.
5. Listen—and keep listening.
6. Be attentive.
7. Have your shit together.
8. Turn her out: sling dick like a pro.
9. Be yourself.
10. Be prepared to leave if disrespected. Man-up.

WAYS WOMEN CAN BREAK THE HOLD OF THE DIZZLE

1. Go cold turkey—cut off the *Oprah* box.
2. Disassociate yourself from bad influences.

3. Hit the gym.
4. Assess yourself honestly.
5. Re-imagine Mr. Right.
6. Stop looking.
7. Try just kicking it. Forget trying to seal the deal.
8. Decide what you need, not just want you want.
9. Stop looking for love in all the wrong places.
10. Be choosy but not picky.

WAYS TO ATTRACT MR. RIGHT

1. Ditch the weave.
2. Less makeup is more.
3. Listen.
4. Be yourself.
5. Try meeting for coffee instead of alcoholic drinks.
6. Wait on giving up the pussy—not a long time, just enough time.
7. Make sure your house is clean—literally.
8. Be certain you are worthy.
9. Smile.
10. Try an attitude adjustment—why so angry?

TEN REASONS TO LOVE ORDINARY BLACK MEN

1. They have nothing to prove.
2. They have everything to offer.
3. They are everywhere.
4. They have the same hopes and dreams that you do.
5. They don't carry the burden of fame and fortune.
6. They are not as ordinary as you think.
7. You can have them all to yourself.

8. Extraordinary men are overrated.
9. No one is perfect.
10. There is only one Denzel Washington.

Black women talk so much about the lack of "good" men, but what I want to know is, who's screening these applications? You know—who's making sure the men you think are so hot actually pass muster? Seems like a lot of young ladies end up with DLs or Fresh Outs who always have all sorts of drama. What up with that?

There used to be a time when young ladies would bring a young man home, leave him alone in the living room, and her menfolk would come in and give the young man the once-over—maybe slap him around a little—essentially screening his application. Those days are long since behind us—whole neighborhoods are inhabited by single mothers. Men only come in long enough to play the doggie game and sneak out before the woman's children wake up to yet another strange man coming out of the bathroom. Some of us, both men and women, haven't figured out that not everyone is appropriate to bring around your kids. Just because you let him hit it doesn't mean you need to move him in. Fathers need to be more vigilant and mindful of who these moms bring around their kids—and vice versa. I can tell you this from experience.

I fought harder than I should have had to in order to be in all my kids' lives, and that has included my getting background checks done on the live-ins. That's right. I figured an IQ test would probably be inconclusive, but I needed to know what kind of man was spending the night in the same house as my kid. That's real talk. If you are a single parent in a shared parenting arrangement, and haven't done a background check on your kid's stepfather, baby-mama's latest boyfriend, baby-daddy's jump-off of the month, or wifey, I'm here to tell you—you're slippin'. Straight up. It's not that any of us are perfect or without sin—every black man I know, and I know a lot of black men—has paper on him of one kind or another. But it's one thing to have a weed ticket, a shoplifting gaffe, or some other kinda dime-store beef and another, as in the case with singer Jennifer Hudson's brother-in-law William Balfour, when dude's got multiple big-ticket, box-store cases. He clearly wasn't someone you should bring around your kid. You can see from the curb that this young man's application wasn't properly vetted.

This goes the other way too, ladies. People that know me will tell you that I laugh and joke, but I'm serious about my kids. I don't bring everyone around them. In fact, hardly anybody, and I'm not alone. I know many single dads who may bang a different chick every night, but their kids will never know. A lot of my boys tend to be reckless. Me? I'm selective. And while I may get a lot of applications, not every app gets reviewed or even filed. Most often, they are thrown away, because I'm grinding away to be a good dad and with kids in the mix, you have to be careful. Any time you are in a relationship, there will be drama. Best if your kids are not involved.

Single parents, we have to get to a place where we are screening applicants. I know—single parenthood can be lonely. But better to get some battery-powered or lubricated love than to find yourself having to talk down your paramour and convince them not to hurt your child. So ladies, if you don't have those menfolk in your life, how do you screen the applicants? I have a few questions that will help you whittle down the candidates, and this list will help the fellas too. I'm not taking applications right now, but these are the questions I used to amass my short stack of preferred candidates.

TEN QUESTIONS SINGLE PARENTS SHOULD ASK WHEN SCREENING APPLICANTS

ARE YOU CRAZY? As in, "Are you psychotic in any measurable way?" I know, it seems too forward. But some people will just come out and tell you that they are not right in the head. We all have emotional problems—it's part of the human condition. But if your prospective mate isn't managing or acknowledging them, cross them off the list. You can't fix people: they have to fix themselves. There's crazy, wacky, and there's crazy, *crazy*. I don't know about you, but I don't need crazy in my life. Crazy, I got.

DO YOU DOPE OR DRINK? I don't want any dopers around my kids—and that means dope of any kind. A glass of wine with dinner and an occasional night of cocktailing is cool, but if you are tipping seriously every night, *pass*.

DO YOU HAVE ANY FELONIES? Yeah. *Any* felonies. Especially violent ones.

ARE YOU ON PROBATION? Again, another nonnegotiable. I'm sure there are a lot of good people on probation out there. I don't want them around my children.

DO YOU HAVE KIDS OF YOUR OWN? How they treat their own kids will say a lot about how they may treat yours.

HOW'S YOUR CREDIT? A lot of us are hit, so I don't hold it against anyone. But it's good to know.

ARE YOU EMPLOYABLE? That is, are you an American citizen, did you graduate from high school, get a GED, and can at least get a job at Wendy's so you can afford a taxi if I have to put you on the curb for acting out around my kids?

DO YOU VOTE? NO? *Next.*

WHAT ARE YOUR INTENTIONS? Are we just dancing, or are we moving toward something? If not, there's no reason for you to meet my kids.

GOT ANY LIFE PLANS? "What's a life plan?" Right. *Next.*

Hell, I bet even Denzel Washington had Pauletta fill out an application.

I know, I know. Don't thank me. I work for you.